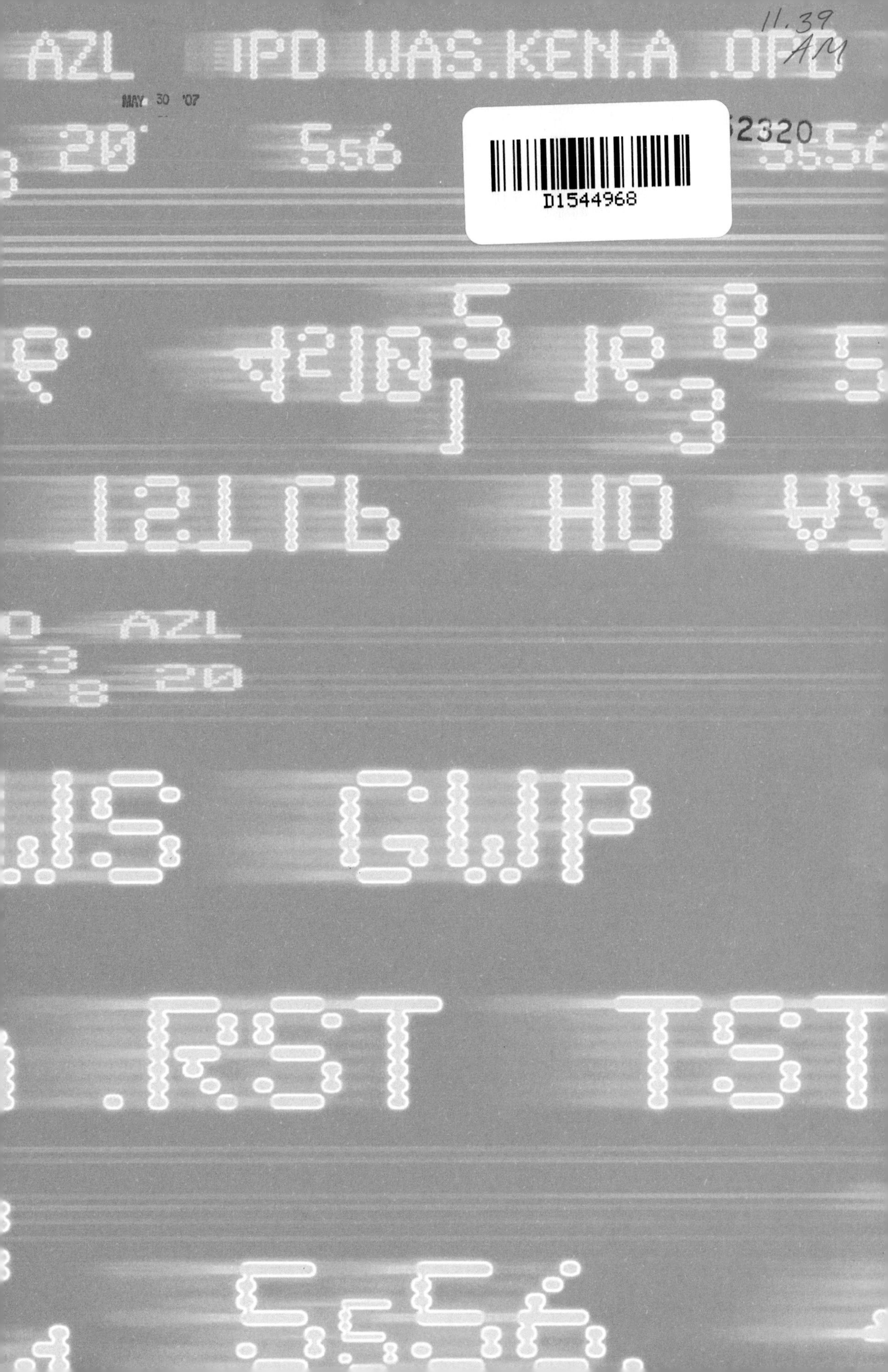
AZL IPD WAS.KEN.A

EQUITIES

AN INTRODUCTION TO THE CORE CONCEPTS

EQUITIES

AN INTRODUCTION TO THE CORE CONCEPTS

Mark Mobius

BICENTENNIAL
1807
WILEY
2007
BICENTENNIAL

John Wiley & Sons (Asia) Pte Ltd

Copyright © 2007 by John Wiley & Sons (Asia) Pte Ltd
Published in 2007 by John Wiley & Sons (Asia) Pte Ltd
2 Clementi Loop, #02-01, Singapore 129809

This publication is designed to provide accurate and authoritative information in regard to the
subject matter covered. It is sold with the understanding that the publisher is not engaged in rendering
professional services. If professional advice or other expert assistance is required, the services of a
competent professional person should be sought.

Other Wiley Editorial Offices

John Wiley & Sons, Inc., 111 River Street, Hoboken, NJ 07030, USA

John Wiley & Sons Ltd, The Atrium Southern Gate, Chichester P019 8SQ, England

John Wiley & Sons (Canada) Ltd, 5353 Dundas Street West, Suite 400, Toronto, Ontario, M9B 6HB,
    Canada

John Wiley & Sons Australia Ltd, 42 McDougall Street, Milton, Queensland 4064, Australia

Wiley-VCH, Boschstrasse 12, D-69469 Weinheim, Germany

Library of Congress Cataloging-in-Publication Data
ISBN-10: 0-470-82144-2
ISBN 13: 978-0-470-82144-2

Typeset in 11points, Galliard by Hot Fusion
Printed in Singapore by Saik Wah Press Ltd
10 9 8 7 6 5 4 3 2 1

CONTENTS

ACKNOWLEDGMENTS

Many commentators and scholars have studied equity markets around the world and their concepts have provided the stimulus for many of the ideas discussed in this book. There are too numerous to mention and to thank individually but I hope that I have been able to accurately reflect the body of knowledge available now about equities

Special thanks go to Dr. Thomas Lanyi, Shalini Dadlani, K. C. Chin and Zita Ng for their valuable assistance and comments as well as John Wiley's Janis Soo and Nick Wallwork for their patience and diligence.

To help us improve future editions of this book, please email your comments to: jmarkmobius@yahoo.com.

THE EQUITY CONCEPT: WHY SHARES EXIST

Shares exist to provide:

1. Capital

2. A means for sharing risks

3. Security of ownership

4. Transferability and negotiability

5. Liquidity

6. Diversification

CAPITALISM AND CAPITAL MARKETS

In order to function effectively, the free enterprise system, or capitalism, requires capital markets. The market for shares, known as the "equity market," is one of the many types of financial markets collectively known as "capital markets."

The idea of free markets was expressed by Adam Smith in his 1776 book, *An Inquiry into the Nature and Causes of the Wealth of Nations*, in which he promoted the idea that economic decisions should be left to the free-play of self-regulating market forces. In the capital markets, a further refinement of the idea of free markets, the profit or excess production is channeled towards further and more efficient production rather than being used in unproductive activities.

Free markets might have found expression in the 18th century, but capitalism was not new. Since ancient times, diverse cultures and religions across the world encouraged wealth creation, the goal of capitalism. Even the relatively newer religious movements, such as the Protestant Reformation in the 1500s, encouraged hard work and frugality. It endorsed the idea that

Figure 1.1 — Adam Smith

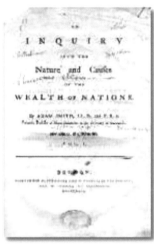

Source: Smith_adam_xbsp...ba.jpg 352x374pixels-54.3kb econclo.bu.edu/GENEC/images/people?M=A.

those who became wealthy through hard work and saving were virtuous and blessed. With the fall of monarchies in Europe, the French Revolution, and other political events, the spread of capitalistic ideas and free markets gathered momentum. Adam Smith's concepts became so popular that by the 1800s, England, France and Germany had adopted the ideas of free trade, strong currencies backed by gold (the gold standard) and balanced government budgets.

Besides political events, other factors that impacted the growth of capitalism were: (1) price inflation, resulting from the increasing supply of gold and silver in Europe; (2) the combination of stagnant wages and rising prices, contributing to rising company profitability and excess savings for capital investment; (3) the rise of strong nation-states, which promoted uniform monetary systems; (4) the enactment of legal codes that made business transactions more predictable and thereby nurtured capital investment and economic development; and (5) the privatization of state-managed enterprises.

However, unfettered capitalism and free markets did not become universal. After the First World War, the global economy and international markets shrank as trade barriers were erected and national managed currencies came to be favored with the abandonment of the gold standard. In the United States (US), the world's greatest capitalist nation, the stock market crash in 1929 and the subsequent Great Depression temporarily damaged the idea of *laissez-faire,* or non-interference by the government in economic matters. The very idea of capitalism was being questioned.

It was then that the ideas of fascism and communism (two sides of the same coin) began growing in popularity. These ideologies advocated the acquisition and control of all the sources of capital and production by the government in the name of the people or the "common good." The Nazis in Germany, the Fascists in Italy and Japan, and the Communists (subsequently, Stalinists in Russia and Maoists in China) promoted these ideas. But since the Second World War, the remarkable economic performance of the US and the United Kingdom (UK) and the transformation of Germany, Japan, Italy and a number of developing countries that adopted free market systems has reinforced the vitality of the capitalist idea.

SHARES AS CAPITAL-RAISING INSTRUMENTS

Companies or corporations raise capital, for investing in equipment, people, know-how and other resources, with a view to increasing profits and productivity. Broadly speaking, they have two instruments for raising capital: bonds (debt) and shares. With bonds or other fixed income securities, they create debt; with equities, they create an interest or part-ownership. (Note: in the UK, the word "stock" often refers to a loan while equities are referred to as "shares." In this book, these two terms are used interchangeably.)

SHARES AS A MEANS OF SHARING RISK

In the early 1500s in England, and later on the Continent, monopolist trading groups (guilds) were formed and chartered by the Crown to promote the government's mercantile policies. The corporation, as we know it today, is a combination of (1) the so-called "joint-stock company" (a type of partnership), and (2) the kind of organization that grew out of the medieval guilds.

SHARES AS SECURE OWNERSHIP

Equities offer written evidence of the security of ownership. This is why equities and other financial instruments are referred to as "securities." A share gives the holder the right to own property which he may not physically possess at that time. It is a stockholder's part-interest in an enterprise.

SHARES AS TRANSFERABLE, NEGOTIABLE, AND LIQUID INSTRUMENTS

Shares can be bought from and sold to other investors via the stock exchange almost daily. This enables investors to value their assets on a daily basis and easily transform the shares into cash. Shares are thus more "liquid" compared to assets such as real estate, private business, art, etc, which are difficult to convert to cash since the markets for these assets may be less organized as well as limited in scope.

Originally, ownership interests in enterprises were not easily transferable or negotiable. But as the popularity of that particular form of ownership grew, it became necessary to make these instruments easily transferable so that they could be passed on from one generation to the next or sold to another person or company. A share thus became an instrument for transferring ownership title. To make the process efficient, a new written evidence of ownership was devised: a bearer form — anyone possessing or "bearing" this form became the rightful owner. This is the reason why robbers steal bearer certificates, mostly bonds, since they then become the owners and no one will ask questions when they go to sell them.

As it became dangerous to have them lying around the house since anyone could pick them up and sell them, the need arose for banks, brokers, or clearing agencies to act as custodians to protect such certificates in strong fireproof, bombproof and thief-proof vaults. This led to a complex transfer agency business where the movement of shares from one account to another was regulated through appropriate bookkeeping entries.

In the US and many other countries, share certificates are registered in the owner's name, in the name of the custodian bank or broker (a "street name"), or in the name of another person or legal entity called a "nominee." When a sale is made, the new owner's name is registered.

In recent years, the practice of registering ownership has spread across the world since many companies have moved to a "paperless" system where names are recorded in electronic form and ownership changes are also done electronically. Such a system offers the benefits of negotiability, transferability, and, if there is a good deal of trading, liquidity.

The share certificate system, therefore, provides one essential ingredient for a free market: an instrument that can be bought and sold at will in the market; in other words, a "negotiable instrument." The greater the number of buyers and sellers, the easier is the process of sale and purchase and the more "liquid" is the share. The buyers and sellers can also assess the value of their holdings on a daily basis since the market price of liquid securities is quoted daily in the newspaper and various electronic quotation systems.

Figure 1.2 — Share certificate

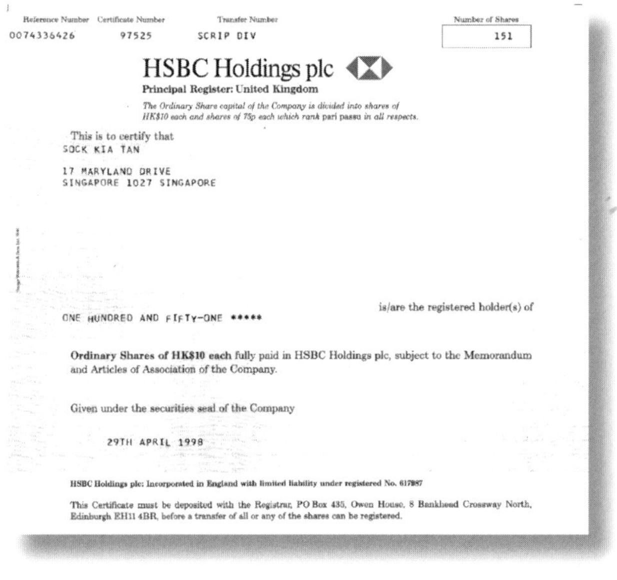

Reference Number	Certificate Number	Transfer Number	Number of Shares
0074336426	97525	SCRIP DIV	151

HSBC Holdings plc

Principal Register: United Kingdom

The Ordinary Share capital of the Company is divided into shares of HK$10 each and shares of 75p each which rank pari passu in all respects.

This is to certify that
SOCK KIA TAN

17 MARYLAND DRIVE
SINGAPORE 1027 SINGAPORE

is/are the registered holder(s) of

ONE HUNDRED AND FIFTY-ONE *****

Ordinary Shares of HK$10 each fully paid in HSBC Holdings plc, subject to the Memorandum and Articles of Association of the Company.

Given under the securities seal of the Company

29TH APRIL 1998

HSBC Holdings plc: Incorporated in England with limited liability under registered No. 617987

This Certificate must be deposited with the Registrar, PO Box 435, Owen House, 8 Bankhead Crossway North, Edinburgh EH11 4BR, before a transfer of all or any of the shares can be registered.

SHARES AS DIVERSIFICATION INSTRUMENTS

Shares enable investors to easily and efficiently invest in a number of different enterprises without committing all of their money to any one enterprise. This diversification characteristic has been facilitated by the development of the modern corporation.

The idea of a "corporation" or "limited liability company" has a long history. It grew out of the fundamental need for people to diversify their investments and thus reduce their risk. Today it has developed into a specific legal form of organization registered with or chartered by the government.

CASE STUDY: THE "NAMES" AT LLOYD'S OF LONDON

Lloyd's of London started in the 1600s in Lloyd's Coffee House in London, a meeting place for imbibing the newly popular coffee beverage and exchanging information regarding the arrival and departure of ships and cargoes. Until his death in 1713, Edward Lloyd encouraged ship captains, merchants and owners to meet at his coffee house. The tradition continued after his death and eventually expanded into a formal society of underwriters. As London became a center for trade, there was an increase in demand for insurance for ships and cargoes. Merchants with ships to insure would ask a "broker" to sell their policies to various wealthy merchants. The broker's knowledge of the financial integrity of those merchants was important, since, in the event of a loss, those merchants would have to pay the claim to the full extent of their personal fortunes. Those wealthy individuals would sign their names one beneath the other on the policy and hence were called "underwriters," and the individuals would be known as "names." As Lloyd's expanded, it gradually outgrew the shipping business and clients started asking for cover on a wide range of risks. In the 20th century Lloyd's even insured the legs of movie actress Betty Grable!

But the partnership structure of Lloyd's with unlimited liability for the "names" resulted in disaster for many. In 2005, after a number of large insurance losses, the names of Lloyd's of London faced mass bankruptcies because of continuing cash calls to meet insurance losses. For example, claims for illness and death from asbestos were estimated to spiral to over US$540 billion.

It is different from the other two major forms of business ownership — the sole proprietorship and the partnership — in the following ways: (1) it is more appropriate for a large-scale business requiring large amounts of capital, since many owners can join rather than a few partners or a sole individual; (2) it entails only limited liability for the investors, so that they are not liable for any amounts greater than their original investment, while sole proprietorships and partnerships most often do not have any such limitation; (3) its shares are transferable, so that the enterprise rights can be transferred from one investor to another easily and quickly; (4) it is recognized as a legal "person" that can enter into contracts, take legal action and hold property; (5) it can survive indefinitely and outlive any or all of the investors; and (6) it provides for shareholder control over its affairs.

Figure 1.3 — Lloyd's of London

EQUITIES: AN INTRODUCTION TO THE CORE CONCEPTS

THE HISTORY OF CORPORATIONS

The idea that a group of people could have a collective identity, independent and separate from each of the individuals in the group, probably started with the Romans. From the 9th century, proto-"firms" were formed in Italy and the Muslim world to finance trading voyages; a wealthy individual could purchase shares in a number of voyages to diversify his risks.

The concept of a "limited liability company" — in which, if the company fails, its shareholders can lose no more than what they have paid for their shares — allowed people to invest "passively" in ventures over which they had no direct control. By the 13th century, shares in such ventures could be bought and sold in major European ports and trading centers. During the 1500s, a system of state-sponsored "mercantilism" developed in Europe that lasted for two centuries. The discovery of the Americas and easier access to other regions of the world brought new raw materials and created new markets.

Commercially oriented states, particularly in northern Europe, benefited greatly. The effects were felt all over the world. For example, chili, native to the Americas, reached the Far East within a few decades of Columbus, voyage of discovery and is now an essential ingredient in Asian cuisine. Special privileges were given to certain towns and to guilds of craftsmen and merchants that stimulated the growth of manufacturing and distribution. International trade had been largely in luxury products, such as spices from the East, but now new "mass markets" were emerging.

Figure 1.4 — A share certificate for the Dutch East India Company, issued in 1606

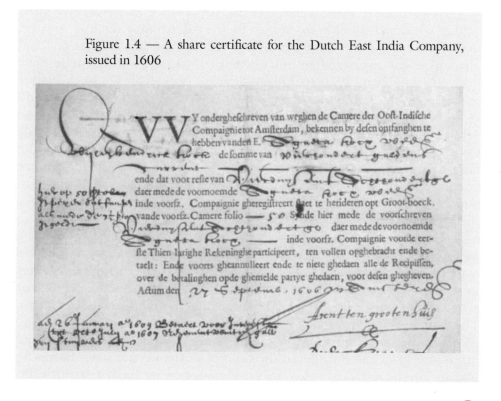

The first chartered joint-stock company was formed in England in 1555 by the famous navigator and explorer Sebastian Cabot and a few other London merchants. It was called the Muscovy Company or the Russia Company. It was granted monopoly on Anglo-Russian trade by Queen Elizabeth I. This company was the first joint-stock company where the capital remained in use by the company rather than being repaid after each voyage, which was the normal practice until then.

The Dutch East India Company, or Dutch Vereenigde Oost-indische Compagnie (VOC), was founded in 1602 to protect Dutch trade in the Indian Ocean. It prospered throughout most of the 1600s in the East Indies (modern Indonesia) as an instrument of the Dutch government with monopoly trading rights. Like the English East India Company, the VOC combined the financing of all its voyages rather than financing each voyage individually. Importantly, each shareholder's liability was limited to the extent of the money he invested. The Dutch formed the first regular stock exchange in 1611 near the VOC's office in Amsterdam.

By the 1800s, "industrial capitalism" had emerged in some Western countries and had developed into a huge and complex system involving large banks, a multitude of joint-stock companies, the efficient organization of factory workers and a well-organized global trade. Although only a few developed Western nations absorbed the largest part of the world's food and raw material exports, industrial development was ubiquitous and growing. By the late 1800s, wealthy people everywhere were holding a wide variety of shares and bonds as a permanent part of their core assets.

Following the First World War, the US, which had pioneered mass market consumerism, was booming. In the "Roaring Twenties," the US stock markets drew in more and more ordinary people as investors, and financial assets, managed by intermediaries, such as equity funds grew from $19 billion in 1900 to $167 billion in 1929. The US stock market crashed in 1929, setting off a chain of destructive events around the world as governments sought to protect their economies by raising tariffs and devaluing their currencies, resulting in the Great Depression. World trade contracted sharply, and investors took their money out of stocks, bankrupting firms and putting millions out of work. By the middle of 1930, US stock prices were a fifth of the levels they had reached in the previous year. Such was the severity of the crash that the Dow Jones Industrial Average (DJIA), the benchmark index, did not regain its pre-crash level until 1955.

The two world wars brought a major shift in world power. The post-Second World War era was, for business, a period dominated by US manufacturing firms and US capital, since the great European powers were bankrupt by the time the war ended in 1945. However, rival politico-economic systems had emerged in the form of communism and socialism. The response of the "capitalist" countries was state-controlled capitalism, protectionism and regulation. In Europe, most countries nationalized their major industries and introduced the concept of the welfare state. European investors were greatly restricted and private share ownership fell dramatically.

CASE STUDY: THE GREAT STOCK MARKET CRASH OF 1929

Figure 1.5 — The Great Stock Market Crash of 1929

The stock market crash of 1929 preceded the Great Depression, a 10-year economic fall which spread across the industrialized world. After a rapid expansion in the mid-1920s, the US stock market reached a peak at the end of August 1929. On October 18, a dramatic fall took place and by October 24 (known as "Black Thursday"), investors panicked. Despite efforts by banks and investment companies to stem the panic by buying large blocks of shares, the precipitous fall in stock values continued, with "Black Monday" and "Black Tuesday" representing a complete collapse.

Causes of the crash of 1929 may be traced to excessive speculation combined with generous financing of stock market trading. Margin trading became widespread so that once the market declined, many speculators were forced to sell in order to meet margin calls from the bankers. This created a "snowball effect" where stock sales depressed stock prices which, in turn, forced another wave of selling.

Source: (*About Business and Finance* http://mutualfunds.about.com/cs/history/l/bl1929graph.htm)

The interventionist ideas of the economist J. M. Keynes, which had been originally developed to help solve the problems of the Great Depression, dominated.

By the 1970s, Europe and Japan had rebuilt themselves, and had created international firms capable of competing with their US rivals. State-controlled capitalism had succeeded in establishing reconstruction and growth, but at the price of extreme rigidity. Flaws in the system were becoming increasingly apparent. Globally, the inefficiencies of large state-run firms and staggeringly bad investment decisions by politicians were exacerbated by the oil crisis of the early 1970s, when the OPEC oil cartel (a group of petroleum products-exporting countries that fix oil prices in unison) hiked oil prices, pushing the developed world into recession.

In the 1980s, the developed nations were transformed again, this time in the direction of the free market economics of the 19th century. Theorists pushed for "privatization," a reversal of nationalization, which, it was hoped, would free up investment and make companies more efficient. Japan boomed as a manufacturer and exporter. In developing countries, the key to progress was seen as industrialization, and some nations, especially in Asia, made great strides in manufacturing and exporting.

During the 1990s, countries in the Far East, such as Hong Kong, Taiwan, Singapore and South Korea, which had emerged as major international players in the earlier decade, continued to outstrip their rivals in the developed world. The advent of personal computers and the internet contributed to the lowering of trade barriers. The collapse of the USSR and other factors ushered in a new era of "globalization" in which obstacles to international investment and trade were greatly reduced. Around the world, millions of people now look to stock markets as a primary means of accumulating wealth, either through direct purchase of shares and other securities, or through the equity investments of institutions such as pension schemes and mutual funds.

INSTITUTIONS AS INVESTORS

A large and important category of investors — the financial institutions — has increasingly impacted financial markets. These institutions include:

1. Pension funds managing retirement benefit portfolios of governments, corporations, unions, etc.

2. Professional asset management groups/companies that manage mutual funds, unit trusts, investment trusts, family trusts, closed-end funds, hedge funds, private equity funds, etc.

3. Banks and finance companies.

4. Brokerage firms that invest on their own behalf and on behalf of their clients.

5. Insurance companies.

ENDOWMENTS

These organizations invest in a wide variety of assets. Principal among them are equities and fixed income instruments, such as bonds. Over the last few decades, the growth in the size of institutional funds has been rapid, while direct private share ownership has also expanded. Although more private individuals hold investments than ever before, much of this is invested indirectly through mutual funds or pension funds, which are professionally managed by asset management or money management institutions. Given the increasing importance of institutional investors, what they buy or sell is closely followed by speculators who hope to benefit from the movement of large money flows.

Figure 1.6 — Growth of funds under management in the US

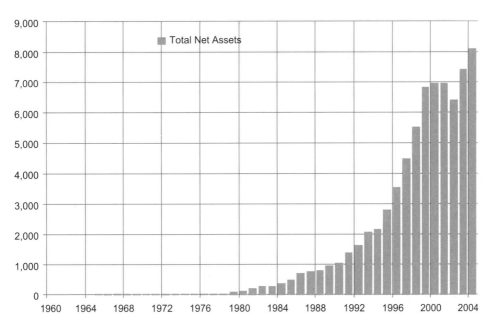

US$ Billion

Source: ICI

SUMMARY

Along with the other capital markets, the equity market provides an efficient way of channeling savings into the most productive part of the economy: growing businesses. Shares, the instrument through which the equity market operates, are liquid, and can normally be bought and sold at any time.

Banking, joint-stock companies and share trading emerged during the Middle Ages. With the development of the great European trading companies in the 16th century, stock markets evolved into a recognizable form. By the 19th century, many industrialized nations had active equity markets. By the late 20th century, rapidly developing stock markets had sprung up in several countries. Share ownership, whether directly or through institutional funds, became widespread across the globe.

QUICK QUIZ

1. Companies existed prior to the development of stock markets (e.g. the English East India Company.) Can companies exist and grow without stock markets now? Give reasons.

2. Can you think of at least five products whose manufacturers could have survived as companies without much change over the last 500 years?

3. Can companies predict what their size and earnings will or may be after twenty years?

4. How do companies benefit from equity markets?

5. What are the reasons why shares exist?

THE REWARDS OF
EQUITY OWNERSHIP

I nvestors do not *have* to put their money into equities; there is a wide range of other options available to them, including real estate, bonds, and cash deposits. Since equities are often regarded as riskier than these other types of assets, at least in the short term, why should anyone invest in equities? The answer is that, in the long term, in most of the world's markets, equities have produced better returns on average than any other type of asset.

Figure 2.1 — Total nominal return indexes, 1802–2001

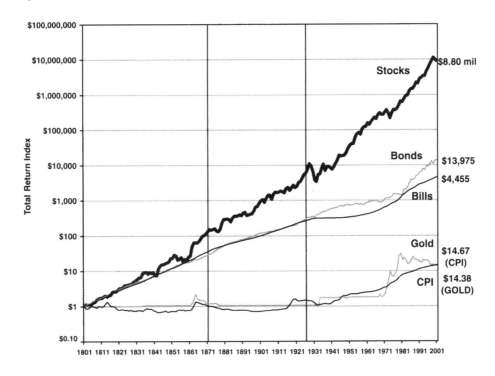

Source: Siegel, Jeremy J. *Stocks for the Long Run (Third Edition)*, 2002, New York, McGraw-Hill

In his book *Stocks for the Long Run,* Jeremy J. Siegel gave definitive evidence regarding how superior stock investments were to other investments such as bonds, bills, and gold. As indicated by Figure 2.1, $1 invested in stocks in 1801 would have grown to $8.8 million by 2001. During that same period, an investment in bonds would have returned only $13,975, in bills $4,455 and in gold only $14.38, worse than inflation.

The proven, superior long-term performance of equities as an asset class matters to institutions and individuals who have a long-term outlook and can afford to wait for many years for their investments to appreciate — for example, when equity investment is used in pension planning. In the short term, however, stock markets tend to fluctuate (a condition described as "volatility"), and investors who cannot afford to wait for better returns in the long term may have to sell their shares at a loss.

ADJUSTING FOR INFLATION

It is evident from Figure 2.3 on page 16 that the countries that were severely affected by the two world wars were poor long-term performers; they were also badly affected by periods of very high inflation. In fact, inflation in Germany was so catastrophic during 1922 and 1923 that since the Second World War the Germans have taken great care to keep it low.

Unless you adjust for inflation, investment returns can be misleading, especially in the long term. Inflation, usually defined as a general increase in consumer or wholesale prices, varies considerably over time and eats into the buying power of money. To establish the true value of investment returns, and to check that the buying power of the original amount of money invested has been retained, inflation-adjusted returns (called "real" returns) are often used. Although most countries have experienced low inflation rates in recent years, any rise in inflation can have a negative effect on returns. So, when you check the performance of investments, always

 TERMINOLOGY

RECESSION – Usually defined as a period of time when the total quantity of goods and services sold ("aggregate output") in an economy declines for two or more consecutive quarters (three month periods).

DEPRESSION – When an economy goes into recession, the expectation is often that aggregate output will rise in the short to medium term. If no rise occurs and the decline continues for a period of years, it is described as a depression. The Great Depression of the 1930s severely affected much of the world; as the world's economy contracted, unemployment rates soared, leading to much social upheaval and distress.

look at "real" (inflation-adjusted) rather than "nominal" (not inflation-adjusted) returns.

The opposite of inflation is "deflation," which is a general decrease in prices; this is much rarer, but has occurred in many countries. The US experienced deflation during the Great Depression of the 1930s. Some parts of Asia have experienced modest deflation since the late 1990s. Over the long term, however, a degree of inflation is considered by many economists to be normal. During the 20th century, most industrialized countries experienced long-term inflation rates in the range of 3% to 4% a year. The oil crisis of the 1970s brought high inflation in many countries, but it gradually fell back to lower levels.

Investors prefer low or stable inflation rates because they make investment returns more predictable. Although some companies may benefit from a sudden rise in the inflation rate — for example, by selling old products at new prices — others suffer because their suppliers' prices rise. Furthermore, high and unstable rates of inflation cause chaos among consumers, changing their behavior and inviting drastic political measures, such as price controls, that can have damaging effects on business growth.

Figure 2.2 — Total real return indexes, 1802–2001

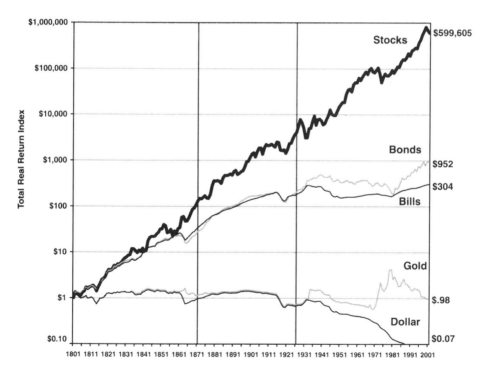

Source: Siegel, Jeremy J. *Stocks for the Long Run (Third Edition)*, 2002, New York, McGraw-Hill

Inflation increases the risks for holders of fixed-income bonds, since a rising inflation rate can wipe out the interest received from those bonds if the bond interest rate is lower than the inflation rate. For this reason, in an inflationary environment, equities are more attractive since asset values (property, inventory, etc) held by companies rise in order to keep pace with inflation. Since companies can raise the prices of the goods and services they sell, their earnings keep up with inflation.

Even if the returns were corrected for inflation during the 1802 to 2001 period, equities still outperformed admirably, as shown in Figure 2.2. After correcting for the consumer price inflation, $1 invested in stocks would have returned $599,605, while bonds and bills would have returned $952 and $304 respectively. The results for investments in gold and the US dollar would have resulted in losses, since that $1 investment in gold would have been reduced to 98 cents and the US dollar to only seven cents.

Figure 2.3 — Real returns on equities versus bonds internationally, 1900–2003

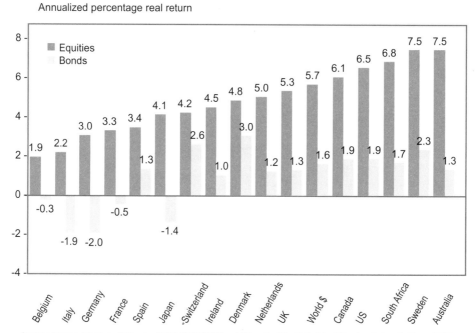

Source: Dimson, Marsh and Staunton (ABN AMRO/LBS) and Triumph of the Optimists, Princeton University Press, 2002.

 TERMINOLOGY ————————————————

REAL RETURN – *The return on investment, adjusted for inflation. For example, a return of 10% in a year of 8% inflation is a "real" return of 2%.*

Figure 2.3 compares the average annual returns on equities and bonds, adjusted for inflation (the "real" returns), for the major industrialized countries during the 20th century (1900–2003). Although there is considerable variation, equities have invariably produced better results than bonds. Until recently, accurate long-term data were not available for countries other than the US. The long-term performance of US stocks has been, in many cases, much better than that of stocks in many other countries, since the US has dominated international politics and the global economy during the 20th century. However, other countries have experienced economic success as well, and so those who invested globally managed better returns than those who invested only in US stocks.

During the stock market boom of the 1990s, investors in many countries, such as the US, the UK, Sweden and Spain, enjoyed much higher returns than what they would have received over the long term on average. These excellent returns led many to raise their expectations, and even to assume that long-term investments, such as pensions, might produce similar high returns. However, after the "dot-com" bubble burst, equities performed much worse in many industrialized countries, actually producing "negative returns" on losses between 2000 and 2003, when bonds outperformed equities in some countries (see Figure 2.4 on page 18).

Few investors expect to hold equities for as long as a century, so they tend to focus on shorter periods. The problem is, a strongly positive or negative trend in a given period may be misleading, since equity returns are highly volatile. Equity performances in the bull market of the 1990s or in the bear market in 2000–2003 are both equally unrepresentative of the long-term potential of equity investment.

IN THE LONG RUN STOCKS ARE THE BEST

For the small investor, equities offer a good way to build wealth out of savings over the long term, when combined with prudent investments in other types of assets.

Regardless of how the investor decides to split his portfolio among stocks, bonds, bank deposits and other forms of investment, a number of studies have shown that, in the long term, stocks perform better than other types of investments. Studies have shown that in the long run, it is a mistake for investors to put money into fixed income instruments such as bonds, bond funds, mortgage-backed securities and other such fixed-income instruments if they want the best long-term returns. Long-term financial data show that although stocks are certainly riskier than bonds in the short run, over the long run the returns on stocks are so stable that they are actually safer than even government bonds or treasury bills.

Contrary to popular belief, the returns on fixed-income assets can pose higher risks for long-term investors while the constancy of long-term, "real" returns on stocks has been surprisingly high. In his studies, Professor Jeremy J. Siegel found that stocks fetched returns at least 5% higher than inflation and higher than cash or bonds in 99.4% of the

Figure 2.4 — Real return on equities, bonds and bills: 1990—2003

COUNTRIES	PERIOD	ANNUALIZED REAL RETURN (% PER YEAR)				
		EQUITIES	BONDS	BILLS	INFLATION	BEST
Australia	2000 - 2003	1.7	4.7	1.2	3.6	Bonds
	1990 - 1999	9.0	10.1	5.1	2.3	Bonds
	1900 - 2003	7.5	1.3	0.5	3.9	Equities
Belgium	2000 - 2003	-6.9	5.8	1.7	1.9	Bonds
	1990 - 1999	9.1	7.8	4.0	2.1	Equities
	1900 - 2003	1.9	-0.3	-0.4	5.5	Equities
Canada	2000 - 2003	-1.4	6.3	1.3	2.4	Bonds
	1990 - 1999	8.3	8.9	4.3	2.1	Bonds
	1900 - 2003	6.1	1.9	1.7	3.1	Equities
Denmark	2000 - 2003	0.3	6.2	1.9	2.1	Bonds
	1990 - 1999	7.5	8.9	5.5	2.1	Bonds
	1900 - 2003	4.8	3.0	2.3	4.0	Equities
France	2000 - 2003	-8.4	6.6	1.8	1.8	Bonds
	1990 - 1999	11.6	8.9	4.7	1.9	Equities
	1900 - 2003	3.3	-0.5	-3.1	7.6	Equities
Germany	2000 - 2003	-12.9	6.1	2.1	1.5	Bonds
	1990 - 1999	9.6	5.6	3.5	2.4	Equities
	1900 - 2003*	3.0	-2.0	-0.4	5.0	Equities
Ireland	2000 - 2003	-2.5	3.5	-0.6	4.2	Bonds
	1990 - 1999	11.8	8.1	5.4	2.4	Equities
	1900 - 2003	4.5	1.0	0.7	4.4	Equities
Italy	2000 - 2003	-8.9	4.9	1.0	2.6	Bonds
	1990 - 1999	6.4	9.8	1.7	4.1	Bonds
	1900 - 2003	2.2	-1.9	-3.9	8.9	Equities
Japan	2000 - 2003	-10.4	4.7	0.8	-0.6	Bonds
	1990 - 1999	-5.2	7.4	1.8	1.1	Bonds
	1900 - 2003	4.1	-1.4	-2.1	7.5	Equities
The Netherlands	2000 - 2003	-15.1	5.2	0.8	2.8	Bonds
	1990 - 1999	17.8	6.0	3.3	2.4	Equities
	1900 - 2003	5.0	1.2	0.7	3.0	Equities
South Africa	2000 - 2003	2.1	11.3	5.1	6.0	Bonds
	1990 - 1999	4.6	7.5	6.3	9.3	Bonds
	1900 - 2003	6.8	1.7	0.9	4.9	Equities
Spain	2000 - 2003	-5.4	4.1	0.3	3.3	Bonds
	1990 - 1999	12.2	8.9	4.7	4.0	Equities
	1900 - 2003	3.4	1.3	0.4	6.0	Equities
Sweden	2000 - 2003	-12.2	5.4	2.2	1.8	Bonds
	1990 - 1999	15.0	11.1	5.1	3.0	Equities
	1900 - 2003	7.5	2.3	2.0	3.7	Equities
Switzerland	2000 - 2003	-6.8	4.5	0.9	0.8	Bonds
	1990 - 1999	14.0	5.0	2.1	2.1	Equities
	1990 - 2003	4.2	2.6	0.8	2.4	Equities
United Kingdom	2000 - 2003	-8.2	2.6	2.3	2.3	Bonds
	1990 - 1999	11.2	9.3	4.4	3.5	Equities
	1900 - 2003	5.3	1.3	1.0	4.0	Equities
United States	2000 - 2003	-6.8	8.3	0.8	2.3	Bonds
	1990 - 1999	14.2	5.7	1.9	2.9	Equities
	1900 - 2003	6.5	1.9	1.0	3.0	Equities
World (USD)	2000 - 2003	-6.5	7.7	0.8	2.3	Bonds
	1990 - 1999	7.8	6.7	1.9	2.9	Equities
	1900 - 2003	5.7	1.6	1.0	3.0	Equities

*For Germany, the mean, standard deviation, and standard error are based on 103 years, excluding 1922-23.
Source: Dimson, Marsh and Staunton (ABN AMRO/LBS)

"rolling" 30-year periods from 1802 through 2001. ("Rolling" yearly periods are calculated by adding one new year and subtracting one old year for each period, for example, 1802–1832, 1803–1833, and so on.) Since 1871, stock returns were higher than cash and bond returns in every rolling 30-year period. His studies showed that 5% higher than inflation was the lowest return for stocks in any 30-year period, and that most of the 30-year periods had returns more than 5% over inflation.

You may ask: "What if I invest in stocks at the top of a bull market? Wouldn't I lose out, even in the long run?" Professor Siegel's study showed that even for those investing in stocks at the worst possible time, such as at the beginning of 1929 (just before the 1929 crash), stocks would have done better than cash or bonds by the end of 1950. For the 30 years from 1929 to 1958, the average return on stocks was 6.8% per year higher than inflation, 5.1% higher than bonds and 7.5% better than bank deposits.

But how long would you have to wait to know that your stock market investments will do better than cash or bonds? Professor Siegel studied holding periods of 1, 2, 5, 10, 20 and 30 years between 1802 and 2001. He found that the longer the holding period, the more likely stocks would perform better than cash or bonds, as shown in Figure 2.5. From 1931 onwards, in some holding periods of less than 10 years, stocks did relatively less well than cash or bonds. But even in those cases, if the holding periods were extended to 11 or 12 years, stocks outperformed.

Figure 2.5 — Holding period comparisons: Percentage of periods when stocks outperform bonds and bills

Holding Period	Time Period	Stocks outperform Bonds	Stocks outperform T-Bills
1 Year	1802-2001	61.0	61.5
	1871-2001	60.3	64.1
2 Years	1802-2001	65.3	65.3
	1871-2001	65.6	69.5
5 Years	1802-2001	70.9	74.0
	1871-2001	74.0	77.1
10 Years	1802-2001	80.1	80.1
	1871-2001	82.4	84.7
20 Years	1802-2001	91.7	94.5
	1871-2001	95.4	99.2
30 Years	1802-2001	99.4	97.1
	1871-2001	100.0	100.0

Source: Siegel, Jeremy J. *Stocks for the Long Run (Third Edition)*, 2002, New York, McGraw-Hill

Conclusion: For a holding period of 10 to 12 years, investments in stocks tend to perform better than bonds or cash. Longer holding periods can reduce risk even more.

Stocks are better than bonds or bank deposits because investing in profitable businesses is likely to have a better investment yield than lending to such businesses, which is what banks and bond issuers do. Stocks represent a share of enterprises that are among the most productive in the world.

Figure 2.6 — Returns on world asset classes, 1900–2005.

| | | Mean returns % p.a. | | | | | Annual returns % | | | | 10-year returns % p.a. | | | |
| | | | | | | | Lowest | | Highest | | Lowest | | Highest | |
Return	Asset	Geometric mean %	Arithmetic mean %	Std error %	Std devn %	Serial Correction	%	Year	%	Year	%	10-yr ended	%	10-yr ended
Nominal	Equities	8.9	10.2	1.6	16.8	0.13	-40.8	1931	70.9	1933	-1.2	1938	20.6	1959
	Bonds	4.7	5.0	0.8	8.6	0.25	-15.3	1919	34.1	1985	-2.3	1920	15.4	1993
	US Bills	4.0	4.0	0.3	2.8	0.9	0	1938	14.7	1981	0.1	1942	9.2	1987
	US Inflation	3.0	3.1	0.5	4.9	0.64	-10.7	1921	20.5	1918	-2.7	1933	8.7	1982
Real	Equities	5.7	7.2	1.7	17.2	0.15	-34.6	1931	70	1933	-6.3	1920	18	1959
	Bonds	1.6	2.2	1.0	10.3	0.32	-26.8	1946	31.8	1932	-9.3	1920	6.1	1930
	US Bills	1	1.1	0.5	4.7	0.62	-15.1	1946	19.8	1921	-5.1	1950	6.1	1930

Source: Dimson, Marsh and Staunton, Triumph of the Optimists: 101 Years of Global Investment Returns, Priceton University Press, 2002 and subsequent research

List of the 17 countries included in the "World" data
Australia, Belgium, Canada, Denmark, France, Germany, Ireland, Italy, Japan, Netherlands, Norway, South Africa, Spain, Sweden, Switzerland, UK and US

Figure 2.6 gives data from studies by Dimson Marsh and Staunton, which confirms the advantages of equity investment on a global scale. Their studies covered 17 countries. The average (arithmetic and geometric means) return data show the superior returns of equities but the annual nominal and real return data also exhibit the key drawback of equities: volatility.

SUMMARY

In the long term, equities are better performing investments than every other class of investment, in most markets across the world. Contrary to popular belief, the returns on fixed-income assets pose higher risks for long-term investors, while there is a degree of constancy about the long-term, inflation-adjusted returns on stocks. Even if the investment is made at the peak of a stock market boom, the long-term returns on stocks are superior to those on bonds. Risks in stocks also diminish over the long-term. For a holding period of 10 to 12 years, investments in stocks hold little risk compared to bonds or cash. Longer holding periods reduce risk even more.

QUICK QUIZ

1. You inherit a run-down house. At present market value, it is worth $70,000. Six months repair work could increase its value by $30,000, but at a cost of $25,000. You can rent out the house in its present condition for $500 a month. Would you sell the house now, rent it out, or do the repair work? Give reasons for your answer.

2. An investment will generate 7.5% a year compounded, guaranteed for the next five years. The inflation rate is currently 4.9%. Assuming the inflation rate remains the same for the period, what will the total value of the sum be in five years time in nominal terms? What will it be worth in real terms (in today's money)?

3. What kind of companies will you choose for your stock market investments if you suspect that inflation is going to increase steeply in the short term?

4. Where in the world will you seek stocks if you want to reap the best long-term returns over the next 20 years? Should you prefer countries which dominated the 20th century economy, such as the US, Germany and Japan, or economies that are set to emerge stronger in the future?

5. If stocks are the best investment option for investors, should one buy bonds at all?

RISKS IN OWNING EQUITY

T he main types of risk faced by the equity investor are:

1. Volatility Risk

2. Political Risk

3. Currency Risk

4. Company Risk

5. Transactional Risk

6. Liquidity Risk

VOLATILITY RISK

As we have seen, share prices fluctuate; even the share price of a strong company that has grown well for many years will usually show many unpredictable changes over the long term. The range of these fluctuations, or volatility, can be used as a measure of the risk of individual shares, industries and markets as a whole. We have seen, for example, that while US stocks produced losses, or a negative return, of -6.8% annually between 2000 and 2003, the long-term average return for US stocks between 1900 and 2003 was a positive 7.5%.

Volatility is not necessarily bad for investors. Many professionals actually attempt to achieve above-average returns by exploiting volatility — for example, by investing in the stocks of a country when they believe valuations to be unduly low, and selling them when they believe them to be too high. Private investors may profit by selling during periods of high prices; for example, individuals nearing retirement age who have flexibility over when to cash in their pension funds may do so when they believe the market to be high relative to its long-term performance. However, this is hard to do in practice, partly because future price movements are difficult to predict, but also because of psychological obstacles: if most other investors are gloomy about market prospects, it takes considerable courage to take an optimistic view.

A powerful argument for holding equity investments for a long period is that investors can "ride out" short-term volatility and achieve results that are closer to the long-term trends. This is a conservative approach to investment, and is appropriate for most private investors and the institutions, such as pension funds, that serve them. However, as one famous economist J. M. Keynes remarked, "in the long run we are all dead." Many investors hope for above-average returns and do not wish to wait for decades to achieve them. There are numerous strategies used in pursuit of above-average returns, but there is considerable doubt over whether they are consistently successful.

CASE STUDY: STOCK MARKET BUBBLES

Even the most knowledgeable people may not be able to recognize a stock market bubble. In December 1928, about ten months before the stock market crash, the then President of the United States Herbert Hoover said: "No Congress of the United States ever assembled, on surveying the State of the Union, has met with a more pleasing prospect than that which appears at the present time." The previous September, the Secretary of the Treasury said that there was no cause for worry and that the "high tide of prosperity will continue." In October, the chairman of a major steel company said: "In my long association with the steel industry I have never known it to enjoy a greater stability or more promising outlook than it does today." In August 1929, Colonel Leonard P. Ayers, Vice President of the Cleveland Trust

Company, said in his monthly economic bulletin: "This is truly a new era in which formerly self-established standards of value for securities no longer retain their old significance." Sounds like the "dot com" boom, doesn't it?

But there were some nay-sayers. In September 1929, Roger W. Babson, a well-known investment letter writer said: "Fair weather cannot always continue. The economic cycle is in progress today, as it was in the past. The Federal Reserve System has put the banks in a strong position, but it has not changed human nature. More people are borrowing and speculating today than ever in our history. Sooner or later a crash is coming and it may be terrific..." Opposing Babson's view in October, Professor Irving Fisher of Yale University, an economist famous for his work on cost of living indices, said: "Stock prices have reached what looks like a permanently high plateau. I do not feel that there will soon, if ever, be a fifty or sixty point break below present levels, such as Mr Babson has predicted." But soon thereafter, on October 29, a stock market panic later called "Black Thursday" hit and the market crashed. The fall continued after that and by the end of 1929, the stock market had fallen 28% from the peak, representing a loss of $25–26 billion. The economy was dragged down and the Great Depression ensued. By 1932, a quarter of the workforce was unemployed and the stock market had fallen by 80%, representing losses of $73 billion. Hundreds of thousands of investors and speculators were either wiped out or suffered tremendous losses. Many banks, railroads, utility companies and industrial firms went bankrupt. With so many suicides and people jumping out of tall buildings, someone joked that a steel umbrella was needed on Wall Street. One popular story was about a hotel clerk who asked a man requesting a room whether it was "For sleeping or jumping?"

"I realize, gentlemen, that thirty million dollars is a lot of money to spend. However, it's not real money and, of course, it's not our money either."

POLITICAL RISK

Political risk includes political instability and poor or discriminatory legal treatment for businesses and investors. A government may, for example, decide to repudiate its debt obligations. At worst, a radical change in government policy could lead to the confiscation of assets and the nationalization of privately owned firms. In any country there is some form of political risk since governments impose taxes of various kinds and regulate businesses. Changes in business regulations or taxation can impact a company dramatically. In addition, there is the problem of corruption. Investors may find that their lawful rights are violated as a result of corrupt law enforcement officials or corrupt courts.

In the area of public utilities, such as electric power companies or water supply companies, for example, a change in the regulations regarding what

OPINION: ELECTRIC POWER OR PROFITS?

"California: land of sunshine, movie stars and rolling blackouts. Unlike power failures caused by earthquakes or storms, California's short blackouts are planned. In recent months, the state has run desperately short of electricity, and authorities have turned to power rationing."

"How did California get into this mess? Until recently, two companies created and delivered all the state's electricity with relatively few problems. But the government decided that Southern California Edison and Pacific Gas & Electric (PG&E) and were monopolizing the energy market in the state. To open up the market to competition, the state legislature passed a law in 1996 that deregulated the industry. The idea was to allow customers to shop for an electricity supplier the same way they shop for long distance phone service. ...The deregulation law required

California utility companies to sell off their power generating plants and just stick to the delivery business. They still own thousands of miles of power lines, but have to buy the electricity itself wholesale from generating companies. In the past few months, wholesale power costs have skyrocketed to more than 10 times the normal price. That means utilities have to pay high prices to buy electricity. But under state law, they can't raise retail prices to customers. The California legislature put price caps on the amount customers can be charged. So while customers' electric bills have gone up noticeably, the higher prices don't even begin to cover the wholesale cost to the utility. Now the state's two major utilities are nearly bankrupt, while power generators enjoy big profits."

Source: *Public Broadcasting Service (PBS)* February 7, 2001

CASE STUDY: JOHN LAW AND THE MISSISSIPPI COMPANY

History is replete with stories of countries that experienced political upheavals resulting in huge losses to investors. In 1716, a Scotsman, John Law, was given permission by the French king to create a bank, the Bank Generale, which could issue paper money. In the following year he founded the Compagnie d'Occident to exploit trade in the resources of the vast French territories in Canada and along the Mississippi River. Law issued shares on behalf of the company and also government bonds. By 1720, Law had monopolies on all French trade outside Europe, the right to mint coins and the authority to collect taxes; he had created the world's first multinational conglomerate.

As speculation in his company's shares grew, Law printed money so that investors could buy more. During 1719, the shares had grown in value by 190%, but began to drop in the following year. Law's bank, now nationalized, promised to exchange its bank notes for the company shares at a specified price, causing rapid inflation. Apparently realizing his error, Law tried to devalue both the bank notes and the share price in an organized manner, but failed. As a result, by the end of the year the share price had collapsed and John Law had to escape from incensed investors.

Source: *The Stolen Prince* by High Barnes

Gannibal (Russian Peter the Great's adopted black African son and ancestor of Alexander Pushkin) while in France at that time invested in the scheme: *"Unwisely the african had bought shares in John Law's 'Mississippi Bubble' - or, more precisely, in his 'Company of the West', which held an exclusive right to develop France's territories in North America. (Ironically, Law's company also monopolised the French trade in African slaves). The use of paper money led to a wild frenzy of speculation in Paris, but the vaunted profits failed to materialise and inevitably the stock market crashed, leaving Gannibal with spiralling debts. Bankrupt, and the nation's scapegoat, Law was obliged to flee France. Soon Gannibal faced the same option but he was adamant that he was not to blame for his misfortune."*

Source: *The Stolen Prince* by High Barnes

tariffs such utilities can charge has a tremendous impact on the earnings of those companies. California power distribution companies were driven to the wall in 2004 when the wholesale market for power was opened but the price the distributors could charge their customers was fixed at a cost below what the utilities were required to pay.

CURRENCY RISK

Investors, whether domestic or international, face currency risks. If they invest only in their own country in their own country's currency, they could face a situation where there is hyperinflation and the currency depreciates against other currencies around the world. If the company in which the investor has invested depends on imported goods to sell directly in the market or on imported commodities to include in the products being manufactured, any depreciation in the local currency could be disastrous. Such companies are paid in local currency for their goods, but they may pay in foreign currency to import products or commodities. If they are unable to increase their product prices in line with the hyperinflation or to switch to locally produced products or raw materials, they could go out of business quickly.

If an investor invests internationally, he must know the relation of his home currency to the currency in the country where he purchases shares. Sometimes, he can benefit from such exchange rate changes, but at other times a change can wipe out all possible gains and can even result in losses. During the 1997 Asian currency crisis, for example, many countries in the Far East suffered sudden drops in the value of their currencies, triggering industrial chaos and huge investment losses.

Also important is the possibility of exchange controls. One of the major risks for foreign investors in such a scenario is that countries may choose to introduce exchange controls that prevent money, including profits, interest and dividends, from being withdrawn from the country. The Asian crisis in 1997 resulted in Malaysia imposing a ban on foreign exchange remittances out of the country. Foreign investors were therefore "locked" in the country for over a year without the possibility of getting their money out.

COMPANY RISK

A company is akin to an individual in many ways. All the risks relating to human behavior are embedded in company behavior, in addition to the

NEWS CLIP
TRANSPARENCY INTERNATIONAL

"The G-8 needs to show that they are in this fight to win. Wealthier countries can hardly call on their poorer neighbors to take the fight against corruption seriously when they themselves are unwilling to act," stated Transparency International chief executive, David Nussbaum.

Source: *Transparency International,* 16 September 2005

various environmental and social variables impacting companies. Johns-Manville was a reputable company providing quality building products, including asbestos insulation materials, for homes and offices. However, when it was discovered that asbestos caused cancer, the company was subject to billions of dollars of class action lawsuits, which resulted in its bankruptcy.

If information about a firm is insufficient or incorrect, investors may suffer unexpected losses from sudden drops in stock prices when any negative information is revealed. The South Sea Company, established in 1711 in England with a monopoly on trade in the South Seas, was intended to exploit opportunities in South America; by 1720 it was engaged in a successful but dishonest effort to drive up its share price, creating a public frenzy for investment, not only in South Sea Company shares but also in other dubious ventures. In August the share price reached 1,000 pounds; in September it had fallen to 175 pounds.

Enron was considered a successful and reputable company with leadership positions in energy supply and trading, not only in the US, but all over the world. Its success was hailed by investors and employees alike. It reputedly spent millions on its annual Christmas party at Enron Field, Houston's sports stadium named after the company.

There are a number of ways that clever company executives or controllers can cheat shareholders. Here are some of them:

MANAGERS HALT MALAYSIAN FUND DEALINGS

"Managers of funds specializing in Malaysia and South East Asia are being forced to suspend dealings after the imposition by the Malaysian government of capital controls. ...The details of the Malaysian controls are far from clear. The initial announcement suggested that the proceeds of share sales could not be repatriated unless the shares had been held for 12 months. However, managers say there are now indications that there will be a 12 month lock-in period from September 1 this year, making it impossible to repatriate funds until the autumn of 1999, however long the shares had previously been held. They are accordingly suspending dealing until the position becomes clear. In open-ended funds, such as mutual funds, SICAVs or unit trusts, investors deal directly with the manager. They face particular problems when markets become illiquid. When investors wish to sell holdings, the managers have to dispose of a proportion of their portfolios to meet such redemptions."

Source: *Financial Times (London)*, 4 September 1998

- **Transfer pricing:**
  It is relatively easy for companies involved in import and export to move cash flows to associated companies, which are outside the home country and which they surreptitiously control.

CASE STUDY: ENRON

In 2001 Enron was the seventh largest US corporation, dominating a global derivatives market in energy, communications and weather that the company itself had developed. A blue chip company with AAA-rated bonds, Enron had grown rapidly from relatively humble beginnings in 1985, when it was a Texas-based seller of natural gas and electricity. Enron had expanded during a period of deregulation of various utility markets across the world, becoming a global intermediary in wholesale energy and offering a wide range of contracts allowing customers to hedge against associated risks such as bad weather and interest rate changes.

Between 1996 and 2000, Enron reported an increase in sales from $13.3 billion to $100.8 billion as it implemented an ambitious business plan to make investments in energy assets, such as pipelines, around the world. Typically these investments required large sums upfront, but were not expected to generate significant cash flows for

many years. Enron now thought of itself as a "risk intermediation" company that was "asset-less," although it did in fact possess substantial assets, because it saw its activities as being essentially trading in risk.

With a large workforce (over 20,000 employees by 2001), Enron's board delegated much of the decision-making on deals to other managers, who had a free hand to make virtually any deal, in any industry, as long as it was thought likely to produce an acceptable return. This led to a series of disastrous investments, including a power plant in India that could not collect from its largest customer; the purchase of Wessex Water in the UK, which found itself hampered by price controls; and a water concession in Brazil that also ran into trouble. These major investments put pressure on Enron's high credit rating, which it needed to sustain in order to continue its energy trading.

In response to these pressures, Enron became increasingly enmeshed in questionable accounting practices. The firm's third quarter earnings for 2001 failed to provide a balance sheet and excluded $1.01 billion of expenses and losses from its earnings figures by describing them as "non-recurring." It later emerged that Enron was using many special purpose entities (SPEs) to conceal losses of over $1 billion and to time or backdate transactions to improve quarterly figures. These SPEs were a means, in effect, to disguise the true picture by keeping many transactions "off-balance sheet," hiding poorly performing assets and managing earnings in line with Wall Street analysts' expectations. Enron was also using a loophole to report the gross value of its derivatives deals as income, rather than their net value, as is normally the case in financial securities deals. This vastly inflated its sales figures. Analysis of sales per employee shows that, in 2000, Enron was allegedly generating over $5 million per employee; a figure that dwarfed the ratio in other successful companies such as Microsoft (just over $600,000 per employee) and Citigroup (just under $500,000).

US "mark-to-market" accounting rules require companies to report securities on the balance sheet at their current market values, rather than their original acquisition cost. For some derivatives, complex mathematical formulae are used to estimate a market value that is often unverifiable. Enron had to make a large number of assumptions about future demand, price variation, interest rates and so on, and typically made optimistic choices that improved cash flow figures.

On November 8, 2001, Enron announced that it had overstated earnings over the prior four years by almost $600 million and had $3 billion in liabilities to SPEs. Enron's investment-grade bonds were downgraded to "junk" and a wave of accounting scandals erupted. Arthur Andersen, Enron's auditor, collapsed after being found guilty of deliberately destroying accounting documents and correspondence related to its Enron account. Enron's stock price dropped from $85 to $0.30 during 2001, while revelations of tax evasion, political bribery and insider dealing led to ongoing criminal investigations.

Figure 3.1 — Six General Counsels or Partners who worked for the Enron Corporation are sworn in before the US House of Representatives Committee on Energy and Commerce on 14 March, 2002, on Capitol Hill in Washington during investigations into the Enron scandal.

Source: AFP PHOTO Paul J. Richards

- **Transfer of assets:**
  Some countries give directors a free hand in how they deal with company assets. In some cases, the assets of listed companies have been transferred secretly into the hands of insiders without the minority shareholders knowing about it.

- **Share dilution:**
  When a company issues more shares, care must be taken to ensure that the new issue does not reduce the value of the existing shares by "diluting" their value. This has been a problem in the US due to the use of stock options, but it also occurs in other countries where insiders have issued new shares to themselves, or to companies they control, at low prices, thus diluting the value and voting power of the existing shares.

- **Service fees or royalty charges:**
  Powerful insiders can charge the company for "administrative" or "service" fees and thus obtain illicit profits. In Brazil, the family controlling a listed company decided to pass a resolution calling for the family to be paid a fee for the use of their name in the company's name.

TWO ARE CHARGED IN CRIMINAL CASE ON STOCK OPTIONS

SAN FRANCISCO, July 20 — Federal prosecutors on Thursday filed the first criminal charges against executives in a mushrooming investigation into the possible manipulation of stock options.

Gregory L. Reyes, the chief executive of Brocade Communications until January 2005, and Stephanie Jensen, the vice president for human resources until 2004, were each charged in a criminal complaint with one count of securities fraud. Prosecutors said the two doctored the minutes of board meetings, job-offer letters and other documents to make it appear that employees were granted stock options at an earlier date, when the share price of Brocade was lower. The Securities and Exchange Commission also filed a civil complaint, which named Brocade's former chief financial officer, Antonio Canova, as well as the other two executives. So far, federal prosecutors in San Francisco, Manhattan and Brooklyn have opened more than 33 cases looking at potential accounting problems or fraud; the Securities and Exchange Commission is examining at least 80 companies. More than a dozen senior executives have been dismissed. "Nearly every company has been reviewing its practices."

An option gives the holder the right to buy shares of stock at a predetermined price in the future, commonly the market price on the date they were granted. Instead of offering higher salaries, companies sometimes prefer to lure potential hires with stock options, conserving company cash. ...

According to the criminal and civil complaints filed Thursday in Federal District Court in San Jose, Calif., Mr. Reyes routinely backdated documents to provide new employees with a larger compensation package. Brocade, a maker of data storage networking products, is based in San Jose.

...The criminal charge carries a penalty of as much as 20 years in prison and a fine of $5 million.

Source: *New York Times* by Damon Darlin and Eric Dash, July 21, 2006

- **Buy low to sell back at a higher price:**
  A straightforward fraud is for insiders to put a viable company into liquidation and then to buy up the shares at distressed prices. In one case in Malaysia, the company's management persuaded the Board of Directors that one of the company's subsidiaries was worthless and it would be best to sell it. The management surreptitiously purchased the assets at a cheap price and then a few years later sold them back to the company for a big profit.

BANKRUPTCY

A company's creditors are usually eager to recoup their money as quickly as possible, so the assets are often sold for a fraction of the price the company originally paid for them. This makes it difficult, at the outset, to estimate accurately the amount of cash that can be raised from liquidation. Payouts may be made in stages as assets are sold off, but stockholders do not usually receive any money until other creditors have been paid in full; as investors in a company, they have taken on the risk that the company may go bankrupt and that their investment may be lost.

In the US there are two main types of bankruptcy: "Chapter 11" and "Chapter 7." If a company files for bankruptcy under Chapter 7, it ceases trading and an official is appointed to sell off (liquidate) its assets. The liquidator uses the money raised to pay off the company's debts in a strictly prescribed order:

- "Secured" creditors, such as banks that have lent money to the company against assets such as buildings, are paid first.

- "Unsecured" creditors, such as trade suppliers and people who have bought the company's bonds, are paid next.

- Lastly, the stockholders are paid. So if you are a holder of shares in the company, you are most likely to end up with nothing.

Chapter 11 bankruptcy allows a company to reorganize itself and escape from costly deals (for example, from leases and other contracts that it cannot afford). Often the company continues to run its business, but under the supervision of the bankruptcy court. Chapter 11 protects a company from its creditors, who cannot foreclose on its assets or take it to court for non-payment. The company must make a plan for how it will settle or escape from its debts, and this must be accepted by the creditors, stockholders, bondholders and the bankruptcy court. The court can overrule the other parties if some of them do not accept the plan.

Under Chapter 11, the court may allow the company's shares and bonds to continue to be traded on the stock market, but often the company no longer fulfils the stock exchange requirements, in which case it is de-listed

A BRIEF HISTORY OF BANKRUPTCY IN THE US

In medieval Italy, when a businessman did not pay his debts, it was the practice to destroy his trading bench. From the Italian for broken bench, "banca rotta," comes the term bankruptcy.

Before the 20th century, rules and practices concerning bankruptcy generally favored the creditor and were very harsh toward the bankrupt. The focus was on recovering the investments of the creditors and almost all bankruptcies at this time were involuntary. In England, the first official laws concerning bankruptcy were passed in 1542, under Henry VIII. A bankrupt individual was considered a criminal and was subject to criminal punishment. Potential punishments ranged from incarceration in debtors prison to the death penalty.

Modern bankruptcy laws and practices in the United States emphasize rehabilitating (reorganizing) debtors in distress.

The Bankruptcy Act of 1898 was the first to give companies in distress an option of being protected from creditors. The company could be put in an "equity receivership." This reorganization provision was made much more formal and extensive in the United States during the 1930s. The economic upheaval of the Great Depression yielded much bankruptcy legislation, in particular, the Bankruptcy Act of 1933 and the Bankruptcy Act of 1934. This legislation culminated with the Chandler Act of 1938. This included substantial provisions for reorganization of businesses.

On October 22, 1994, the Bankruptcy Reform Act of 1994 (Public Law 103-394, October 22, 1994), the most comprehensive piece of bankruptcy legislation since the 1978 Act, was signed into law by President Clinton.

Source: *The 2001 Bankruptcy Yearbook & Almanac, BankruptcyData.com.*

and removed from the stock market. A company's securities may, however, still be traded on the over-the-counter market.

Occasionally a company will offer a restructuring plan to its creditors and shareholders before going bankrupt; this is registered with the Securities and Exchange Commission (SEC) if new securities are to be issued and, if

CASE STUDY: CAN INVESTORS PROFIT FROM BUYING DISTRESSED STOCK?

In general, this is a risky undertaking that is only suitable for specialists. Although some companies do eventually emerge from Chapter 11 bankruptcy, usually it is the creditors who own the new shares as a partial compensation for their losses. The plan for reorganization that a bankrupt company prepares often cancels all existing shares, and even if the old shareholders do receive some shares, they are likely to be diluted by the creditors' new holdings.

Some situations do offer opportunities for specialist investors, however, because they are able to purchase stock at rock-bottom prices. Companies that are making profits before interest charges, for example, may be attractive because if they restructure their financing, they may become viable concerns.

In general, investors in such companies look for:

- A good underlying business that can be revived and sustained.

- Managers — possibly a new team — who can make the necessary changes and see the recovery process through.

- An estimated recovery time that is acceptable — this depends on the price paid for the stock, but normally it would be no more than two or three years.

- A very low stock price; this increases the potential gains from success.

- Distressed stock, however, tends to be highly illiquid and would be difficult to sell if the new investors change their minds, so risks are high and hard to estimate accurately.

successful, it substantially reduces the period and the costs of bankruptcy. For example, some leveraged buyouts (LBOs), which were popular in the 1980s, subsequently came to grief because of the enormous burden of debt they had taken on. Some troubled LBOs were able to restructure their debt voluntarily by persuading creditors to accept losses.

As mentioned earlier, companies in Chapter 11 bankruptcy temporarily suspend all payments to creditors — this includes interest payments to bondholders and dividend payments to shareholders. Most publicly quoted companies in the US choose Chapter 11 because it allows their securities to continue to be traded and gives them more control over the efforts to reorganize. If their securities are still listed, they must continue to file company reports with the SEC. Such reports may be of some value to the concerned investors.

LIQUIDITY RISK

"Suspension" means that trading of the shares in the market is stopped. The idea is to level the playing field when there is uncertainty about a company, giving time for all investors to find out what is going on without giving some investors advantages over others.

 CASE STUDY: **CRAZY EDDIE**

Crazy Eddie Inc. operated more than twenty electronics stores in the New York area in 1986. Heavily advertised on TV, the company had caught Wall Street's attention; its stock had risen from $4.50 in late 1984 to $37.50 in mid-1986. The firm did not own its stores but leased them — some of them from Crazy Eddie Antar's relatives. It had also conducted extensive business with other companies owned by relatives, even making them loans. Prior to going public in 1984, the firm had also made sizeable interest-free loans to some of the Antars who were officers of the company, including Crazy Eddie himself. There was a very generous stock option plan for the CEO and some other family members.

When Crazy Eddie announced that he was moving into the TV home shopping business, the stock price jumped to $40. Analysts recommended the stock as a buy, and continued to anticipate rapid growth. In October, Crazy Eddie warned that third quarter earnings might be below estimates, and shortly afterwards the second quarter's figures were released, showing revenues up by 42% but also a heavy increase in inventory holdings and more stock options for insiders.

In early January 1987, Eddie Antar resigned from the company. The stock price collapsed to $10, and when the fourth quarter figures for 1986 were released in April 1987, it was clear that earnings were dropping and margins had shrunk. The next month, Eddie Antar made a takeover bid for the company, offering $7 a share, only to have it topped by another entrepreneur. Antar's bid collapsed as more damaging information appeared in time-delayed SEC reports, revealing, among other things, that Eddie Antar had continued to receive his salary after he had resigned.

The company was taken over by the rival bidder, Elias Zinn, in November 1987, who immediately audited the inventory; inventory worth some $65 million was missing. The new owners accused Eddie of false accounting, building an illusion that the company had been far more profitable than it really was. The company filed for bankruptcy in 1989, by which time Antar was on the run.

Crazy Eddie Inc. had:

- Produced false invoices reporting fictitious sales

- Encouraged employees and suppliers to lie to auditors

- Inflated inventory figures by borrowing merchandise from suppliers

- Concealed debts

- Altered auditors' worksheets without their knowledge

The danger is that the suspension can last for years, which means that you are stuck with a shareholding that you cannot sell and that you cannot claim as a tax loss. However, suspensions are sometimes used in happy circumstances too, such as when a bid is in the air, to allow time for all the information to reach the investors.

Some majority controllers deliberately set out to reduce liquidity by purchasing the company's shares in the market, reducing the "free float" and liquidity of the market. Investors are thus left with no one to sell the shares to, except the people who control the company, without giving some investors advantages over others.

TRANSACTIONAL RISK

The functioning of a stock market depends heavily on smooth, well-run systems for processing the buying and selling of securities. Settlement processes and money transfers by share custodians and share registrars must be efficient and accurate. Errors in the records can result in losses to investors. To prevent fraudulent activities, many investors now demand "delivery against payment" (DVP) terms when buying or selling shares. In other words, the shares must be delivered at the same time as the payment is made and vice versa, so that both sides in the transaction are protected. This is to avoid the problems experienced in the past where brokers completed a share purchase and accepted the money for the trade, but then were unable to deliver the share scrip because their bookkeeping was not in order or because the counterparty seller failed to deliver the shares to them. There have been instances where brokerage companies went bankrupt, transactions worth millions of dollars were stymied and client assets frozen.

CASE STUDY: SAVED FROM THE COLD CALLING BROKER

NEW YORK — James Pipoly admits he was suckered once by the cold-calling broker with "a real exciting tone in his voice." The 47-year-old novice investor said he felt duped again when that same broker suddenly went belly-up, without the slightest heads up. It was as if, in one fell swoop, someone had snatched away his pride — and his $70,000-plus portfolio. "And the worst part," he added, recalling his stunned reaction at the time, "is that there isn't a damn thing you can do about it."

Pipoly, a Youngstown, Ohio, businessman, wondered the same thing on the day in November 1997 when a bankruptcy trustee appointed by the Securities Investors Protection Corporation (SIPC) phoned him out of the blue with the sobering news that a bankruptcy court had declared his onetime broker legally insolvent. Striking a solicitous note, the caller told Pipoly not to fret; the SIPC had a salvage crew at the ready. All he needed to do was fill out a claim form for his wayward stock. And wait. And hope. "I was kind of surprised, because when I talked to my attorney, he said, 'you'll have to pay $8,000 to $10,000 (in legal fees to get the shares back)," Pipoly said. "I never knew anything like this was available out there."

Neither do most jilted investors. Yet the SIPC, a federally chartered non-governmental and non-profit agency, has been out there since 1971, helping customers left in the lurch by bankrupt brokers to get their cash and securities back.

Born of the 1970 Securities Investors Protection Act, the industry-sponsored SIPC functions much like the Federal Deposit Insurance Corp. (FDIC), except it bails out stockholders instead of banks. The SIPC covers customers for a maximum of up to $500,000 each, including $100,000 in cash held in accounts for the purpose of buying securities.

The agency owes its existence to a grim Wall Street reality — securities occasionally outlast the brokers entrusted with their safekeeping. Hence, when brokers go bust, they run the risk of bequeathing a sizable stack of blue chips to oblivion.

Unless reclaimed, these orphaned securities exist only as electronic blips, gathering virtual dust in some computer database, or, more quaintly, as dog-eared paper documents languishing in some forgotten vault. Even an aboveboard broker can go under. Reasons for bankruptcy can range from a failure to meet standard requirements for net capital to book-entry problems or a simple computer glitch.

Source: *Cnn.fn*

 SUMMARY

Industries, economic systems and countries have risen and then fallen in ways that were not foreseen. For most investors, the essential challenge is how to protect and add to their wealth in a steady and stable manner. For businesses, it is how to survive and prosper in the unpredictable and ever-changing market conditions.

The investor who purchases a share in a company provides risk capital and thus takes the risk of losing all his investment, just like the other shareholders. Share prices can go down as well as up and they are affected by numerous risks. The ultimate possibility for shareholders is total loss.

1. You are the CEO of a company. A customer firm tells you that they would like to increase their orders by 100% a month, but they will need to take 90 days credit from now on. Do you agree immediately, ask for special conditions, or refuse altogether? Explain your reasons, stating what conditions you might impose, if any.

2. Do you think the collapse of Enron could have been prevented if the wrong-doings had come to light earlier? At what point could it have been saved?

3. As a newly appointed CEO of a chain of retail stores, you discover that the company is losing thousands of dollars every month because of stock "shrinkages" in the warehouse and items "disappearing" from stores. Who might be responsible? What measures would you take to reduce these losses? Can you eliminate them entirely?

4. Your boss owns a group of companies, all with slightly different accounting dates. He uses different auditors for each company and is constantly changing accounting methods. What could be his motive?

5. Do investment strategies have to be necessarily short-term in countries where the political risk is high?

REDUCING RISK

E quity is inherently riskier compared to many other assets. However, several tools help mitigate the risk of investing in stocks.

RESEARCH

Along with the growth of the stock markets in various countries, the global financial services industry has also grown rapidly. As more and more countries liberalize their financial markets, thousands of new employees are being hired by growing financial services firms such as brokers, investment banks, financial news services, and equity research companies. They hire some of the world's smartest and well-trained people, compensating them well, both through high salaries and generous bonus schemes. Their knowledge and skills are now available to investors. Some investors have made fortunes in equities by using this storehouse of knowledge and combining it with their own disciplined investment approach.

SHAREHOLDER RIGHTS

Normally, shareholders have certain rights, such as the right to part of the profits in the form of dividends. In many countries, companies are required to treat their shareholders fairly and non-preferentially. Every shareholder should be able to:

- Obtain company information easily and examine company accounts

- Be protected from company "insiders" or controllers who may take advantage of their inside knowledge or control

- Participate in major decisions and vote at shareholder meetings, if the shareholder has voting shares

- Share the profits of the company through dividend payments

- Approve directors' and auditors' appointments/dismissals by majority vote

- Vote on any action that might dilute the value of their shareholdings, such as the issue of new shares

In addition, shareholders also have "pre-emptive" rights in certain situations, such as when a new share issue is contemplated. This enables them to have equal rights to purchase the new shares, thereby ensuring that there is no dilution of the economic or voting rights of the existing shareholders.

All of these conditions are not only often embedded in the by-laws or the charter of the company, but are also often defined in the laws of the country where the company is incorporated or chartered. But it must be noted that corporations can have different types of shares with different rights.

Protecting shareholders' rights, in the widest sense, is the essence of corporate governance and proper management of firms. Unfortunately, some governments around the world stifle efforts to protect shareholder rights.

One example of how government bodies restrict the rights of shareholders can be seen in the European Community's law for mutual funds, the UCITS (Undertakings for the Collective Investment of Transferable Securities) III of December 20, 2002, which prohibits a fund from investing in companies in order to influence the management of that company. Art. 48(1) of this law expressly states that: "...an investment company or a management company acting in connection with all of the common funds which it manages and which fall within the scope of Part 1 of the law, may not acquire any shares carrying voting rights which would enable it to exercise significant influence over the management of an issuing body."

In Luxembourg, the leading venue of mutual funds in Europe, the rule-making body is the CSSF (Commission of Monitoring of the Financial Sector). The Luxembourg authorities interpret the provisions of the UCITS directive in a more limited way so that an investment company may not acquire a specific percent of a company's shares carrying voting rights that will enable it to exercise "significant influence" over the management of a company in which it is invested.

DOLLAR COST AVERAGING

Since the short-term movements of equity markets are largely unpredictable, one clever mechanism for avoiding the pitfall of buying too high or selling too low is to engage in what is called "dollar cost averaging." This is simply a program of purchasing or selling shares at regularly spaced time intervals using the same amount of money each time. So, for example, if an investor wanted to purchase $10,000 worth of Company A shares, he would decide to purchase the shares over a 10-month period and then use $1,000 each month to purchase the shares at whatever price was prevalent at that time.

The average cost would thus even out and there would be no risk of purchasing only at the high point of the market when everyone (including the investor) was optimistic.

FINANCIAL PLANNING AND PROFESSIONAL HELP

For the majority of private individuals who are able to invest part of their assets in the stock market, the most realistic approach is to devise an investment program, if necessary with the aid of financial advisers, which is tailor-made for the investor's personal circumstances. This should aim for capital growth over a period of, say, 10 to 20 years during the working life of the investor, who can then weight the portfolio towards gaining income after retirement. This approach seeks not to accumulate vast riches, but to amass a capital sum by retirement age that can generate sufficient income to pay for most or all of the investor's living expenses during retirement.

The great advantage of this approach is that it is relatively safe; small private investors who seek to make large gains through a series of high-risk, unplanned speculations often perform far worse in the long term than the "steady" investor who saves what she can out of her monthly income over many years and puts it in a sound investment program. Most often, such programs make extensive use of professionally managed mutual funds, which offer numerous advantages for the small, part-time investor.

DIVERSIFICATION

Investors have a number of strategies available to them to reduce the risks of investment, and chief among them is diversification. The world of share investing today is very large, with many markets and companies available to investors. Therefore, the opportunity to diversify is greater today than ever before.

Diversification is the process of spreading the total investment money available across different asset classes, countries, industries and individual companies. Diversification also entails choosing investments that are, as far as possible, negatively correlated, which means that when investment A is performing poorly, investment B is likely to be performing well.

CORPORATE GOVERNANCE

Probably the most effective but least used tools to reduce risk when investing in publicly listed companies is corporate governance. For any investor, one of the most obvious risks that presents itself when making an investment

> **OPINION**
> # BASKETS AND MONEY
>
> *The best way to be safe is not to put all your eggs in one basket. But if you want to make a lot of money and have the time and intelligence, then you can put all your eggs in one basket... but watch that basket carefully!*

Figure 4.1 — Former Enron CEO Ken Lay listens to opening statements on 11 February 2002 before the Senate Committee on Commerce, Science and Transportation on Capitol Hill in Washington, DC. Lay took the 5th amendment and refused to answer any questions.

Source: AFP PHOTO/ Shawn THEW

decision is whether the company will be honestly managed and, more importantly, managed in the interests of all the shareholders, particularly the minority shareholders. Senior managers of any firm, but in particular of large, publicly listed companies, are often in powerful positions—which enables them to act in their own interests rather than in those of their company's shareholders.

For investors and fund managers, the primary concern is how companies treat shareholders, particularly minority shareholders. Ideally, an investor should be able to purchase shares with confidence, and without fear of loss through corruption or mismanagement. In this narrow sense, corporate governance will continue to remain a matter for serious concern indefinitely, since legislation and self-regulation can never completely eradicate the potential for abuse. Nevertheless, various studies have demonstrated that well-governed companies attract investors and have improved performance; so much so, that one can say there is often a share price premium for good governance.

Over the many years that corporations have been in existence, a structure has been established that attempts to provide safety and security for the various shareholders so that the company is managed according to their collective wishes, and so that they may obtain the maximum benefits from the company's operations in the short, medium and long term. With the spread of financial deregulation and globalization over the last 25 years, there have been increased efforts to find ways to improve voluntary codes of corporate governance practice.

In 1997, the Asian economic crisis revealed serious flaws in corporate governance and financial reporting that had contributed to the collapse of several economies in the region. More recently, corporate scandals in the US, such as Enron, WorldCom and AIG, demonstrated that even the most financially sophisticated countries have problems with corporate governance. On June 25, 2002, for example, WorldCom announced that it had overstated its earnings by more than $3.8 billion during the previous five quarters, mainly by improperly accounting for its operating costs.

These scandals led to extensive investigations and prosecutions by New York's Attorney General, Mark Spitzer, and the passage of the Sarbanes-Oxley Act in the US, which laid down strong requirements for company officers and directors with heavy penalties for violations.

As globalization progresses, the stakes are increasing and there are fears that the long-term credibility of the free market system could be seriously undermined if better standards of corporate governance are not established internationally. In 1999, the OECD (Organization for Economic Cooperation and Development) issued the OECD Principles for Corporate Governance, which is probably the most comprehensive and authoritative exposition of good corporate governance principles. These principles were ratified by 29 member states. The main elements of these principles are as follows:

- **Fairness:**
  Shareholders should be treated fairly, especially foreign and minority shareholders.

- **Transparency:**
  Sufficient company information should be disclosed for investors to make informed decisions.

 TERMINOLOGY

TRANSPARENCY – Transparency is used to mean greater openness in the way institutions work. In finance, for example, there are calls for greater transparency in many areas, such as company statements, brokerage fees, banking charges and stock pricing. Governments, too, are promoting greater transparency in national and international organizations, emphasizing the need for better public access to information and better explanations of how agencies work. While many people think that maximum transparency is desirable, some argue that it is in the nature of any organization, administrative or commercial, to seek to conceal information; it remains to be seen if the current fashion for greater transparency can succeed in the long term.

CASE STUDY: SARBANES-OXLEY

The Sarbanes-Oxley Act was enacted by the US government in July 2002 in response to a series of major corporate financial scandals, including those affecting Enron, Tyco International, and WorldCom. It is intended to provide better protection for investors by tightening up the regulations on company disclosures to improve their accuracy. The Sarbanes-Oxley Act, also known as "SOX" and "Sarbox," is widely seen as the biggest reform of US securities law since the New Deal was introduced in the 1930s to address the problems of the Great Depression. SOX is a combination of two bills that had been introduced independently by Representative Michael G. Oxley in April 2002 and Senator Paul Sarbanes in June 2002.

The main provisions of SOX are:

- CEOs' and CFOs' compensation and profits must be fully reported

- CEOs and CFOs must certify the accuracy of financial reports

- Legal trades by insiders must be reported more quickly

- No insider trades are allowed during pension fund blackout periods

- No executive officers or directors may borrow personally from their company

- All public companies must provide independent annual audit reports on the existence and reliability of internal controls on financial reporting

- Measures must be taken to improve the independence of auditors, including the mandatory rotation of auditors every five years

- Auditors are banned from providing other services to companies, such as actuarial, legal and consulting services

- Increased and extended penalties for securities violations

- Longer prison sentences and other penalties for corporate executives who knowingly make false financial statements

OPINION
WHY INTRODUCE SARBANES-OXLEY?

"At the margin, the U.S. system of mandatory corporate governance regulations appears to contribute little, or nothing... Take for example, the (mandatory) provision in U.S. law that requires public companies to produce financial statements that have been audited by independent accounting firms... Independent accounting firms are thought to be unlikely to permit (or acquiesce in) fraud because it is not in their economic interests to do so. The gains from participating with a client in any such fraud are, in theory, greatly outweighed by the losses to the accounting firm's reputation that would follow from being implicated in a fraudulent accounting scheme. Unfortunately a combination of factors, including: (a) the consolidation of the accounting industry into a highly concentrated cartel-like structure; (b) the elimination of accounting firm partners, incentives to monitor their firms due to the transformation of accounting firms from general partnerships to limited liability partnerships; and (c) the organization of accounting firms into audit teams comprised of auditors who serve only one corporate client, led to the demise of the public firm as gatekeeper...

...Sarbanes-Oxley was a measured and appropriate response to the abject failures in U.S. corporate governance typified by Enron... The corporate governance crisis in America, with Enron as its poster child, represents a failure of both our system of mandatory rules, and of the contracting processes, which, together, constitute the infrastructure of the U.S. corporate governance system."

Source: Jonathan R. Macey, *Washington University Law Quarterly, Summer 2003. vol 81*

- **Accountability:**
  The responsibility for governance should be clear, and efforts should be made to align the interests of company managers and their shareholders.

- **Responsibility:**
  Companies should comply with the other laws and regulations in the countries within which they operate.

SHAREHOLDER ACTIVISM

As the number of shareholders has grown, it has become more and more difficult for shareholders to exercise control over corporations. With thousands of shareholders, coordination of control by the rightful owners of the corporation has become difficult, if not impossible. With the introduction of proxy voting (where the voting share of absent shareholders is given to another party, in many cases the management), professional managers often take control and exercise their own discretion over the corporation. This has resulted in continuing debates regarding who controls the corporation and how shareholders can exercise their control.

Many shareholders are now becoming more active in demanding their rights, with the result that there has been a gradual change in management attitudes. With the rise of private equity funds and hedge funds with large assets under their management, the strength of minority shareholders and their influence on management has grown.

Figure 4.2 — Nicolas Miguet, a French investment adviser who led the rebel shareholders, flashes the victory sign on 7th April 2004 upon his arrival in Villepinte, outside Paris, where Channel tunnel operator Eurotunnel's mainly French minority shareholders gathered for their general assembly. The shareholder revolt at Eurotunnel resulted in the sacking of the board and the installation of new directors to revamp the business, its pricing structure and debt arrangements. The company's debt could lead, theoretically, to bankruptcy at the beginning of 2007.

Source: AFP Photo

CASE STUDY: THE GILBERT BROTHERS

One example of shareholders fighting for their rights can be seen in the famous Gilbert Brothers, Lewis and John. Lewis, who died in 1993, first attended an annual shareholders meeting in 1932. When the management refused to answer any questions, he was angry and became an activist. He and his brother, who has also since died, together went to as many as 100 annual meetings a year challenging corporate directors and executives on behalf of shareholders. A number of shareholder rights now embedded in laws and regulations can be attributed to their activism. For example, they urged the SEC to allow shareholders to distribute their management criticisms at the company's expense by submitting shareholder proposals to be included in proxy voting. They also battled for shareholder approval of auditors, confidential voting so that shareholders could not be coerced, cumulative voting so that minority shareholders could elect one director to the board and holding annual meetings in places where it was convenient for shareholders to attend. They were among the first to object to excessive CEO pay packages.

Institutional investors, such as pension funds, mutual funds, endowments and insurance companies, are estimated to hold as much as half of the stock of many publicly traded companies. Many, if not most, have the attitude that they do not want to take the time or resources to monitor corporate governance violations. But attitudes are changing and there are notable examples of major institutional investors putting more emphasis on corporate governance and taking action. There is, of course, the problem of conflicts of interest. For example, a pension fund manager for an automobile company pension might not want to take action against a major part supplier of the auto company. Institutional investors are happy to reap the benefits of activism, but with some exceptions they normally don't want to take the leading position. Therefore, individual investors can play a very important role since they do not normally have to worry about conflicts of interest or appearances. With the Internet, shareholders can communicate with each other and form powerful groups to protect their shareholder interests. One example of this occurred in 2000, when individual shareholders of Luby's, the Texas cafeteria chain, used a Yahoo! message board to mount a campaign to oust the chief executive officer of that company.

"This is the part of capitalism I hate."

RISK AND REWARD

Risk and reward are linked. Investing in equities that have high risk or volatility relative to the market average can bring better-than-average rewards to the investor. Although in the very long term (holding stocks for a century, say) the volatility of stocks "regresses to the mean" and approaches the long-term average, the performance of stocks with high volatility can be very different from the average. For example, investors who invested in the most volatile stocks (the "top decile," or top 10%, in Figure 4.3) achieved substantially better or worse returns than the average, even if they held for relatively long periods (10–20 years).

Although the investment results tend to converge to the mean in the very long term, those investors who follow riskier investment strategies by investing in the most volatile stocks may obtain better returns during their investing lives than those who pick less volatile or less risky stocks. Of course, that all depends on the investor's ability to pick stocks that are likely to do well. If the investor picks the wrong stocks and they are highly volatile, the results will be worse than the average. One advantage in picking the highly volatile stocks is that they may tend to be less closely researched and examined by investors, so well-informed investors who take the time to look at such stocks may be able to more easily pick overlooked winners.

THE SAFETY OF LISTED COMPANIES

Companies that are listed on stock exchanges are easier to examine and study because it is mandatory for them to give critical information to regulators

Figure 4.3 — Dispersion of real returns on US equities over periods of 10–105 years

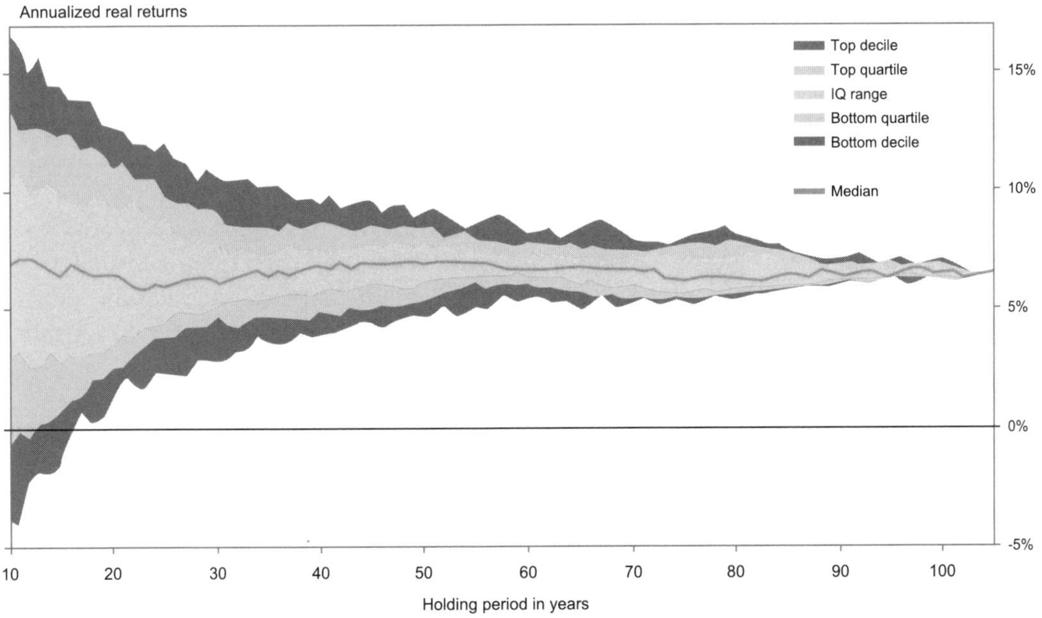

Annualized real returns

Source: Dimson, Marsh and Staunton, Triump of the Optimists: 101 Years of Global Investment Returns, Princeton University Press, 2002 and subsequent research

and investors. Therefore, it is easier to spot problems in such companies. Of course, there is no guarantee that investors in listed companies will not be cheated. It is just that the opportunities for investors to protect themselves are far greater with listed companies than with private, unlisted companies where disclosure obligations to the public or to the shareholders are much fewer, if they exist at all.

Any company can go bankrupt, but the warning signals may be easier to detect in public companies than in private companies. Although the data regarding the safety of investments in private and public companies are sketchy, indications are that private companies go bankrupt more often than public companies. Consulting firm PricewaterhouseCoopers found that in 2001, 257 public companies and 9,928 private companies filed for bankruptcy under Chapter 11. The odds of losing money by investing in a private company are higher than those of losing by investing in a public company simply because there are more private companies to choose from. Of course, this does not mean that private companies are of lower quality than public companies. It is just that various, and often stringent, requirements for listing a company on a stock exchange usually translate into better critical variables such as stronger balance sheets and a history of profitability for such listed companies. Studies also indicate that if they go bankrupt, public companies are more likely to survive and return to viability than private companies. In the PricewaterhouseCoopers study, a higher percentage of public companies emerged from bankruptcy than did private companies.

SUMMARY

Shareholders face many risks. How can they protect themselves against them? History has shown us that there will never be complete protection. Human nature and company behavior have foibles, many of which cannot be predicted or anticipated.

Equities, by definition, carry risk. For an investor in equities, risk cannot be eliminated altogether. However, it can be contained through tools such as research, professional advice, diversification, financial planning, shareholder activism through the application of shareholder rights and investment tactics such as dollar cost averaging.

A number of scandals involving some large corporations have led to concerted efforts aimed at promoting better corporate governance, a key risk reduction tool. While risk and reward are linked, investing in highly volatile stocks that are likely to do well could boost returns even in the long term.

A close examination prior to investing is one of the best preventive measures. Investors must remember four valuable words: Investigate before you invest!

QUICK QUIZ

1. Why does the world still not have a set of universally acceptable "Principles for Corporate Governance"? What will it take to have one?

2. Does diversification indicate lack of adequate research or lack of confidence in one's judgment? Should one diversify investments when one knows what surely the "best" investment is for one's goals?

3. What prevents every investor from becoming a shareholder activist like one of the Gilbert Brothers?

4. If you bought 10 shares for $1,000 this month through dollar cost averaging, how much money would you invest next month, if the share prices move up 20%?

5. Your brother lives in an economically troubled, politically unstable country. Recently it has decided to privatize a government company. The company's bonds have been rated below investment grade. A local banker has advised your brother to invest his life savings in these bonds because he says they are safe, although they offer a relatively low return. Would you invest? Give reasons.

6. Would you advise your grandmother, who is 90 and is keen on investing in equities, to invest in A, a low volatility stock of an average company, or B, a high-volatility stock of a well performing company?

5

UNDERSTANDING CORPORATE BEHAVIOR

Corporate behavior includes an entire range of activities: planning, management, ownership, control, customers, staff, etc. Serious investors spend a lot of time trying to understand corporate behavior, which might reveal what financial statements or other reports do not. For example, it may appear that the managing director of a company is making all the key decisions; but there may be a majority or even minority shareholder who is actually directing the company from behind the scenes. We have to understand such people and their motives. Is the majority shareholder directing the company towards a sale to competitors? Would he like his son to take over? How many family members are involved in the company? Are there conflicts of interest? Who does the company buy from? Is it a related party? Who does it sell to? Who are its customers? What is the distribution system? Is the company selling through a distributor owned by the majority shareholder? Is the staff happy? Are the unions getting ready to strike? Answers to these questions would help an investor gain a better insight into a company, and would therefore lead to better decisions.

COMPANY STRUCTURES

In the Anglo-Saxon corporate model followed in the US, UK and many other nations with historical British or American influences, every listed company has a Board of Directors, which is voted in by the shareholders. Unfortunately, not all shareholders always have equal voting rights. Therefore, it is possible that one group of shareholders may gain control of the board. Even if all shareholders have equal voting rights, in many companies the concept of proportional board representation does not operate. This means that the shareholders with the most votes have the power to select the entire board rather than only a part of the board proportionate to their shareholding size.

In publicly traded companies, the board should include non-executive directors (people who do not either work for the company or do business with the company) so that they can be independent and look after the interests of all the shareholders. Under most legal jurisdictions, companies must hold annual general meetings in which shareholders can vote on major issues, either in person or by proxy, and must issue detailed financial statements. These financial statements must comply with the requirements of the regulatory authority of the stock exchange on which the company is listed, and also with company law of the country where the company is based. This information is vital for investors to monitor the firm's performance, since they are not privy to the day-to-day running of the company.

In Continental Europe and countries influenced by Continental law, the concept of a Board of Directors differs from the Anglo-Saxon model. In Europe there is a two-level system of company control: a Management Board, which is responsible for the actual daily operations of the company, and a Supervisory Board with responsibility for overall supervision of the company. The Supervisory Board does not necessarily include shareholder representatives but includes, in addition to large shareholders, other stakeholders such as banks, politicians, and trade unions. In some European countries, companies must have a "workers council" that has authority comparable to the Board of Directors.

SHAREHOLDER VOTES

The theory of one share one vote is good, but does not always apply in practice. In countries that do not allow votes posted by mail or through the Internet, shareholders who are unable to travel to the meeting lose their rights. In Japan and South Korea, some groups controlling a number of listed companies would hold all their firms' shareholder meetings simultaneously on the same date at venues spread around the country, thus preventing shareholders from attending and voting at more than one meeting.

Peter B. E. Hill, author of *The Japanese Mafia: Yakuza, Law and the State*, cites examples of Japanese culture creating an environment where illegal transactions can blossom. He mentions the role *yakuza* (Japanese gangsters) play in meetings of shareholders, which has no counterpart in Western society. Purchasing shares of stock in a publicly traded Japanese company gives the buyer a right to attend stockholder meetings, which is no different from United States' practice. But there the resemblance ends. *Sokaiya* (corporate blackmailers) extort money by threatening to reveal sensitive information about the financial status of the company or the private lives of management.

Yakuza also demand payments from corporations for protection against extortion by other groups, as well as to prevent protestors from disrupting meetings. Unique to the Japanese culture is the expectation that stockholders' meetings should last no longer than 30 minutes. If a meeting extends beyond a half-hour, the additional time is assumed to indicate the company is in trouble and the stock's price will fall. Thus, based on cost-benefit analysis, many companies believe that it is in the company's best interest to pay the sums demanded. Recent laws have been passed in Japan to counteract the *yakuza* corporate activities, but implementation of those laws is not comprehensive.

CASE STUDY: LEGAL DIFFERENCES AROUND THE WORLD

The laws protecting investors' rights vary significantly around the world, which explains the differences in the ways in which companies are owned and financed in different countries. For example, while large companies in the UK and US are generally publicly listed and ownership is widely dispersed, only a small percentage of Italian companies are publicly owned. One recent study points out that the commercial laws of most countries can be grouped into four "families" — English, French, German and Scandinavian — that treat investors very differently. The French, German and Scandinavian families are derived from civil law, based on the Roman legal system, while the English system is based on common law. Most of the newly developed economies derive their systems from one or more of these families; for example:

English system is followed in:

- Hong Kong
- Malaysia
- Singapore
- India
- Pakistan
- Thailand

German system is followed in:

- Taiwan
- South Korea
- Japan

French system is followed in:

- Brazil
- Greece
- Indonesia
- Mexico
- Italy
- Turkey
- Spain

The study found that the English legal structure gave the best protection to shareholders. For example, in most cases shareholders are allowed to vote through the mail. The French system offered the least protection, for example by restricting the voting rights of minority shareholders. The civil law countries often "block" shares for a period before and after shareholder meetings to prevent shareholders from selling their shares during this time.

The competitive nature of business is often at odds with attempts to have perfect corporate governance. In an ideal world, corporate officers would always adhere to generally accepted norms, but an overly rigid system of control enforced by the government is likely to be inefficient and wealth-destroying. In the current era of deregulation, looser controls based on self-regulation are seen as more desirable, although this inevitably leads to the occasional scandal.

Major failures of corporate governance often come to light at the end of a sustained bull market; as the famous investor Warren Buffett puts it, "it's only when the tide goes out that you learn who has been swimming naked." One possible explanation for this phenomenon may be that during a bull market investors are satisfied with their profits and do not wish to probe too deeply into how companies achieved them, while after a crash all parties are horrified to discover that the true value of many investments is significantly lower than previously reported.

The principles of fairness, transparency, accountability and responsibility are generally accepted. However, as the former chairman of the US Federal Reserve Alan Greenspan has remarked, some human beings have "...enviable standards, but others continually seek to cut corners." There is no doubt that standards of corporate governance have evolved and improved over the last 100 years, and the relative prosperity of the modern world could probably not have been achieved without this. Corporate governance, overall, is in sufficiently good shape for equity markets to function at a high level of efficiency. The challenge for investors is to remain vigilant for potential violations, and for companies, to make continuous efforts to maintain high standards.

STAKEHOLDERS

Stakeholders are individuals and organizations who may not have an ownership interest in the company, but are impacted by the company in some way or another and want their interests considered by the company's management. An environmental protection group wants to make sure that a logging company is not decimating the virgin forest. A union wants to make sure that a hotel company is practicing fair labor practices for its workers. A local community wants to stop the local company from polluting the local river with its chemical waste. A bank wants to ensure that the company adheres to sound financial policies so that the bank can recover the loans it has extended to the company. Governments, too, are concerned that companies are managed honestly and, especially, that they do not harm their employees or society at large. Other stakeholders, such as lenders, suppliers and customers, also need to be confident that a company is behaving honestly and ethically. Obviously, conflicts will arise among these different interest groups, the shareholders and the company management. In order to manage these differences, clear corporate governance guidelines are required. Therefore, the governing structure of companies requires careful examination.

CASE STUDY: UNFAIR GOOGLE VOTING RIGHTS

SAN FRANCISCO — A union pension fund has proposed that Google Inc. eliminate a two-tier voting structure, which would dilute control of the company's top three executives, who hold a privileged class of stock, the company said in a regulatory filing on Wednesday. The one share, one vote proposal by the Bricklayers & Trowel Trades International Pension Fund will be put to Google shareholders at the company's annual meeting May 11. Google's triumvirate — co-founders Larry Page and Sergey Brin and Chief Executive Eric Schmidt — hold overwhelming voting power through a two-tier voting structure. Page and Brin hold around 28.8% and 28.7%, respectively, of Class B voting shares, giving them majority control of Google. Schmidt holds 11.3% of votes. Collectively, the three retain more than two-thirds of all votes, the filing said. Under the current structure, each Class B Google share has 10 votes, while Class A shares carry only one vote per share, giving insiders absolute control. In a filing with the U.S. Securities and Exchange Commission, Google said it opposed the proposal by the pension fund, a holder of 4,735 shares of Class A common stock, to force Google to accept a new structure in which each share held, no matter what its class, would represent one vote. "Most institutions frown on dual-class stocks," said Charles Elson, director of the Weinberg Center for Corporate Governance at the University of Delaware. "Two-tier stocks lessen accountability" of management, he said. He was referring to institutional investment funds, which typically represent the biggest class of company shareholders. "When your voting interest is divorced from economic interests you have potential problems," he said, pointing to corporate governance scandals at media companies Adelphia Communications Corp. and Hollinger Inc. where insiders manipulated company finances at the expense of shareholders of non-voting common stock.

Source: *Reuters*, Eric Anchard, April 13, 2005

SPECIAL PURPOSE ENTITIES

Special purpose entities (SPEs), or special purpose vehicles (SPVs), are legal entities or companies that a company may create to hold assets it sells to them or to undertake a number of other operations that are designed to improve the balance sheet of the company. The legitimate need for SPEs emerged in large-scale international projects where investors wished to limit their risks to the project itself, avoiding participating in any other risks associated with the sponsoring company. Typically, an SPE was set up as a joint venture between a company and outside investors, and was restricted by its charter to specific activities, with the income generated being returned to the investors.

By the 1970s, however, the use of SPEs spread to other types of business. For example, a brewery that owned a number of bars might set up an SPE for the purpose of purchasing those bars and issuing bonds secured against the value of the bars. The bond proceeds could then be used to pay the parent firm for the purchase of the assets. This enabled the parent company to free up capital without losing control of the assets or diminishing the value of the brand. It also protected against insolvency risk.

In the 1980s, the financial services industry was attracted to SPEs as a way of "securitizing" illiquid assets such as bundles of mortgages. Since the mid-1980s, the use of SPEs has grown enormously, and by 2003 their total global value was thought to be $544 billion. SPEs are often set up in low-tax, offshore jurisdictions, such as the Cayman Islands and the island of Jersey. They can be established as charitable trusts to show that the SPE is not part of the parent company's group, but rather is truly independent.

The legitimate uses of SPEs can be beneficial to all, since they can improve the marketability of certain assets and can be used to ring-fence the risks on large projects. However, as mentioned in the Enron case study in chapter 3, SPEs may also be used to distort accounting information. This may be done for the following reasons:

- Off-balance sheet financing – A company may be able to conceal its debts by having an SPE borrow money if the SPE's accounts are not required to appear in the company's consolidated statements. For example, many firms arrange "synthetic leases" of assets such as aircraft through SPEs so that no liability appears on the company's balance sheet.

- Disguising poor performance – A company may transfer a badly performing business to an SPE to conceal the facts from outside investors, thus making the parent company look healthier than it really is.

- Manipulating "related party" transactions – Most countries have accounting rules that prevent groups of companies from making inter-group transactions at artificial prices; such deals are supposed to be fixed at "arm's length" market prices. Enron and other companies used SPEs to avoid these restrictions. In the case of Enron, the SPEs were very complex in order to hide risks and the trail of millions of dollars. It is important to note, however, that the majority of SPEs in the world are legitimate and answer a specific need. They were created as a result of pressure from banks and leasing companies to avoid capitalizing or booking special types of leases when the accounting rules of leasing were made more stringent. Although there are some financing and tax benefits of SPEs, the primary objective is most often to achieve off-balance sheet financing.

CREDIT RATINGS

A credit rating is a score as expressed by letters or numbers that investors and lenders use to determine whether an individual or company is creditworthy. In the US there are a number of credit rating firms offering credit ratings for individuals. These include such firms as TransUnion, Equifax, and Experian. The formula used by these agencies to rank individuals' credit scores is called the FICO (Fair Isaac Credit Organization), which is based on the formula used in the 1950s by one of the first companies in the business. A FICO score ranges from 300 to 900, with 300 considered extremely high risk, and 900 considered virtually no risk.

In the corporate world, there are a number of major international credit rating agencies (CRAs), including Fitch Ratings, Moody's and Standard & Poor's. The primary orientation of these agencies is to rate bond issues. Investors, issuers, investment banks, broker-dealers and governments all use these services. Issuers of bonds and other financial instruments must rely on credit ratings to gauge how their creditworthiness is ranked, allowing them to assess their ability to raise capital. If they want to issue a bond, it is necessary in almost every case that they obtain at least one rating from a respected CRA. Investors use credit ratings to calculate the risk of their investment portfolios.

Credit rating agencies have sometimes been criticized for unduly causing a decline in creditworthiness as a result of a vicious cycle created when they lower the credit score of a company. This causes a rise in the interest rates that the company must pay, which in turn weakens the balance sheet of the company and again results in a lower credit rating. In certain situations it can cause the company's bankruptcy when the banks holding the company's loans have "ratings triggers" that enable the banks to call back their loans if the company's credit rating is lowered. In such cases, the loans are payable immediately in full, thus resulting in a "death spiral" and bankruptcy.

In addition, large corporate rating agencies have been criticized for being unduly influenced and misled by the companies they are rating, since the agencies have frequent meetings with the companies and advise them on how to maintain their credit rating.

Some studies have shown that yield spreads for corporate bonds often expand before an actual rating downgrade occurs. This indicates that the market leads a downgrade, rather than following it. The whole value of a credit rating is thus called into question. Why not just use the credit spreads to assess the safety of loans and bonds rather than relying on a CRA?

Of course, rating agencies have not always detected danger. Before their collapse, Enron and Worldcom had AAA-rated bonds. Rating systems are run by human beings and are subject to human error. By its very nature, fraud is hard to detect. In situations where company managers and accountants conspire to cheat or mislead shareholders and regulators, there is little that rating agencies can do.

SHORTCOMINGS OF CREDIT RATINGS

For any serious investor, rating systems are only a starting point and a useful reality check. The key element of any credit assessment and monitoring process has to be your own analysis, not someone else's view. Credit assessment needs to be bottom-up, forward-looking and cash flow focused. There are no short cuts! The main drawback of a rating system approach is that it aims for an output that is user-friendly and easily comparable. This usually results in a company's credit profile being boiled down to a few common denominators. Key clues to changes in the ability and willingness of a borrower to repay are often missed.

Here are a few shortcomings of ratings:

- **Oversimplification** – Standard credit models often fail to take into account structures that prevent creditors from accessing cash. Only by making company-specific adjustments do you get a real sense of available cash balances and cash-generating ability.

- **Inability to Assess, Willingness to Pay** – Often determines whether or not a company defaults. Credit scoring systems are not designed to capture such qualitative information as the company management's attitude and moral character. These conclusions are a judgment call, based on your ongoing dialogue with market sources and the company's management, competitors and counterparties.

- **Inability to Stress-test** – Rating systems are given a "snapshot" of a company's ability to pay — they are not set up to convey the issuer's vulnerability to external pressures. Only by doing your own financial models do you get a sense of a company's ability to withstand credit shocks.

- **Dated** – At best, credit scoring and rating systems reflect a company's ability to generate cash as at their last reporting date. Workload constraints usually prevent new information from working its way into credit assessments until well after the results are posted. This is particularly an issue for companies that issue financial reports only once or twice a year.

- **Backward-looking** – Credit modeling is still mostly based on historical financial information. Explicit forecasts and assumptions are still not part of the credit assessment process. However, this area has seen some improvement in recent years.

MERGERS AND ACQUISITIONS

Mergers and acquisitions (M&A) are ostensibly about growth; they are a means for companies to expand by acquiring an external business. M&A occurs for other reasons too, such as reducing risk by diversifying into different industries, or gaining financial advantages, such as better borrowing power or tax breaks. For many years, governments have attempted to control M&A activity, principally in order to prevent the development of giant monopolies, but it is unclear whether such "anti-trust" legislation consistently has the effect of promoting trade; in some cases, antitrust laws may actually restrain trade.

A company can grow either by developing internally ("organically") or by acquiring or merging with another company ("acquisitively" or "inorganically"). M&A encompasses various types of transactions:

- **"Friendly" mergers and consolidations** – This is where two companies combine, usually with the agreement of the boards and the majority of the shareholders of both companies.

- **Tender offers** – A company offers to buy the outstanding stock in another firm from individual shareholders. This may override the wishes of the board and senior managers of the target company.

- **Purchase of assets** – A company buys assets (which may include standalone businesses) from another company, but does not take it over in its entirety.

- **Management buyouts and leveraged buyouts** – This is where control of a company is purchased by its managers, perhaps with a group of investors; the buyout is "leveraged" if it is funded primarily by debt taken on by the purchased company, which usually then becomes a privately-owned business.

For the investor, the main lessons seem to be that acquisitions need good, value-adding business reasons to justify continuing to hold equity in the acquiring company, and that selling the shares of a target company to a bidder may often be a good move. M&A activity is glamorous, and intermediaries charge high fees. Often senior managers in a merger benefit personally, not only financially but also by way of enhanced status from the associated publicity and the attainment of power in an enlarged firm. The managers of the company being taken over are often given "golden parachutes," which are large termination bonuses that many regard as excessively high. From the shareholder's point of view, these managerial benefits may be seen as legitimate incentives, but only if the merged company "adds value" by enhanced performance.

There is considerable disagreement over whether M&A activity "adds value" to the combined businesses and benefits shareholders. The rationale given for a merger or acquisition, which may not reflect the true picture, generally falls into one of the following types:

- **Purchasing a bargain** – The acquiring company may believe that the target is worth more than its purchase cost. For publicly traded companies, the price paid is usually higher than the market price and there is a danger that the market price rises considerably during the acquisition process. Purchasers are more likely to find undervalued companies in private hands or in inefficient markets.

- **Diversification** – The main reason to diversify is to reduce risk. Many family-owned companies have expanded to become conglomerates, possibly for this reason.

- **Business synergy** – This is the idea that an acquiring company may be able to add overall value by purchasing competitors ("horizontal" mergers) or suppliers and customers ("vertical" mergers). Such a merger may increase market power; for example, if there is legislation to prevent companies from cooperating to set prices, a merger could enable the merged company to keep prices high. If the acquiring company has better management, it may be able to enhance value by improving the efficiency of the target company. It may be possible to add value through economies of scale, such as increased purchasing power, better production coordination or streamlined distribution channels.

- **Financial synergy** – This may be related to taxes, leverage or return on assets. In terms of tax-related synergies, the acquiring company may gain a tax advantage through the purchase if the target company's country of domicile has a beneficial tax regime. Or the acquired company may be loss-making, so that taxes could be reduced by setting off the losses against profits of the acquiring company. Also, there may be potential to increase depreciation charges after the acquisition, resulting in tax savings. Another area of financial synergy could come from an increased ability to borrow, and at better rates, since the merger could improve the stability of earnings, making the combined company a better credit risk in the eyes of lenders. Finally, a merger could result in a better return on excess cash if the acquiring company has plenty of cash but few business opportunities. The acquiring company may operate in a mature or

Figure 5.1 — GE Chairman and CEO Jack Welch announces that GE has agreed to acquire Honeywell for US$45 billion in stock during a press conference on 23 October 2000 in New York. Welch said he would postpone his retirement until the end of 2001 to oversee the transition. The merger ultimately failed.

Source: AFP PHOTO/Doug KANTER

dying market, but may purchase a company with more opportunities for high returns but insufficient cash.

The phenomenon of M&A has been studied extensively, but remains one of the unsolved problems in theoretical finance, and much remains to be explained. Studies suggest, however, that:

- Shareholders of the acquired companies generally do well; the share price in the acquired company tends to rise before the takeover attempt is announced and shareholders earn returns over those they would expect to earn after adjusting for risk and market performance.

- The stated reason for a merger is most often "synergy," but various studies have concluded that most mergers and acquisitions do not add lasting value to the combined business. Often the merged company earns returns that are less than its cost of capital and does not outperform its market competitors.

- Many merged companies reverse the merger within a few years, often because the hoped-for synergy did not occur or because the acquisition price was too high.

- Synergies derived from immediate cost savings tend to be more lasting than those based on hopes for growth.

- Takeovers of private companies are more successful than takeovers of publicly listed companies, possibly because the acquisition prices are better value.

- Hostile takeovers perform better subsequently than friendly mergers, perhaps because of more rigorous assessments by the acquiring company.

SPIN-OFFS, SPLIT-UPS

A large company may separate part of its business and create a new publicly traded company from it in a number of ways:

- **Spin-off** – A portion of a company's existing business is separated to create a new business, with the existing shareholders given shares in the new company in proportion to their existing holdings.

- **Split-up** – The original company divides into several new companies and then ceases to exist. As with the spin-off, the original shareholders are given shares in the new companies in proportion to their existing holdings.

Spin-offs, split-ups and their variants may not generate cash for the parent company, but they may add value for shareholders for the following reasons:

- If the existing parent company is not managing a particular part of its business well, by separating it into an independent unit the operations could improve as a result of receiving more attention and funding from the new managers or existing managers who are given proper incentives.

- If the parent company suffers from regulatory restrictions, antitrust litigation or other problems that prevent it from optimizing its performance, splitting up the company or spinning off the problem operations can minimize the problems.

- Existing shareholders may be able to obtain tax benefits (in the US, spin-offs are tax exempt if they meet certain tests).

ANTITRUST REGULATIONS

The US, the European Union and many other governments around the world often want to prevent large companies from achieving market monopolies or near-monopolies through mergers and acquisitions. In the US, the focus is primarily on protecting consumers from monopolies. This stance originated in the reaction to the development in the late 19th century of conglomerates known as "trusts" that dominated major industries. For example, Standard Oil, formed in 1870, created a cartel in the oil industry that set high prices for consumers. In 1911, the Supreme Court decreed that Standard Oil should be broken up.

Many of the 19th century monopolies were thought to have been bad for consumers and to have allocated resources inefficiently. A monopoly may lead to poor product quality, poor service, and lack of innovation. However, "natural monopolies," which arise from practical requirements, such as in the case of electric utilities, may be the best solution for consumers. It would be a waste of resources for a number of competing electric power distribution companies to lay multiple power cables to the same homes and businesses. Such natural monopolies, however, must be regulated to ensure that consumers are not disadvantaged and that the monopolies get a fair return on investments.

The main aim of the extensive antitrust regulation in the US is to weigh the effects of M&A in terms of whether a given transaction may "restrain trade," and to prevent possible abuses. Cases against firms such as Microsoft have focused on that company's efforts to monopolize software and thus exclude competitor companies offering new applications from entering the market.

CASE STUDY: ANTI-COMPETITIVE ACTIVITIES: MICROSOFT

Hours before Microsoft is due to ship the next version of its Windows operating system, the US Government is expected to join 19 or more states in the most serious legal challenge in the company's history.

The Attorney General Janet Reno and a number of state attorney generals are reported to be planning a news conference in Washington DC on Thursday announcing plans for a wide-ranging attack on Microsoft's alleged anti-competitive practices. .... In a separate action on Tuesday, Sun Microsystems asked a federal court to block shipments of Windows 98 unless the components in it that rely on the Java programming language were modified to be compatible with Sun's version.

Microsoft is expected to vigorously defend its position. "We think a lawsuit would be bad for consumers and bad for the future of the software industry, and we don't believe there's any legal basis for a lawsuit," said spokesman Mark Murray. ...The anti-trust Sherman Act, enacted in 1890, had its most recent success and most striking failure in 1982.

In that year, US telecommunications giant AT&T agreed to break itself up (though some parts have since re-assembled). It was also the year that the government dropped its case against IBM.

Conservative and anti-trust scholar Robert Bork reportedly likened the latter case to Vietnam because it started in 1969 and the government could not get out of it.

Mr. Bork is now helping Netscape in its battle with Microsoft.

Probably the most well-known and successful example of anti-trust action in the US is the dismantling of John D. Rockefeller's Standard Oil in 1911, after a five-year court battle.

The author of a new biography of Rockefeller, Ron Chernow, has called Mr. Gates a "clever and resourceful monopolist" whose strategy is similar to Rockefeller's own.

A lengthy series of courtroom clashes seems inevitable. It could be years before it is clear whether Microsoft will follow the path of Standard Oil or IBM.

Source: *BBC News,* 14 May 1998

In the US, the Banking Act of 1933, known as the Glass-Steagall Act, was an attempt to restore confidence in the financial system. It forced banks to choose between two businesses — taking deposits and underwriting securities — and gave birth to the investment banks, which specialize in stock market business, as distinct from commercial banks, which take customers' deposits, give loans and so on. Further measures were taken over the years to restrict banking monopolies and place legal walls between different areas of the financial services industry. More recently, however, the trend for deregulation has begun to reverse this process, and once again large financial conglomerates that own companies actively across the whole field of financial services have developed.

OPINION
IS ANTITRUST POLICY JUSTIFIED?

It is not at all clear that monopolies and cartels are damaging to consumers and competition in the long term. The main criticisms of any antitrust policy are:

- *Instability – Most cartels do not last for long because there are strong internal incentives to cheat. For example, in a price-fixing cartel, individual members may be tempted to cut prices in order to increase sales and profits, and this can lead to the collapse of the cartel. The oil cartel OPEC, which held the world to ransom during the oil crises of the 1970s, subsequently lost much of its control of the world market.*

- *Market changes – As consumer demand changes and new technologies appear, a monopoly may lose its power. IBM's domination of the computer business in the 1970s, for instance, was broken by the emergence of personal computers.*

- *Does concentration in an industry always lead to higher prices? – There is no consensus among economists on this question.*

- *Antitrust policies may be driven by anticompetition motives – Groups such as labor unions, business competitors and lobby groups may seek to prevent a large merger even if it promises to be beneficial in terms of economic efficiency and lower prices because of their own anticompetitive agendas.*

In other countries, antimonopoly legislation is often intended to protect existing industry structures, especially from foreign buyers. In the European Union (EU), individual member states and the EU's European Competition Commission play regulatory roles, making it difficult for large firms to obtain clear guidelines on whether a cross-border merger will be permitted. A number of international mergers have been approved by the US authorities but banned by the EU. For example, in 2000 General Electric and Honeywell announced that they intended to merge; the Department of Justice approved the proposal, but several months later the European Commission declared that it was "incompatible with the common market," and the two firms had to abandon their plans.

 SUMMARY

Understanding corporate behavior is important for better assessment of a company's stock. This means finding out who make and influence decisions, and what their motives are. In other words, understanding "off-balance sheet" risks is crucial before investment decisions are made. Laws protecting investors' rights vary significantly across the world. Protection of the rights of all those who have a stake in the company, (i.e. stakeholders) has emerged as a new concept. Credit rating companies aim to offer assessment of risk on a continual basis, but the efficacy of their analysis is debatable. Companies resort to M&A, spin-offs and split-ups for growth, and investors should be aware of the potential of such activities for more accurate valuation of a stock. Governments have enacted laws against monopoly, but it is not certain if antimonopoly movements are necessarily consumer-friendly.

QUICK QUIZ

1. If Microsoft had been forced to split, how would it have helped the consumer? Would either/any of the new companies grow into a monopoly in its restricted area of operation?

2. Should the government of a country have the power to ban the hostile takeover of a domestic company by a foreign company?

3. Why did credit rating agencies fail to foresee Enron and Worldcom?

4. Can we assume that at any point in time, a company's share price reflects most of the key risks? Why or why not?

5. Can there be a logical process to assess all the "off-balance sheet" risks of a company?

6. Company A has been on a three-year acquisition spree, and has enjoyed an extraordinary rate of growth in earnings. It is bidding for a company in which you own shares. You are offered 30% over the pre-bid price for your shares. Just as you are about to accept, a friend advises you to keep the shares, on the grounds that if the bid is successful, you will own shares in the merged company, which will continue to grow at a rapid pace. What do you decide to do? Give your reasons.

6
TYPES OF SHARES

All shares are <u>not</u> created equal. Companies issue different types of shares with different rights. When raising finance, a public company may issue equity securities as well as debt securities such as bonds.

COMMON STOCK

The most common share type is, in fact, called common stock. These stocks are also referred to as ordinary shares. They shares represent a share in the earnings and assets of a company equally divided among all the common shares. Dividends paid on common stock vary with earnings and are normally decided by the company's directors.

PREFERRED STOCK

Preferred stock is a stock that has certain rights different from those of ordinary stock. For example, preferred stock may have the right to receive higher dividends than ordinary stock or may have first access to dividends (when dividend payouts are limited). Such stocks may also have higher priority in obtaining a share of the company's assets in case of the dissolution of the company. In some cases, holders of preferred stock are guaranteed a fixed dividend rate or return.

Often when a company is financially weak, it is forced to offer preferred stock to induce investors to risk their money. Such preferred stock can be entitled to specific dividends and can also have other conditions such as redemption dates like those given to bonds, as well as certain conversion privileges.

Preferred stock can also differ from ordinary stock in regards to voting rights. In some cases, in return for the extra benefits, preferred stock may have some restrictions such as not being allowed to have votes equal to those of common stockholders. In other cases, preferred stock may have greater voting power than ordinary shares. For example, one preferred share might have two votes while an ordinary share could have only one vote.

Many kinds of preferred stock assure their owners of a steady stream of predetermined dividends that are not related to company performance. In these cases, the stock begins to look like a bond because of the steady income. The revenue from preferred stock with assured dividends is, however, more risky than bonds, because a company can decide not to pay the dividend without incurring the legal liabilities inherent in defaulting on payment of a bond coupon.

Dividends from preferred stock can be either cumulative or non-cumulative. If in a given year a company does not pay dividends on preferred stock with cumulative dividends, it will have to do so in the following years. With non-cumulative preferred shares, the unpaid dividend is not carried forward. In most cases, owners of preferred stock have the right to receive a dividend before any holder of common stock.

SHARE CLASSES

In addition to preferred stock, a company may decide to issue different classes of common stock with different dividends and voting rights. For example, class A stock may have full voting rights and cash dividends, while class B stock may have no voting rights, or only a fraction of a vote per share, and may only offer stock dividends. The decision on how to structure the different classes of stock is often based on their marketability to different types of investor; for example, Warren Buffett's Berkshire Hathaway issued "B" stock with no voting rights to give small investors, who could not afford the high price of the "A" stock (tens of thousands of dollars per share), access to the company while retaining control of the company in the hands of the existing shareholders. Wealthy investors may be attracted to share classes that do not pay a cash dividend because they avoid income tax.

WARRANTS

In addition to the different types of shares, there are also derivatives of shares. The most prevalent are warrants. A stock purchase warrant is a type of option contract allowing the investor to buy stock at a specific price and in a specific ratio. So, for example, a warrant could have a ratio of one to two, meaning that one warrant allows the purchase of two shares at a specific price.

"Covered" warrants are issued by third parties, usually financial institutions, that give an option to buy existing shares that the issuer already owns or is obliged to purchase (hence the "cover"). Since no new shares are issued, covered warrants can be viewed as call options and not as an equity instrument issued by the company.

The prices of warrants can be more volatile than those of common stock. Consider Company A, which is currently traded at $50 and issues a warrant at a price of $10, allowing each warrant owner to buy two shares of the company at $60. If the market price of Company A rises from $50 to $70, then an investor who purchased one share of common stock at $50 will have made $20 — a 40% gain. The owner of the $10 warrant, on the other hand, will have made a profit on the difference between two shares that have appreciated from $60 (the exercise price of the warrant) to $70, which is $20 less the $10 cost of the warrant. This yields a gain of $10 (100%).

The price of warrants is of course derived from the price of the underlying stock and tends to be higher when the stock price is highly volatile.

Fisher Black, Robert Merton and Myron Scholes developed the Black Scholes Model in 1973. It is widely used today to determine the price of options and, with certain modifications, of warrants. The model assumes that the prices of heavily traded options or warrants normally follow a geometric Brownian motion with constant drift and volatility. The model uses the constant price variation of the stock, the time value of money, the option's strike price, and the time to the option's expiry in a formula. Unfortunately a number of assumptions must be made which may not hold true in real life situations. Therefore, blind reliance on the model can be dangerous. (The term *Brownian motion* — named after the botanist Robert Brown — refers to the random movement of minute particles in a fluid and the mathematical models used to describe those random movements, such as stock market fluctuations.) Merton and Scholes were awarded the Nobel Prize in Economics in 1997 for their work.

If the company believes that the stock market overestimates the risk of the company, then it is in its interest to issue warrants, since their price will be higher. Warrants are often issued by companies to make a new share issue more attractive to the buyers. It is a way to "sweeten" the share issue by giving the buyers the right to purchase more shares in the future at a given price, normally higher than the current price. However, warrants expose their owners to decisions by the company's board over which they have no influence, since they only have the option to buy shares and no voting rights. If, for example, a company decides to pay a large dividend to existing shareholders before the warrant can be executed, it could substantially reduce the value of the outstanding warrants.

STOCK OPTIONS

Stock options are basically rights to buy stock at a certain price, called the exercise price, after a certain date. The options are said to be "vested" once the employee can exercise the options. Employee stock option plans (ESOPs) originated in the US in the 1950s and 60s as a way of keeping and incentivizing a company's workforce — usually to help a company in distress. Subsequently they were, and still are, used as an incentive for top management. In the US especially, stock options constitute a significant part of executive compensation, particularly for the company's top management such as the Chief Executive Officer (CEO) or the Chief Financial Officer (CFO). The theory is that stockholders want the company's top executives and even the Board of Directors to have their interests aligned with their own.

Employee stock options are most often not transferable and have a number of restrictions. Since they are used to persuade the employee to stay in the company, they may "vest" (become usable) after one, two, three or more years. The options allow the employee to purchase shares in the

SEC PROBING STOCK OPTION "BACKDATING" SCANDALS

WASHINGTON — The newest intrigue in corporate America, the apparent backdating of stock options to boost top executives' compensation, is rapidly taking on the dimensions of a major scandal. The number of public companies under investigation by the Securities and Exchange Commission or federal prosecutors has grown to more than 30 and executives at several companies have been fired. ...At issue is whether company insiders manipulated the timing of stock option grants to bring big payoffs to executives by improperly backdating the grants to coincide with low points in stock prices. As first noted in a series of groundbreaking articles in The Wall Street Journal, these patterns of almost too-good-to-be-true timing took place in the late 1990s and early years of this century. Stock options become more valuable as the market price rises above the exercise price, so backdating fattens the spread — and executives' payoff when they eventually sell their stock. Unlike the byzantine financial schemes concocted by Enron and other poster companies of the corporate scandals of recent years, options backdating is fairly easy to comprehend and goes straight to the issue of whether executive remuneration is out of control. ...The SEC, with power to impose civil fines and sanctions, is looking at whether plans to backdate options to a specific date were properly approved by a company's board and disclosed to shareholders in regulatory filings. Some options backdating is legal, and even is touted by companies as an incentive to executives they seek to recruit, securities experts say.

Source: *Associated Press*, Marcy Gordon

company at a specified price, often at the current price, so the employee has the incentive to work for seeing the share price rise.

Stock options can be an effective part of an employee's compensation and incentive package if the stock is rising. But if the stock is performing poorly or the exercise price is substantially higher than the market price (making them decline in value), they can, understandably, be a source of considerable friction. If the company performs well, they can be expensive for the company's ordinary shareholders. This is one of the reasons why some companies prefer to issue restricted stock instead, because it typically costs much less, while giving the employee the assurance of some gain even if the stock declines.

"I don't want stock options. I want you to pay your tab."

In some countries, stock options are often heavily taxed, making it more difficult to create schemes that provide real incentives, and so are less widely used. There are many variations in ESOPs, most of which are directly linked to the way these options are taxed in the company's country of domicile.

RESTRICTED STOCK

Restricted stock is stock that cannot be transferred or sold for a given period of time. Such stocks can be used in a variety of financial transactions, but most often are used as an employee incentive. If a company wants to persuade an employee to stay and work hard to increase the price of the company's share, they may issue to the employee shares in the company that may not be sold or transferred for a number of years. In this way the employee is given the incentive to (1) stay with the company and (2) work hard to increase the price of the company's share. Such a stock may also have other restrictions or conditions. For example, the vesting or transfer of ownership of the restricted stock may be tied to certain performance conditions, such as attainting specific profit targets.

DEPOSITORY RECEIPTS

These are certificates representing the ownership of shares deposited with a bank or depository. The most well known type of depository receipt is the American Depositary Receipts (ADRs), first issued by the J.P. Morgan Bank in the 1920s as a way of allowing American investors to purchase shares in

Europe more efficiently. At that time, American investors had to send money by sea and wait for the actual share certificates to be returned. To facilitate the process of purchasing foreign shares, the bank introduced a system where it would instruct its branches in Europe to purchase shares of foreign companies wanted by American investors. Those shares were deposited in the vaults of J. P. Morgan's European branches. Then depository receipts were issued in New York to the American investors indicating that the investors' shares were held in deposit with the bank in Europe and were at the disposal of the investors. When the investor wanted to sell or redeem his investment, instructions to sell the shares would be cabled to the European branch and, once sold, the equivalent value would be issued to the ADR holder in New York. As the system developed and grew, ADRs were traded on the market just like the underlying stocks and, in some cases, were even more liquid than the underlying stocks. The system has grown today to the point that you can purchase the ADRs of many little-known foreign companies. ADRs are more attractive to smaller investors, particularly in the US, than purchasing shares on the company's home stock exchange, which can be expensive and complicated.

" OPINION
ARE ADRs BECOMING REDUNDANT? "

ADRs still serve important purposes. For instance, if a country has foreign exchange restrictions, buying and selling ADRs of that country's shares can avoid those foreign exchange restrictions since the shares are traded in the US in US Dollars without the need for conversion into the local country's currency. Also, an investment or pension fund may have restrictions on investing in foreign company shares, in that they may be allowed to invest only in shares or certificates issued in their home country. In such cases a depository receipt may be purchased, giving the fund access to a foreign stock. This is one of the reasons why ADRs survive in the US. Certain regulations preventing US-based funds from investing directly in certain countries can be surmounted through the use of ADRs.

Other types of depository receipts can be found in various parts of the world, including Global Depositary Receipts (GDRs), European Depository Receipts (EDRs) and Inernational Depository Receipts (IDRs). ADRs are normally traded on US stock exchanges such as the New York Stock Exchange and the American Stock Exchange, while GDRs, EDRs and IDRs are traded in European stock exchanges such as the London Stock Exchange.

It is important to note that the rights of a depository receipt (DR) holder should be the same as those of the holders of the underlying shares, so that the depository receipt holder also becomes entitled to dividends and voting rights of the underlying shares. The price of the DR should be the same as the underlying shares, but sometimes there are discrepancies, which can be utilized by traders to do cross-border trades and make profits. This activity on the part of arbitrage traders and brokers normally results in the DR and the underlying stock reaching parity or coming in close relation to each other.

CONVERTIBLES

A convertible security allows the holder to exchange it for another security. Most common is the convertible bond, where the bond may be converted into company shares at a certain time and under certain conditions. Another type of convertible security is the convertible preferred stock. Most often, the convertible is exchanged for the common stock of the issuing company, but in some cases they may be converted into securities issued by other companies.

For the investor, the attraction of convertibles is that they generally provide greater security than the common stock and produce a larger income stream. Companies with lower credit ratings may issue convertibles as a cheaper way of obtaining finance than if they issued bonds.

Convertibles may have a number of different characteristics. For example, some may be "callable," which means that the issuer may "call" or redeem the issue whenever they wish by giving, say, thirty days' notice. Or they may be "non-callable," which means that the issuer has no right to redeem them and must continue to meet the convertible's conditions such as payment of a fixed dividend. This can be disadvantageous in an environment where interest rates are falling. The issuing company may find that with lower interest rates, it is able to borrow money at a cheaper rate than what it is paying on the convertible. Of course, if interest rates fall, the convertible holder will find his investment rising in value.

RIGHTS

Rights issues are made by companies to raise more capital from existing shareholders. The existing shareholders are given the "right" to purchase more shares in the company, normally at a price below the market price. It is thus considered a privilege granted to existing shareholders. Like warrants, rights shares can be sold and transferred. They allow the shareholder to purchase additional shares in the company in proportion to their current holdings. They normally have a shorter life than warrants. The new shares issued in a rights offering may have the same voting rights and dividends as the existing shares, or they may offer different rights, which usually affect their price.

When a rights offer is made, shareholders must decide whether or not to "take up" or exercise their rights. If they choose not to take up their rights, they may yet be able to sell their rights to others. Once market dealing begins, the price of new shares that have the same dividends and conditions as the existing shares will usually fall between the old market price and the amount of discount on the issue price, so the price of the old shares will drop a little and that of the new shares will go up.

BONUS ISSUES

A variation on rights issues is the "capitalization" or "bonus" issue, when a company offers new shares to shareholders in proportion to the number that they already own, but without asking for more money. This is done to increase the total number of shares in the company, so that there are more shares in the market and they can be bought and sold more easily, and also so that the company can transfer some of its reserves into capital on its balance sheet. The company needs the approval of its shareholders to offer a bonus issue. The result will be that the company has more capital on its balance sheet, though it is not worth more, and there are more shares available, but with a lower nominal value. Generally, the market reacts positively to bonus issues and share prices can increase.

TRACKING STOCK

Tracking stock is issued by public companies as a means for investors to "track" the value of one part of the company. In this way, investors can value different segments of the company differently.

One example of how tracking stock can be used would be if a company producing automobiles has a new division involved in Internet gambling, which is growing faster than the automobile business. While the automobile business has a price/earnings ratio of only 10, similar to other automobile companies, the Internet gambling industry, which may be "hot" and fast-growing, is valued at 30 times earnings. The automobile company therefore decides to issue a tracking stock for the Internet division. By issuing the tracking stock rather than spinning off the Internet gambling subsidiary, the company is able to keep control of the subsidiary and also raises more capital at a lower cost.

When a company issues a tracking stock, it may sell the stock in the market (in the form of an initial public offering) or it can distribute the new shares to existing shareholders. The advantages of issuing the tracking stock rather than separating the subsidiary completely from the parent company are as follows: (1) the parent company is able to keep control over the subsidiary; (2) if the subsidiary gets into difficulty, it still has the support of the parent company; (3) the parent is able to obtain capital at a lower cost by obtaining a better credit rating; (4) the subsidiary and the parent can continue to share expenses such as marketing, administrative support, etc; and (5) if the market price of the tracking stock rises, the parent company can use that stock to make acquisitions and pay in stock rather than cash.

THE INSIDE TRACK ON TRADING STOCKS

It seems like everyone's doing it. Walt Disney Co. (NYSE: DIS) is planning to launch a tracking stock for its go.com Internet assets, and Microsoft (Nasdaq: MSFT) is considering a similar move for its MSN.com properties. ...

Take AT&T (NYSE: T) for example. With the company's acquisition of cable TV operator TCI, the telecom giant ended up with two tracking or letter stocks: New Liberty Media Group Class A (NYSE: LMG.A) and New Liberty Media Group Class B (NYSE: LMG.B). The two track what were formerly TCI and Liberty Media's programming, non-cable, and international assets... AT&T explains rather eloquently the difference between asset ownership and having economic interest in those assets: "Consider this illustration. You and your brother own a house together and rent out the top floor, sharing the rent equally. After a time, your brother thinks you could charge more rent by redecorating the apartment. You're not interested, though, because your money is tied up in pork bellies. So you reach an agreement. Your brother pays you to give up part of your claim to income from the apartment. He,

in turn, is free to spend on new wallpaper, carpeting, and anything else, knowing that a bigger chunk of income from renting the top floor is his to keep. So while you still both own the underlying asset — the house — more of the apartment's economic risk and reward belong to your brother.".... Some investors like tracking stocks for such characteristics as high revenue growth and being part of an emerging industry. Other investors prefer sticking to reliable performers that pay a regular dividend and deliver steady earnings growth. For companies that opt to do so, setting up tracking stocks is a way to appeal to different investors.... Tracking stocks are like internal spin-offs. So why don't companies just go ahead and spin off or spin out (a partial spin-off) a business unit? .... Well, tracking stocks allow companies to keep certain tax advantages, and it can help the tracked businesses to remain grounded to less risky corporate entities with solid credit ratings. In other words, the tracked businesses are given some room to maneuver but can also lean on their parent for support.

Source: *Motley Fool*. September 7, 1999

Of course, there are certain disadvantages to tracking stock for the investors. The most important disadvantage is that holders of tracking stock do not have the same voting rights as the holders of the parent company's stock. Tracking stock holders may have only a portion of the vote or, in some cases, no vote at all.

SUMMARY

Shares come in many types, each designed to suit a particular need of the issuing company. A company may use a particular type of share as a tool to manage adverse situations. Stock options may prevent high attrition rates among employees and may improve productivity. If the company believes that the stock market overestimates the risk of the company, then it may issue warrants. Tracking stock may help a company unbundle valuations for different business streams. Bonuses reward existing shareholders and rights seek to tap them for more funds. Depository receipts make intercontinental investments hassle-free. Preferred stocks help a company that is perceived to be financially weak to attract investments.

QUICK QUIZ

1. As a CEO, you find an alarming number of junior employees leaving the company. Would you issue a restricted share or a stock option scheme to retain them? What will your decision be based on?

2. If it is not difficult to invest in a company's stock listed on a stock exchange in a different country, would you still prefer to invest in a depository receipt of the company in your country?

3. What kind of shares should a company look at in the following situations:

   • Rising interest rates. Company has a large number of satisfied, wealthy shareholders.

   • High attrition among senior managers.

   • Company starts a new division. Existing core business may be hived off to a buyer and the new division may become the core business.

4. Can you think of a new type of share for a specific situation (beyond what we have discussed), assuming that it will get regulatory sanction?

5. Would you sell a company's share since it has risen steeply and has met your price target when you know for certain that there is a rights issue in the offing? You don't yet know the price at which the rights shares will be issued. What will your decision be based on?

6. A company has a class of common stock outstanding and a class of preferred stock outstanding that converts on a one-to-one basis into common stock. The company issues

you 50 shares of common stock and 10 shares of preferred stock. As a result the company has 1,000 shares of common stock and 500 shares of preferred stock outstanding. What percentage of the common stock and preferred stock do you own?

7. You are the CEO of a company that is issuing shares on the stock market for the first time. Your underwriter calls you to tell you that the issue has been massively oversubscribed. Is this good news or bad news? Why?

7

INITIAL PUBLIC OFFERINGS (IPOs)

Initial public offerings (IPOs) are the first step in the process of becoming a company listed on a stock exchange. Because of the various regulations imposed by stock exchanges and government regulatory agencies, in addition to the requirements of banks and stockbrokers involved in this process, a number of steps are involved in the IPO process.

FINANCING GROWTH

The options open or available to a company for raising funds vary according to its stage of development. A new small business has very few options; its founders can invest what cash they have available, a few other individuals may be persuaded to purchase shares, and the company may be able to obtain a trade credit or a bank loan. Without substantial backing or a good track record, it will not be able to issue shares on a stock market or raise money from bonds at a reasonable price. To grow, it will have to reinvest as much of its profits as possible. While reinvesting profits ("internal financing") allows the owners to retain control, this could set quite a low limit for growth, since the young company's profits are normally a small proportion of its future sales. Some private companies have prospered by sticking to this self-financing method, but many companies have found it a long and arduous road to growth. Without access to the capital markets, a firm may have to abandon many promising business opportunities because it lacks the funds to make use of them.

VENTURE CAPITAL

Some private firms seek a solution to this problem by turning to venture capital. Venture capitalists are professional investors who specialize in funding private firms that show promise. While some fast-growing industries, especially in the US, have attracted substantial investments from venture capitalists, in other parts of the world, venture capital is generally difficult to obtain. Venture capitalists see themselves as being in a high-risk business and thus require a high reward — which often translates into a demand for a controlling interest, or at least a strong voice, in the firms in which they invest. For a venture capitalist, the best chance for a profit is to nurture a fast-growing firm in a "hot" industry to a point where it can be taken public, allowing the venture capitalist to sell out.

As a firm becomes established and builds its customers, its access to credit improves, but until it has reached a point where it meets the listing criteria of a stock exchange, its choices remain limited to self-financing or loans. Exceptions to this general rule may occur when a particular sector, such as the "dot coms" in the 1990s, is popular; or when foreign investment is pouring into a region following political changes, such as Eastern Europe after the collapse of the USSR; or when an individual entrepreneur is regarded as having a "magic touch," such as a venture capitalist who became involved in a number of successful start-ups in his past and is thus able to raise large sums from professional investors for other ventures largely on the basis of his reputation.

CHANGES AFTER LISTING

If a firm reaches the stage where it is able to make a public offering of its shares, profound changes often ensue. The founders may lose control or willingly sell out to enjoy a happy retirement. The heavy regulatory burden on public companies could make the firm more bureaucratic. Professional executives who have no shareholdings may be hired to run the company. In some cases, this may cause the company to "lose its soul" and business direction; in others, the increased professionalism and formality may be very beneficial.

Once a company is able to issue shares on a stock exchange, its opportunities may expand. With access to large amounts of capital, it may be able to roll out its products and services across the country or even the world, and transform itself into a much larger organization. As long as the firm can sustain earnings growth, it will usually be able to raise capital, but its reinvestment needs are likely to outstrip its profits and it may turn to warrants and convertible debt to feed the appetite for capital.

Companies that have been publicly listed for a long time may eventually find that their original businesses have matured. While they are still earning healthy profits, there will be fewer opportunities requiring substantial investment. Their need for new capital may decline, and the majority shareholders may prefer to issue bonds when the company needs capital, rather than to dilute their control by issuing more shares. Mature, profitable companies with good cash flows are often attractive to acquisitive companies, and may be swallowed up in a merger.

Some businesses will decline as the market for their products changes in such a way that they are unable or unwilling to adjust. Consider, for instance, the makers of horse-drawn carriages in the 19th century. At their height, they were producing the main mode of transport, but today such a product is in a tiny niche market. Although some 19th century mass-market companies, such as Coca-Cola, have been able to survive and prosper by selling the same basic product with different packaging and marketing techniques, some companies find that they must eventually move into other businesses or sectors in order to survive. As industries mature, they often consolidate until there are a few giants dominating a declining market. At this stage, companies are often producing substantial cash flows but have few investment opportunities. Thus they no longer need to raise capital, and may begin to buy back shares and retire debt. If this process continues, such companies are in effect liquidating themselves.

UNDERWRITERS

Normally when a public flotation of securities is made, investment bankers become involved in either underwriting the issue or acting as sales agents. In some cases they may actually purchase the securities in the expectation of subsequently on-selling them at profit at a higher price. When it is a very large issue, a group of competing investment bankers or brokers may be invited to participate so that the risk is dispersed. It is called "underwriting" because the investment banker(s) guarantee(s) to the company issuing the shares that the money will be raised, so if the bankers are unable to sell the shares, they will themselves buy them and take on the risk. Of course, some bankers and brokers use the "book-building" process where they take orders for shares in advance so their risk is reduced or even eliminated.

The investment bank conducts a "due diligence" investigation into the company to verify all statements and discover any subjects that may be relevant to potential investors. Such subjects may become the subject of a heated debate over whether or not they should be disclosed. Due diligence involves visiting company operations; interviewing company managers, employees, lawyers and accountants; and analyzing company financial data and information about the industry, markets and competition. The investment bank not only has a duty of care towards investors since it is underwriting the issue, but it must also ensure that it has verified and understood the company's business very thoroughly, since it is also taking on some risk.

DISCLOSURE

When there is a new issue of shares or an IPO, one stringent requirement is full public disclosure in a prospectus document of audited balance sheets, profit and loss figures, and all other information that may have an impact on the firm's health. See Figures 7.2A and 7.2B for a sample first page and index of a prospectus.

The prospectus gives details of the business, its accounts, its future plans, the various risks, etc. Topics include:

- General information about the company, including its history, activities, management and future prospects

- A description of the offer and details of how the company will use the money it raises (the "proceeds" of the offer)

- Details of the firm's directors, auditors, advisers, underwriters, lawyers, bankers and stockbrokers

- The risks involved

- The company's share capital and existing debts

- Details of the company's products, brands, trademarks, important customers, research and development, manufacturing, major suppliers, competition and employees

- Information about major stockholders

Figure 7.1 — 19 August, 2004: Google's Dr. Eric E. Schmidt (2nd-L), Chairman of the Executive Committee and CEO, and Larry Page (C), co-founder and President, Products, at the opening of Google's public offering on the NASDAQ. Google shares soared in a hectic launch on the NASDAQ Thursday, a spectacular comeback from the humiliation of its cut-price initial public offering (IPO). Google, the biggest Internet float since the 1990s technology bubble, soared 18.0% to close at US$100.33, valuing the entire company at US$27 billion.

Source: AFP Photo

- Directors' shareholdings and other interests, and their employment contracts

- Subsidiary and associated companies

- Important contracts

- Pending litigation

- Financial statements

Much of the material in the prospectus is descriptive, and will be drafted initially by a company executive with help from legal advisers and investment bankers. The auditors must check the financial data, and also the accuracy of any statements about business operations, such as the number of customers for a certain product. The challenge for the writers of the prospectus is how to show the company in the best light, while at the same time conforming to the regulatory requirements of full and fair disclosure. They must also take care not to disclose sensitive information that might be useful to competitors. Legal considerations are very important, because the company must avoid possible lawsuits arising from any misleading claims or disclosure failures.

Preparing such a large and detailed document usually requires the participation of a sizeable group of people, including:

- Company personnel, principally from the legal and accounting departments, but also some from business operations

- The company's external legal advisers

- The company's auditors

- Representatives from the investment bank/underwriting firm

- The investment bank's legal advisers

- Various experts

In most jurisdictions, a prospectus must give details of relevant risks. These tend to be particularly detailed in the US, where they are described under the heading of "Certain Risk Factors." These risk factors may include information directly affecting shareholders, such as "dilution," risks relating to the company's markets and businesses, regulatory risks and the risk of losing key personnel. Many of them are standardized "boilerplate"

Figure 7.2A — A sample first page of a prospectus

TABLE OF CONTENTS

No dealer, salesperson or other person is authorized to give any information or to represent anything not contained in this prospectus. You must not rely on any unauthorized information or representations. This prospectus is an offer to sell only the ADSs offered hereby, but only under circumstances and in jurisdictions where it is lawful to do so. The information in this prospectus is current only as of the date of this prospectus.

In connection with this offering, the underwriters or any person acting on their behalf may over-allot or effect transactions with a view to supporting the market price of the ADSs at a level higher than that which might otherwise prevail for a limited period of time after the issue date. However, there is no obligation on the underwriters or their respective agents to do this. Such stabilization, if commenced, may be discontinued at any time, and must be brought to an end after a limited period.

Figure 7.2B — A sample index of a prospectus

THE OFFERING

The following information assumes that the underwriters will not exercise their option to purchase additional ADSs in the offering, unless otherwise indicated.

Offering price .... We currently estimate that the initial public offering price will be between US$11.00 and US$13.00 per ADS.

ADSs offered by us .... 7,500,000 ADSs.

ADSs outstanding immediately after this
   offering .... 7,500,000 ADSs.

Common shares outstanding
   immediately after this offering ...... 141,111,111 shares.

ADSs to common share ratio .... Each ADS represents four common shares.

Listing .... We have applied to have the ADSs listed on the New York Stock Exchange under the symbol "EDU." The ADSs will not be listed on any other exchange or traded on any other automated quotation system.

The ADSs .... The ADSs will be evidenced by American depositary receipts, or ADRs.

- The depositary will hold the shares underlying your ADSs. You will have rights as provided in the deposit agreement.

- If, however, we declare dividends on our common shares, the depositary will pay you the cash dividends and other distributions it receives on our common shares, after deducting its fees and expenses.

- You may turn in your ADSs to the depositary in exchange for common shares. The depositary will charge you fees for any exchange.

- We may amend or terminate the deposit agreement without your consent. If you continue to hold your ADSs, you agree to be bound by the deposit agreement as amended.

To better understand the terms of the ADSs, you should carefully read the "Description of American Depositary Shares" section of this prospectus. You should also read the deposit agreement, which is filed as an exhibit to the registration statement that includes this prospectus.

Depositary .... Trust Company.

disclosures that appear on most prospectuses. Entries such as "Lower Demand for Our Customers' Products Will Result in Lower Demand for Our Products" or "Defects in Our Products Could Increase Our Costs and Delay Our Product Shipments" are obvious and could apply to almost any manufacturing business; but it is still worth reading them closely as the explanation may reveal insights into the nature of the business. The "Certain Risks" section is thus valuable to investors, but should not be taken completely at face value. Certain items will have been included at the insistence of lawyers or the underwriters merely to protect themselves against any possible blame, and these items may give an alarmist view of the risks the company faces. In other cases, the true nature of a risk may be disguised by legal jargon and caveats.

Particular attention should be paid to risks that directly affect investors, such as:

- **Dilution** – A private company that is issuing shares on a stock exchange for the first time is often raising its share price substantially. Suppose the founders of the company paid $5 per share three years ago when the company started, and the book value per share is now, say, $8, including the money to be raised by the issue. The IPO may offer new shares to the public at a much higher price — say, $22, far above the original value or the present book value. If the issue is successful, the original shareholders may be able to sell their shareholdings at a huge profit. To protect the interests of the new investors, there may be clauses restricting the ability of the original shareholders and the key experienced operator/owners to sell their shares during or soon after the IPO.

- **Anti-takeover clauses** – If you are a shareholder in a listed company that is acquired, you could receive a higher-than-market price for your shares. In many companies, the managers and major stockholders often want to prevent takeovers and stay in control indefinitely, since they are enjoying the prestige and income that comes from managing the company. There is a potential conflict of interest, therefore, between the "insiders," who may resist any takeover bid, and outside investors who might be delighted to gain a windfall profit by selling out. Many companies now have rules restricting shareholders' influence in takeovers, putting the power firmly in the hands of the insiders.

- **Insider control** – Statements such as "Our Principal Stockholders Have Significant Voting Power and May Take Actions That May Not Be in the Best Interests of Our Other Stockholders" are a warning that even if the main stockholders do not own a controlling interest in the company, they may still be able to influence board decisions in ways that outside investors may not like.

- **Goodwill** – "Goodwill" is that part of a company's value in excess of the book value of its "real" assets, such as buildings, machinery, inventory and cash. A "Certain Risks" clause that tells you that, say, 80% of the company's assets consists of goodwill, is a warning that a very large part of your investment will not be backed up by tangible assets, so you will be relying on continued growth and positive market sentiment to keep the share price up.

Once the company, the investment bank and the lawyers have finalized the prospectus, it must be submitted to the stock exchange and the regulatory agency for approval, along with supporting documentation that will not be made public. Further changes and clarification are often requested, and new drafts of the prospectus must be drawn up and submitted until approval is given.

FEES AND EXPENSES

As we have said, the issue of new common stock for a company involves a number of procedures and processes requiring the services of investment bankers, lawyers, analysts, brokers and other experts. This means that when companies issue new common shares, not all of the money raised from the sales of the new shares goes to the company, since there are fees involved. The most important fee is the underwriting fee, or placement fee, charged by the investment bankers. Such fees can range between 3% to 7% of the amount of money raised.

PRICING

The price at which shares of an IPO will be issued is often a bone of contention between the underwriters and the company management and/or control group. The existing shareholders want the highest price possible, while the underwriters want to ensure that they will be able to sell all the stock offered. They want to please their clients, the existing shareholders, but they also want to give full and fair value to the new buyers. Eventually, they reach an "offering price" that they estimate will be acceptable to investors. Then the marketing of the issue begins. If the reaction in the marketplace is not positive, they may decide to lower the price. There is a fine balance between the risk of selling the company too cheaply and the risk that the issue "flops" because investors think that the price is too high. If the issue is a "flop," the institutions that have underwritten the shares must take them on their own books and hope to sell them off gradually in the market to recoup the cost.

DISTRIBUTION AND OFFERING METHODS

There are two main ways to offer the stock:

- General offer: Shares are offered to anyone who wants to buy them. In some new issues there is a minimum price for the shares, but applicants are invited to tender a higher price. After the closing date for the applications, the sponsors decide on the "strike price" for the shares, which all applicants who tendered it or anything higher must pay. Applicants who tendered a lower price receive no shares. In some tenders, applicants pay the amount they tendered, as long as it is equal to or higher than the strike price. Very often the underwriters will have a so-called "Dutch auction" (which is more accurately called a Vickrey Auction after William Vickrey, winner of the 1996 Nobel Prize for Economic Sciences), in which there will be a closed bidding by interested buyers with each bidder ignorant of other bids. The strike price is then set at the point where the greatest number of shares could be sold, not at the highest price.

NEWS CLIP

LEADING SCIENTISTS TO PROVIDE TECHNICAL DUE DILIGENCE SERVICE TO INVESTORS

A new venture, Bio Life Technical, including leading researchers within Nanotechnology and Personalized Healthcare, such as Professor Chris Toumazou and Professor Sir Magdi Yacoub of Imperial College, London, is being launched in London, UK providing independent due diligence services to investors, globally. Bio Life Technical is structured to aid venture capital groups, investment banks, business angels and institutional investors by providing a single contact point and managing the technical due diligence reporting process on behalf of prospective investor clients.

In addition, Bio Life Technical can estimate a quantitative commercial value for a device, even though it is at a pre-development stage without the usual financial inputs to rely on.

By specializing in Nanotechnology and Personalized Healthcare, Bio Life Technical is concentrating upon areas of high contemporary and future importance to the investment and financial community.

Source: *Bio Life Technical LLP*, September 1, 2005

- Private placement: The shares are not sold to the general public but only to a selected list of buyers. This is a low-cost, low-risk option, but it may not yield as high a price as a general offer. Since a general offer for sale is very costly, smaller companies often prefer private placements, but can only choose this option if they can locate enough major buyers who are willing to invest.

Generally, if the number of shares applied for exceeds the total number of shares to be issued, the offer is considered "oversubscribed,"

NEWS CLIP

WHIZKIDS' BLUNDERS BLACKEN IPO'S EYE

Wednesday night — after a one-day delay and considerable back-pedalling — Google said it is selling 19.6 million shares at $85 each in an initial public offering that values the company at $23.1 billion. Google had predicted the IPO would sell for up to $135 a share, giving it a $36.6 billion market value.

Using a "Dutch auction," Google had investors submit bids on how many shares and at what price they would be willing to buy, so it could use that information to price the IPO. The IPO will not exactly be a flop, raising $1.7 billion for the company and its selling shareholders.

The company's missteps included:

- A lofty suggested share price, which Google set at $108 to $135.

- Two classes of stock. The founders get stock that gives them 10 times the voting power of the masses. Google had said it wanted to be democratic.

- A trail of legal missteps - the most embarrassing was the publication of an interview with Playboy magazine just as the company was about to start its auction. Google was forced to add the text of the interview to its registration document.

- Google's IPO doesn't require insiders to hold on to their shares for six months. "Lockup periods" are designed to protect buyers from a price decline caused by a insiders unloading their stock.

Source: Adapted from Matt Krantz, *USA Today, September 29, 2005*

HONG KONG ELITE SCORE ON IPOS TYCOONS RECEIVE STAR TREATMENT; BIG ALLOTMENTS ARE NOW CRITICIZED BUT ONCE HELPED DEALS GET DONE

HONG KONG — Back in the days of the technology-stock boom, U.S. investment bankers were criticized for handing out all-but-sure-money IPO shares to favored clients like candy. In Hong Kong, a similar feeding frenzy is happening with China's hottest initial public offerings of stock.

Take Bank of China Inc.'s IPO, which had a strong debut Thursday. The deal is expected to raise as much as US$11.2 billion, making it the world's biggest IPO in six years. The marketing document for the shares cites 12 "corporate investors" which each were given a chance to buy the stock at the IPO price, as long as they don't sell for a year. Among the lucky few are some of Hong Kong's celebrity tycoons or companies they control, including the flagship businesses of the bluest-blood of them all, Li Ka-shing.

This is the way business has been done in Hong Kong for years, mainly because investment banks felt they needed to use star power to boost the credibility of the IPOs of Chinese enterprises that weren't household names to global investors. The tycoons' names and cash attract more capital, increasing the IPO's chances of success.

But critics say the practice has outlived its original purpose, given that China is one of the hottest investment opportunities in the world. Far from being an obscure backwater company in need of name recognition, Bank of China has drawn tremendous demand globally and locally for its new shares. The banks overseeing the deal — Bank of China affiliate BOC International, Goldman Sachs Group Inc. and UBS AG — received applications to buy shares from more than 10% of Hong Kong's population. Including international and institutional demand, offers to buy totaled $150 billion — well over 10 times the value of the available shares. Not surprisingly, the shares popped 15% on their debut.

Source: *The Wall Street Journal*, by Kate Linebaugh, June 2, 2006

and the company has to decide how to allocate the shares. If the number of applications is less than the number of shares to be issued, the offer is "undersubscribed"; the underwriters must buy the remaining shares.

SPECULATION ON NEW ISSUES

If the market expects a new issue to be popular, investors may attempt to make short-term gains by applying for shares in the hope of selling them soon after at a profit (this is known as "staging" in some countries). Although profits can be attractive, the conditions for application are often complex, and many small investors fall afoul of them, either failing to receive any shares at all or suffering losses by omitting to calculate the interest cost of borrowing deposit money for the purchase.

Suppose a small investor decides to apply for shares on the morning of the closing date and applies for the maximum number of shares her budget allows. The investor must submit part or all of the cash with the application. If the issue is heavily oversubscribed and she receives far less than what she applied for, she may have paid out more money than the cost of the shares that are eventually allocated. In the meantime, her money is tied up and often not earning interest. If she has borrowed money to make the deposit, the losses can be considerable and more than any increase in the stock price in the aftermarket.

Figure 7.3 — Sri Lankan officials process applications for shares in the Indian Oil Company (IOC) in Colombo, 29 November 2004. IOC has offered 100 million shares in an Initial Public Offering (IPO) by which they hope to raise some US$34 million.

Source: AFP Photo

The application rules can often appear confusing and opaque to the uninformed investor. For example, the investor may be allowed to apply for shares in amounts of 200 shares up to a total of 1,000 shares, then in amounts of 500 between 1,000 and 5,000 shares, and then in amounts of 1,000 above 5,000 shares. If the investor applies for, say, 5,200 shares, she may be disqualified from receiving any shares because the terms state that applications for more than 5,000 shares must be in amounts of 1,000 — she should have applied for 5,000 or 6,000 to qualify.

 TERMINOLOGY

THE GREEN SHOE – *When there is an over-allotment in a new share issue it is referred to as the "green shoe option." This allows the underwriters the right to sell more shares than originally planned by the issuer if the demand is higher than expected. In a case where there is very high demand, this option puts more supply in the market and helps to prevent excessive volatility in the aftermarket once the stock starts trading. The Green Shoe Company was the first company to have such an option; hence the name.*

OVERSUBSCRIPTION – *When there is excess demand for the shares (i.e. more subscriptions than the supply of shares). This is generally welcomed by investors because the share price will usually rise when market dealing starts.*

UNDERSUBSCRIPTION – *When there are fewer applications for shares than the supply. This is usually bad for investors in the short to medium term, because although they will receive all the shares they wanted, the price will often stay low as the underwriters slowly sell their shares into the market.*

NEWS CLIP
A PIECE OF THE ACTION: WHY INVESTORS ARE FIRED UP BY CHINESE IPOS

Relieving the tedium of the 627-page prospectus for Bank of China's initial public offering is a section euphemistically entitled "Special Events". Over three pages, the bank and its underwriters detail the embezzlement of funds totalling

$737m (£393m, £574m) from BoC's branches in Kaiping in southern Guangdong province, Heilongjiang province in China's north-east and Beijing. Alongside such daring thefts, perpetrated by branch managers, staff and clients, the six senior BoC executives who netted a mere $8.9m through bribery and other frauds - also noted for the record - appear un-ambitious.

If any of the institutional and retail investors clamoring for a piece of BoC's $9.7bn offering made it to these revelations on page 160 it is unlikely that they dwelt on them for very long. Each disclosure is spectacular either for the amount involved or the seniority of the executives implicated — including a former BoC chairman and a former chief executive of its Hong Kong operations. Yet the offering, which priced at the top end of its range, was heavily subscribed last week even as global capital markets tumbled.

"With Chinese IPOs you have to ride the momentum," says Yang Liu, a China fund manager at Atlantis Investment Management. "As long as you get out before it becomes too expensive, you will be fine."

Ms Liu estimates she has made an average 30 per cent return on her China IPO investments over the past six months, including a 60 per cent gain on Dalian Port, which listed in April. She reckons BoC, which debuts today in Hong Kong, is a sure thing because it has been priced at 2.18 times book value. That compares favorably with the valuations of its Hong Kong-listed peers, China Construction Bank (CCB) and Bank of Communications (BoCom), which are trading at 2.5 and 2.7 times book respectively.

Investors such as Ms Liu win only if they get in early on a hot IPO or time the latest China fever cycle well. For longer-term investors, it is a different prospect entirely. The largest companies in China's state-owned "pillar" sectors — such as energy, finance and telecommunications — sell investors a small stake while the government keeps an iron grip on their boards. Dividend yields are paltry, with only two of China's 10 largest Hong Kong IPOs paying out more than 2.7%

Source: *Financial Times*, Justin Lau and Tom Mitchell, June 2006.

Figure 7.4 — Traders at work shortly after opening at the Hong Kong Stock Exchange, 15 December 2004. Shares of Air China Ltd., the nation's biggest international carrier, ended the day at 3.225 Hong Kong dollars (41 US cents), up eight percent from their IPO price of 2.98 Hong Kong dollars. The stock had opened the day at 3.15 dollars.

Source: AFP Photo

 SUMMARY

Listing a company on a stock exchange begins with an initial public offering (IPO). Prior to that, a company might need venture capital for growth, particularly if it is a relatively high-risk venture. IPOs are usually governed by a number of disclosure norms. The company issues a prospectus that gives enough details to potential investors, without disclosing sensitive information that might help rivals. The company also needs to conform to the statutory norms of "due diligence." The company has choices in distribution and offering methods of IPO.

1. You have US$10,000 to invest. Would you:

   - Give it to a venture capitalist who has promised a hefty return? He has a good track record.

   - Invest in a company that is in a great business, offers steady appreciation over the long term, but nothing much can be expected in the short term?

   - Invest in the IPO of a firm which is perceived to be "hot," is in the news, and post-IPO you can expect a decent appreciation in the stock?

   You are not sure of the company's long-term prospects.

   What factors would guide your decision?

2. A recently listed company, in which you hold shares, is seen to be deviating from much of what is said in the prospectus but seems to be all right financially. Would you sell its shares?

3. Why are companies required to explain how they will apply the proceeds of an issue?

TRADING IN SHARES

8

ORIGINS

The idea of trading and exchange has a long history. As civilizations developed, the exchange of goods and services became more sophisticated and graduated from barter trade to the use of currency by which goods and services could be sold more efficiently.

In the Middle Ages, traders at fairs required the use of credit and thus documents such as drafts, bills of exchange, etc. By the 11th century, bills of exchange (in essence, an IOU that can be sold at a discount to a third party) were being traded actively in France. Efforts were made to regulate the business by the French king Philip the Fair (1268–1314). He started the *courratier de change* (change agent), the forerunner of the modern stockbroker.

During that same period in Bruges, then the trading center for the Low Countries (Netherlands, Belgium and Luxembourg), merchants met in front of the house of the Van der Buerse family to trade. The family name Buerse became *bourse* and was identified with stock exchanges in the 1500s and 1600s. Similar developments followed in other major trading centers in Holland, England, Denmark, Germany and elsewhere.

 TERMINOLOGY ─────────────────

BILLS OF EXCHANGE – *Bills of exchange originated as documents signed by a creditworthy person ordering payment of a sum of money to the bearer, either on presentation or after a specified date. They could often be used for making payments to third parties, who could cash them at will. The "acceptor" of the bill — such as a bank — is obliged to pay when the bill is presented. Today, the principal use of bills of exchange is in international import and export.*

As the markets developed for commercial bills and notes, there was an easy transition to stock exchanges in securities. The Dutch East India Company shares were traded in Amsterdam in the early 1600s. In London, stock dealers who previously had met in coffeehouses moved into their own building in 1773, and by the beginning of the 19th century securities trading was widespread in industrialized countries.

STOCK EXCHANGE TRADING AND OPERATIONS

Stock exchanges are designed to enable their participants to trade equities in an orderly and fair manner. Every exchange has a governing body that lays down extensive rules and supervises procedures for business. To participate directly, a person or an organization must be an approved member of the exchange. Acquiring membership can be an expensive process. For this reason, many stockbrokers are members of only one major exchange, so a private investor wishing to trade internationally on several exchanges may have to employ several different brokers, all at different rates and operating under different constraints. However, increasingly, major financial institutions, led by banks, have acquired or developed global brokerage and investment banking operations. Their vast financial strength has enabled them to purchase memberships on stock exchanges around the world.

In addition to providing a venue for share trading, stock exchanges also carry out the following key functions:

- They regulate the listing of companies on the exchanges to ensure standards.

- They operate a settlement system for the payment of share transactions. Some exchanges operate a rolling system where transactions are paid for within a fixed number of days (three days, in the case of the NYSE). Other exchanges operate an account date system where all debts for a period of, say, two weeks, are settled on a fixed date.

- They collect and disseminate company news and information about transactions for the benefit of their participants.

THE WORLD'S STOCK EXCHANGES

Figure 8.2 on page 104 shows the market capitalization of major stock exchanges around the world. The New York Stock Exchange (NYSE) is by far the world's largest, representing 30% of the world's market capitalization, which totals US$46,351 billion. Next largest are the Tokyo Stock Exchange with a 10% share, NASDAQ in the US with an 8% share, and London with a 7% share. The daily average turnover of the various markets differs in rank from the market capitalization. For example, NASDAQ has a higher turnover than Tokyo, and Euronext has a higher turnover than its market capitalization might suggest.

Figure 8.1 — In the early 19th century, a stock exchange building was erected in St Petersburg Russia. The Stock Exchange, designed by the French architect Thomas de Tomon, was inspired by Ancient Greek and Roman architecture.

Source: www.saint-petersburg.com/virtual-tour/stock.asp

As indicated by Figure 8.2 on page 104, the market capitalization in the United States dominates the equity markets worldwide, with the New York Stock Exchange topping the list with US$14,000 billion (US$14 trillion) in market capitalization as of July 2006. The second largest market in the world is Japan's Tokyo Stock Exchange at a little more than US$4 trillion, followed by NASDAQ, the London Stock Exchange and Euronext, all at about US$3 trillion each. After those markets, others such as Hong Kong, Australia and Korea pale in comparison. At the time of writing, the Chinese markets in Shanghai and Shenzhen were not freely open to foreign investors, thus they are not included, but their combined size is about equal to that of the Hong Kong market.

Figure 8.3 on page 104 shows the average monthly turnover of various markets around the world as of July 2006. As with the market capitalization figures, the NYSE dominates with about US$1,700 billion in turnover per month, followed by NASDAQ with a little less than half the NYSE turnover of about $800 million. Next in turnover size is the London market. Although the Tokyo exchange has a greater market capitalization than NASDAQ or London, in terms of market turnover, it follows those two markets.

The market capitalization of stock markets around the world has shown steady growth in recent years, although there have been fluctuations as a result of price declines. As indicated by Figure 8.4, between 1995 and 2004 the world market capitalization grew from approximately US$18,000 billion (or US$18 trillion) to US$38,000 billion (or US$38 trillion), or almost equal to the world's total GDP of $44 trillion.

Figure 8.2 — Stock market capitalization

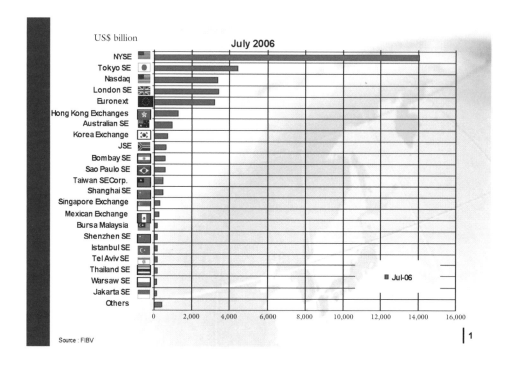

Source : FIBV

Figure 8.3 — Stock market monthly turnover

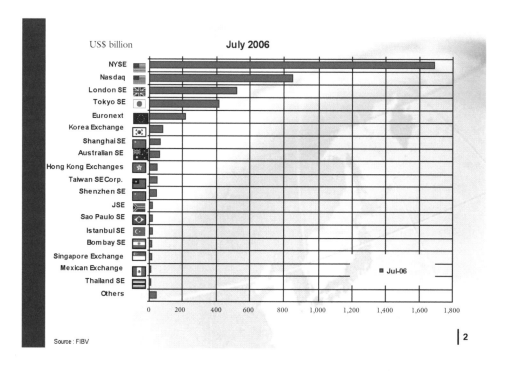

Source : FIBV

EQUITIES: AN INTRODUCTION TO THE CORE CONCEPTS

Figure 8.4 — World stock market capitalization

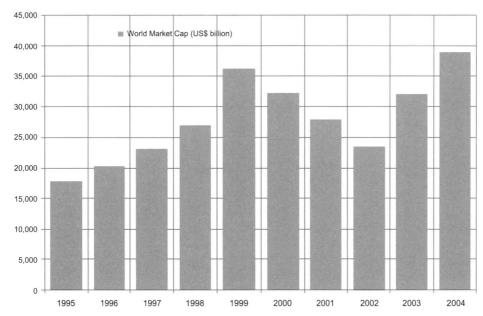

Source: S&P/IFC

 TERMINOLOGY

TOTAL MARKET CAPITALIZATION – *This is the total market value of all the companies in a given market or group of markets. It can be calculated for each company by multiplying the market price of each share by the number of shares outstanding. The sum of those individual market capitalizations is the market capitalization of a stock market.*

REGULATION AND ORGANIZATION

Each exchange has a unique history. Some were started as private organizations of traders while others originated by government mandate. Therefore, each exchange has its own organizational structure and operating environment. Regulation of the early stock exchanges varied. The London Stock Exchange regulated itself, but in France the stock exchanges were for the most part regulated by the government, although there initially was an unregulated market in unlisted securities. In Belgium, exchanges were government-controlled in the early 1800s but the controls were removed in the latter part of the century, only to be imposed again after the 1929–34 economic crisis. In Switzerland, the exchanges were regulated by cantonal, or state, law.

"I'd love to ask you in, Howard, but they start
trading in Hong Kong in ten minutes."

At present, regulations and organizational structure vary from one stock exchange to another and from one country to another. In some countries stock exchanges are independent entities with their own constitutions, boards of directors and rules, with little government intervention. In other countries government regulation and control predominate. Some stock exchanges are even listed on the stock exchanges themselves and their own shares are also traded just like those of other companies. As communications improve all over the world, however, exchanges are likely to become more similar than different.

In the UK, the London Stock Exchange is an independent entity with its own constitution, operating rules and regulations. In the US, there are a number of securities regulations starting with the Securities Act of 1933, then the Securities Exchange Act of 1934 and more recently the Sarbanes-Oxley Act. The Securities and Exchange Commission (SEC) supervises the exchanges in addition to supervising other securities, but generally the exchanges operate autonomously. In other parts of the world stock exchanges are organized as independent organizations but have varying degrees of government control, either through SEC-type organizations or under the ministry of finance or central bank. For example, the Amsterdam Stock Exchange is a private organization, but the Dutch Minister of Finance supervises the exchange. In Switzerland, the Zurich exchange has a board of elected members who determine policy, but the Finance Department of Zurich state is involved in regulating dealings on the exchange floor. In Germany, the Frankfurt Stock Exchange is supervised by a Board of Governors elected by the members of the exchange, but the exchange rules must be approved by the authorities of the Hesse state. In Brussels, the Ministry of Finance participates in the appointment of major committees.

In the Paris bourse, the policy-making Exchange Commission is headed by the Governor of the Banque de France and the regular members are chosen by the Ministry of Finance, and the *agents de change* in charge of supervising trading are semi-government officials. The number of *agents de change* is limited to 85. They supervise the trading and order execution while their employees and employees of the exchange carry on the actual trading. The *agents de change*, after passing a written examination and meeting certain education and experience requirements, must be nominated

NEWS CLIP
AUSTRALIA: CHINESE WALLS

The Australian Securities and Investments Commission's decision to bring broking firm BBY to heel over its failure to maintain a "Chinese Wall" between its corporate advice department and its research department is a sign that the regulator is coming to grips with real-world problems raised by a single, new paragraph in the Corporations Act.

Last year's CLERP 9 corporate law reform package was the Howard Government's main response to the corporate governance shambles that was exposed by the collapse of the dot.com boom.

Among many other things, it amended the Corporations Act to require financial service licence holders to "have in place adequate arrangements for the management of conflicts of interest that may arise …" The lawmakers left it up to ASIC to define conflicts, and whether they should be managed or avoided entirely.

The uncomfortable fact is that modern investment banks are designed to harness services that produce conflicts.

The standard industry defence is that such conflicts can be avoided, or managed away by structures such as Chinese Walls — invisible "don't ask, don't tell" barriers meant to quarantine key departments from each other.

Source: *The Age*, September 26, 2005

by a retiring member or the heirs of a deceased member. After crossing these hurdles, one must deposit guarantee money and be formally appointed by the Ministry of Finance.

OVER-THE-COUNTER MARKETS

Over-the-counter trading refers to the way goods or commodities were traded in a general store when goods were passed over the store counter. Now the term refers to all securities transactions that are not handled on the formal exchanges. In some countries over-the-counter securities trading is prohibited and all securities transactions must take place on the approved exchanges. Some exchanges provide for trading of unlisted securities or securities that have not been formally approved by the stock exchange or the government authorities. Others, like those in Japan, have a second "section" to provide for trading in over-the-counter securities.

In the US and the UK, many unlisted securities have traditionally been traded outside the official stock exchanges in the "over-the-counter" (OTC) markets. Much of the OTC trading activity is in corporate debt, but there are also a large number of shares being traded, including the shares of very small or troubled companies. In the US, the OTC exchange is very large, both in terms of the number of shares traded and the total number of dollars that change hands.

Traditionally, many people regarded shares traded on the OTC as speculative, in contrast to the perceived high quality of the "blue chip" companies listed on the official exchanges. "Penny share" stocks of companies with few tangible prospects were often — and still are, despite efforts to protect smaller investors — promoted by unscrupulous dealers to naïve investors who thought — and think — that their low share price (hence the name "penny stocks") meant good potential profits.

US EXCHANGES

In the US, securities trading started with debt issues of the new government, and then in 1791 the first stock exchange was formed in Philadelphia. Soon after, as New York grew in prominence, a group of brokers established an exchange association in 1792, with a great deal of the trading taking place under a tree at 68 Wall Street. Initially most of the trading was in government securities, but later shares of banks, insurance companies and then road and canal companies were traded. Finally in 1817 a New York Stock and Exchange Board was formed, which changed its name to the New York Stock Exchange (NYSE) in 1863. Later, the forerunner of the current American Stock Exchange and others were formed.

The NYSE is one of the world's most important stock exchanges, with the shares of thousands of companies listed. NYSE-listed companies include many of the great names of American business, such as Coca Cola, IBM and GE, often regarded as "blue chip" companies. Each year, some companies are "de-listed" for various reasons, sometimes because they are failing, but more often because they have merged with other companies or have changed their corporate structure. New companies also enter the market, often coming from other, smaller exchanges. Many large foreign companies are also listed on the NYSE to gain access to American investment capital, but most of them do so through American Depositary Receipts (ADRs). The main exceptions are Canadian companies, which are listed in the same way as US firms.

The NYSE has stringent criteria for listing, mostly relating to the size and strength of the company. These include:

- Size of annual earnings

- Market value of the shares

- Number of publicly held shares

- Number of shareholders

The main purpose of these standards is to ensure that there is a fair and liquid market for the shares of companies listed on the NYSE; if, for example, the vast majority of a company's shares is held by insiders, outside investors might be disadvantaged at times.

In NYSE there is no corporate membership; only individuals may be members, although they can be partners or shareholders in companies that deal with the public. Those companies are known as member companies, and all individuals with a 5% or more interest in them must be members or allied members of the exchange. Allied members cannot transact on the floor of the exchange. Since the number of "seats" on the NYSE is limited, in order to become a member a person must acquire it from a current member or a deceased member's estate after passing a securities examination and with the approval of the board of governors, who investigate the applicant's record and financial position.

The NYSE has an unusual broker structure, with different types of brokers: the commission brokers execute orders at or near the market price; the specialist brokers specialize in certain stocks and executes orders for other members; the dealer brokers deal on their own account; the floor brokers (also called "two-dollar" brokers) work orders for other brokers (but not the public) at a commission; the odd-lot brokers buy and sell in quantities that are not the standard 100-share lot; and the "registered traders" buy and sell for their own account.

The specialist broker plays a unique stabilizing role in the market, since he has the responsibility for creating a market in the stocks he is assigned to. He will buy and sell for his own account as well as represent other brokers who are buying or selling but who have orders than cannot be immediately or easily executed. Of course, in times of panic buying, or particularly panic selling, the specialists are often nowhere to be found since they must abdicate their stabilizing role or face bankruptcy.

In early 2006, the Securities and Exchange Commission (SEC) approved the merger of the New York Stock Exchange with the Archipelago organization. That merger added to the NYSE, at that time the world's largest stock exchange, the high-tech trading capabilities of Archipelago. This transaction also transformed the NYSE into a for-profit, publicly traded company, the NYSE Group, so that the NYSE and Archipelago became divisions of the Group. The Group's new stock is now listed on the NYSE. Previous disclosures of widespread violations and a scandal in 2003 about the $188 million pay package of a former NYSE chairman raised concerns regarding the traditional self-regulation system of stock exchanges. A publicly traded vehicle seemed to promote better corporate governance.

The change also reflected the strong competitive pressure from electronically based stock exchange rivals such as the NASDAQ and other electronic trading platforms. One of the strengths of the NYSE was its auction system, which tended to reduce price volatility, but NASDAQ and other electronic trading systems have higher transaction speeds. Ironically, the merger of Archipelago has made it possible to deal in NASDAQ-listed and over-the-counter stocks through the NYSE Group, through Archipelago's electronic trading system. The deal also increased the exchange's market share in exchange-traded funds and derivatives trading.

THE AMERICAN STOCK EXCHANGE (AMEX)

AMEX is also based in New York. Most of the companies listed on AMEX are large or medium sized, but either cannot meet the NYSE's higher criteria for listing or do not wish to migrate to the NYSE. In recent years, however, some of its larger firms have moved across. The number of companies on Amex fluctuates more widely than those on the NYSE, and although its total market capitalization is dwarfed by its larger rival, most of its companies are substantial concerns.

NASDAQ AND THE OTC

The National Association of Securities Dealers (NASD) is a self-regulating body created in 1939 to impose rules on broker-dealers. In 1964, as a result of a number of scandals, the US Congress widened the scope of securities regulation to include the larger over-the-counter firms so as to impose rules on reporting, proxy solicitation and insider trading. Computerized systems have been established to facilitate such trading. NASDAQ, established by NASD in 1971, is a computerized trading system for several thousand of the more important OTC shares. It boasts some of America's largest newer enterprises, including Microsoft and Intel, and became a household name around the world during the dot-com boom of the 1990s, when many new high technology enterprises were able to raise massive sums from the public by listing on NASDAQ.

NASDAQ, together with most of the rest of the OTC market, is a "principal" market, where dealers "make a market" by holding an inventory of shares and offering continuous prices at which they will buy ("bid") or

Figure 8.5 — New York Stock Exchange: value of shares traded (1990 to 2004)

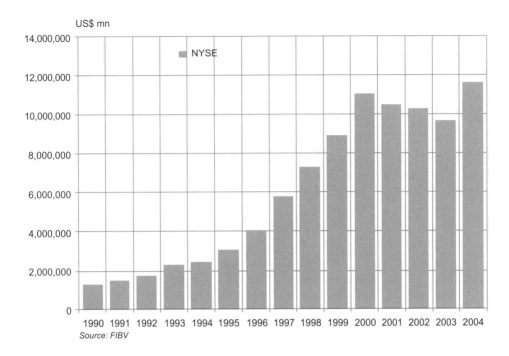

Source: FIBV

sell ("offer") a given stock. The difference between the bid and offer price is known as the "spread," which is the dealer's profit. If a company has a large capitalization and is widely traded, the spread should normally be low and the shares should be liquid; however, companies with low capitalization and little institutional interest may be illiquid, meaning that they are difficult to buy and sell (often they are more difficult to sell than to buy), and spreads may be very large, to reflect the dealer's risk. In some cases, a dealer may opt not to bid for certain stocks at all, making them unsalable for long periods. To protect investors, NASDAQ has introduced "Rules of Fair Trading" that limit the spread in most cases to plus or minus 5% and require dealers to warn customers if the bid prices they quote are not "firm" (guaranteed).

NASDAQ has been a big success, despite the occasional crisis, and has made the OTC a realistic option for professional and private investors from all over the world. As official exchanges move towards computerization, NASDAQ has served as the model for success, and in the future the distinction between it and the other exchanges may become negligible.

The OTC Bulletin Board (OTCBB) was introduced in 1990 as a computerized system for trading in over 4,000 OTC equities that are not listed on NASDAQ. It is an improvement on the Pink Sheets, as firm (binding) prices are more prevalent. Traders may post requests for quotations — e.g. "offer wanted" or "bid wanted." Like other parts of the OTC market, the OTCBB has been vulnerable to fraud in the past, and efforts are being made to regulate it more closely. The OTCBB was created in response to

DO SPECIALISTS HAVE AN UNFAIR ADVANTAGE?

"Specialists compete with limit orders for the provision of liquidity at the New York Stock Exchange. Though the Exchange uses a variety of mechanisms to regulate this competition, specialists have a unique advantage. They know the expressed trading interest of all traders, while a limit order trader only knows about his own order. If the aggregate order information is valuable, then specialists can profit from it through selective participation in trades, thereby exacerbating the adverse selection problem for limit orders...

"We find strong evidence that the specialist uses information from option values more than from quantities in his decision to stop a market order, or trade with

it. This suggests that individual order properties such as duration, price relative to the market, and order size have information content of which only the specialist is likely to be aware. These results are particularly relevant now as the NYSE opens its limit order book by displaying only aggregate quantities to the public. We also find strong evidence for such actions to be more likely in low-priced stocks than high-priced stocks...

"...It may be the case that the specialists are given this advantage, as compensation for meeting their Exchange obligations such as providing liquidity when there is none available."

Source: *L.E. Harris, V. Panchapagesan: Journal of Financial Markets 8 (2005) 25–67 31*

 TERMINOLOGY

PINK SHEETS – *In the US the name derives from the fact that the information was originally printed on pink paper. The sheets have information on OTC shares that are considered "penny stocks" and may be very speculative. The information is produced by Pink Sheets LLC, a private company based in New York. Since 1999 it has operated an electronic price quotations service for OTC securities, available at www.pinksheets.com.*

the Penny Stock Reform Act of 1990, which required the US Securities and Exchange Commission (SEC) to set up an electronic quotation system. All foreign securities and ADRs that are fully registered with the SEC can be quoted on the OTCBB. The OTCBB is a separate entity from NASDAQ and the Pink Sheets, and only lists stock quotations from subscribing market markers (currently over 200).

MAJOR NON-US EXCHANGES

Although the US remains the largest and most important center for dealing in equities, there are many other stock exchanges located in other countries. The most important of these are located in Europe and the Asia Pacific region, reflecting the economic importance of these areas in global business. As investment interest has shifted to developing countries enjoying high growth, such as China and India, and countries in Latin America and Eastern Europe, exchanges there are gaining importance, but are still markedly less developed. These are attractive only to professional investors who have the capacity to cope with the many practical difficulties they inevitably encounter.

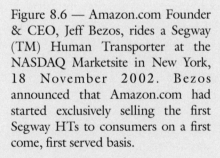

Figure 8.6 — Amazon.com Founder & CEO, Jeff Bezos, rides a Segway (TM) Human Transporter at the NASDAQ Marketsite in New York, 18 November 2002. Bezos announced that Amazon.com had started exclusively selling the first Segway HTs to consumers on a first come, first served basis.

Source: AFP Photo

LONDON STOCK EXCHANGE (LSE)

The LSE is a major international financial center; many non-UK companies are listed here and there is a vigorous managed-fund sector making investments all over the world. Deregulation during the 1980s opened the doors to foreign purchasers of UK securities houses. The exchange continues to outstrip its continental rivals, despite predictions that it could eventually lose its pre-eminent position to Frankfurt.

EURONEXT

Euronext N.V. is a holding company that was formed in 2000 under Dutch law. It was formed when the Amsterdam, Brussels and Paris exchanges merged, and was expanded in 2002 when it acquired LIFFE (the London International Financial Futures and Options Exchange) and merged with the Portuguese BVLP (Bolsa de Valores de Lisboa e Porto) exchange. Today it is the leading cross-border exchange in Europe. It integrates trading and clearing operations on both regulated and non-regulated markets for stocks as well as derivatives. In December of 2003, the London Clearing House and Clearnet merged to create LCH Clearnet, Europe's largest provider of clearing and central counterparty services.

GERMAN EXCHANGES

Germany has eight regional exchanges that together make the largest market after New York, London and Tokyo. As an industrial giant, Germany is of substantial interest to foreign investors. Investors need to be aware of the important differences between the German and the "Anglo-Saxon" models in the reporting of accounts, financing of companies, etc, as well as of the domination of German banks in financial services.

PARIS BOURSE

France is one of the world's leading economies, but historically it has favored strong state involvement in big business over privately funded and controlled enterprises. The Paris Bourse lists the stocks of France's top companies, which can be freely traded by foreigners, but local private investors have little involvement in equities, as they prefer to invest in bonds and state-backed investment schemes.

TOKYO STOCK EXCHANGE (TSE)

The TSE is Japan's largest stock exchange, listing most of the largest Japanese firms. The TSE also has a section for non-Japanese companies, but some limitations exist for foreign investors, and it remains primarily the means for investing in Japan, rather than a truly international exchange.

STOCK EXCHANGE OF HONG KONG (SEHK)

Hong Kong's stock exchange was established in the 1800s, and it is widely seen as the most important, sophisticated and internationalized financial center in Asia, attracting investors from all over the world. Since Hong Kong's return to the People's Republic of China in 1997, there have been fears that its importance will be eclipsed by the growing markets in mainland China, such as Shanghai. However, its sophistication, openness and cosmopolitan approach have so far allowed it to maintain its status as the first port of call for foreign investors in Asia.

INTERNATIONALIZATION AND MERGERS

With the growth of international investing, stock exchanges have increasingly seen the need to expand their operations beyond their original borders. By mid-2006, the "urge to merge" between American and European stock exchanges moved apace. The New York Stock Exchange planned to spend $10 billion to purchase Euronext, which itself was the result of a series of mergers. This would be the first transatlantic exchange capable of offering equities, options and futures. But there was opposition to such a merger, as some preferred a merger of Euronext with the Deutsche Borse. At the same time the London Stock Exchange was being courted by the Deutsche Borse, NASDAQ and others.

One of the reasons for the desire to merge was the increasing competition. As a result of technology that was creating more efficient trading methods than the traditional ones, commissions were declining and more trading volume was taking place off exchanges in banks and in alternative networks. Also, there was reduced opposition from stock exchange members who were traditionally organized as mutual trading clubs and resisted greater efficiency that promised to benefit customers but at the expense of their own profit sources. But with demutualization, members voted to turn their exchanges into for-profit firms. Those members then sold their shares or became shareholders and thus were interested in maximizing the value of their firms rather than serving the narrow interests of members. By 2001 the three major European exchanges, the London Stock Exchange, Euronext and Deutsche Borse, had demutualized, and later the NYSE joined the club and listed its shares. There is also a push from hedge funds, which account for an estimated 40% of the volumes on the US exchanges. Those funds often use automated algorithmic trading methods that involve large quantities of electronic limit orders designed to take advantage of opportunities that may exist for only a second. Since building trading platforms for large and fast order flows is an expensive exercise, entailing capital expenses, economies of scale are important. According to a European Commission document, Europe's total cost of trading clearing and settlement could be cut substantially as a result of consolidation.

TRADING SYSTEMS

Stock exchanges normally conduct business using the auction process, where there is open and public buying and selling, bidding prices until the bids can be matched. Securities are bought from the broker offering the lowest price and sold to the broker offering the highest price. For large markets, this auction process is continuous throughout the daily trading sessions. In smaller markets where the volume and activity are not so great, a rotation system, or "call market," may be used where each stock is taken one at a time and then auctioned.

Orders on stock exchanges are treated in different ways according to the size of the order and the liquidity of the particular stock. Normally in the NYSE when a customer gives an order to a broker member the order is transmitted to the exchange floor where the clerk receiving the order takes it to the post where the stock is traded and starts to bid or offer in the auction depending on whether he is buying or selling. In cases where the order is not a market order (where immediate action is required at the prevailing price), the broker's clerk takes it to the specialist in that stock and gives him the order at a specified price. The specialist will then execute the order when the indicated price is reached. In the case of large orders from such institutions as insurance companies, mutual funds and pension funds, the challenge is to execute big blocks of orders. One way to do this is to break them up into smaller orders and execute them gradually over a period of time in order to avoid having an impact on the market. Another way is for brokers to assemble, buy and sell orders off the market and then "cross" them so that the traditional auction process is bypassed. In some cases the broker may take a position and purchase the block from the selling institution and then sell it over a period of time. There are a number of variations to this theme where various operations are undertaken off the floor of the exchange in order to execute large orders.

The NASDAQ market is a negotiated market compared to the auction market. Investors trading over-the-counter securities give their orders to brokers who search for other brokers to obtain the best price. For large blocks of listed securities, some firms who are not stock exchange members have established a "third market" of over-the-counter trading in those blocks, but based on prices of the formal exchange. A "fourth market" also exists, where large investors trade amongst themselves without an intermediating broker.

On the London Stock Exchange, brokers act on behalf of their customers, while the jobbers do not deal with the public. The jobbers in London are similar to the specialists in New York. They are principals buying and selling for their own account and deal only with brokers and other jobbers. It is the broker's job to get the best possible price from the jobbers. While the brokers receive a commission on these transactions, jobbers try to make profits by increasing the difference or spread between their buying and selling prices. In New York, the specialists are under an obligation to create an active market and support prices; in London, the jobbers have no such responsibility.

In the US, electronic trading became formalized in 1980 when the SEC passed a rule that allowed New York Stock Exchange member firms to trade listed stocks off the exchange floor in an "over the counter" (OTC) market. Unfortunately, since it was a closed group of brokers involved in the market, the bid-offer spreads were so wide that "...you could drive a truck through them...". However, the situation changed when two professors from Vanderbilt University published a study in the Journal of Finance that highlighted the absence of "odd-eighth quotes" (quotes in odd-eighths of a dollar) in the OTC. From this they surmised that there was collusion among the market makers to ensure that spreads remained high. As a result of the study, the Justice Department charged the dealers with antitrust violations. This stimulated a number of class-action lawsuits by the clients of those dealers. By 1999, the dealers had paid $910 million to settle private lawsuits and agreed to pay the SEC nearly $27 million in fines.

ORDER TYPES

There are a number of different ways that orders to buy or sell stocks are made. The different types are as follows:

Market Order:

The most common type of order is a "market order," where the investor instructs the broker to buy or sell at the best prevailing price available, when the order reaches the stock exchange floor or trading system. For very liquid stocks with heavy trading turnover this is the most efficient, since the best price prevailing for the buyer or seller will be used by the broker. For illiquid securities, such orders can be dangerous since price fluctuations could be high and the order may be executed at a bad price.

Limit Order:

The buyer or seller gives a specific price at which he is willing to buy or sell and the order must be executed at that price or better. (Middle price orders: In some markets the "middle price" mechanism is used, where an investor giving a limit order before the stock exchange opening will have it done at the day's median level or a price better than the limit, whichever is better for the client.)

Stop Order:

These orders are used to protect or take advantage of sudden price turns. A **stop-loss order** is an order to buy or sell a security as soon as a specific price is reached. As soon as that price is reached, the customer's security is placed in the market and the order becomes a market order. Such stop-loss orders protect customers from market reversals and, as the name implies, prevents or stops losses. Of course, in rapidly changing markets no one knows at what price the orders will be executed and the losses could be greater than expected.

A **stop-sell order** is an order to sell at a specified price below the current market price, while a **buy stop order** is an order to buy a share if it reaches a specified price below the current market price. If the specified price is reached, the stop order becomes a market order, and is executed as soon as possible. The idea of using stop orders is to protect the frequent trader at times when she is not watching the market and ready to react; however, there are two major problems: (1) in a market crash, it may not be possible to execute the stop order at the specified price, and (2) a very short-term fluctuation may trigger a stop order, but prices may then reverse for a long period, leaving the investor feeling that they have set the stop price too near to the market price.

Immediate-or-cancel (IOC) – This is a rare form of the limit order, enabling the broker to fulfill part of the order and cancel the rest if the desired price is restricted by the specialist to a certain number of shares.

Fill-or-kill (FOK) – This is another variation on the limit order, requiring the broker either to execute the entire order immediately at the desired price or to cancel it.

Good-till-cancelled (GTC) orders – These widely used orders may use a limit, stop, or stop-limit, and their acceptance is at the broker's discretion. Normally a GTC order must not be excessively far away from the current price.

Day orders – Many exchanges require that any order that is given without a specified time limit (which is common because investors assume they will be fulfilled rapidly) must be treated as a "day order" and resubmitted the following day if unfulfilled. Some financial institutions use day orders in preference to GTC orders (which are registered with a specialist) to prevent others from guessing their aims.

Good-through-this-week (GTW) orders – GTW orders, and a variant, good-through-this-month (GTM) orders, are often used by investors who will be away from the market for some time. GTWs and GTMs are banned on some exchanges, and many brokers refuse them because of the extra record keeping required.

Odd lots – Most orders on the NYSE are for "round lots" of 100 shares or multiples of 100 shares, but it is also possible to buy or sell lots of less than the standard "round lot" size; these are known as "odd lots." In the past, odd lots were mostly used by people who could not afford to purchase a round lot, but since the mid-1970s the volume of odd-lot transactions has grown, partly because many stock option schemes and other investment plans use them. Transaction charges tend to be a little higher for odd lots, but investors sometimes prefer to purchase an odd lot if they can obtain faster execution of the order. The range of orders available varies on other major exchanges; London, for example, does not use odd lots and round lots, but brokers may require a minimum order size in money terms, or charge a minimum commission fee that effectively creates a minimum order size. Generally speaking, some of the non-US exchanges, particularly in Europe, are not eager to encourage small investors to indulge in the short-term trading that a very wide range of orders may encourage, and the more obscure order types may only be available to larger investors.

BROKERS/DEALERS/JOBBERS

Brokers buy and sell stocks on behalf of their clients, earning a commission on the transaction. Dealers and jobbers buy and sell stocks on their own account. Although a broker may also be a dealer, they cannot be both in the same transaction, since there could be a conflict of interest.

Securities houses may own brokers, dealers, market-makers, investment analysts and investment banks, while operating mutual funds and other financial services aimed at retail customers. For such financial conglomerates, there is considerable potential for insider dealing and other abuses of the system. Regulatory bodies, such as the SEC in the US, go to great lengths to minimize the opportunities for such abuse, using the "Chinese walls" system. Although the origin of the term is uncertain, it appears to derive from the enormous length of the Great Wall of China, the largest man-made border in the world. The idea is to keep the different activities segregated from one another. For example, if a firm's investment banking arm is underwriting a share issue or arranging a merger, it will possess privileged "inside" information; Chinese walls are intended to prevent, say, the firm's brokers from gaining access to this information and taking advantage of it in the market.

Market-makers (known as "specialists" on the NYSE) are "wholesale" dealers in specific stocks who guarantee to buy or sell these stocks at all times to ensure liquidity, although they are not required, for example, to buy up every stock in a collapsing market. They make their profit on the spread between the bid and offer prices, and in theory the spreads on larger, more actively traded stocks should be lower than on less popular stocks. On the NYSE and many other exchanges, the market-maker/specialist is the sole market-maker for designated stocks. This differs from NASDAQ, where there are many market-makers for the same stocks. Market-makers make extensive use of short sales using borrowed stock to help keep the market liquid.

TRANSACTION COSTS

According to studies of transaction costs around the world, the total cost of transactions varies widely among the world's exchanges, from a high of nearly 150 basis points (1.5%) of the transaction value to as little as 22 basis points (0.22%). See Figure 8.7 for a list of transaction cost from around the world. Private investors, who generally deal in far lower quantities than

Figure 8.7 — The cost of executing trades across the world - 2005

Country	Average 07/03-06/04 total (basis points)	Average 2003 total (basis points)	Average 2002 total (basis points)
Argentina	50.25	49.91	141.29
Australia	30.83	32.11	33.61
Austria	28.87	31.58	32.30
Belgium	29.96	27.73	35.24
Brazil	45.59	46.42	45.12
Canada	25.35	30.15	32.62
Chile	72.42	82.28	102.00
Colombia	111.21	75.27	91.39
Czech Republic	63.02	51.60	61.90
Denmark	28.41	33.98	38.88
Finland	36.34	39.20	38.10
France	28.36	26.06	31.86
Germany	32.17	32.99	30.11
Greece	55.55	61.45	59.33
Hong Kong	42.11	44.72	47.10
Hungary	62.03	57.17	62.11
India	51.49	54.15	64.32
Indonesia	67.43	67.70	85.86
Ireland - Buys	129.41	126.35	141.32
Ireland - Sells	36.04	41.57	40.25
Italy	31.48	31.85	33.46
Japan	20.57	19.15	21.77
Korea	57.58	61.03	64.05
Luxembourg	27.84	38.27	59.98
Malaysia	53.78	58.11	60.06
Mexico	35.66	36.84	42.87
Netherlands	29.08	28.68	28.28
New Zealand	40.91	47.49	32.13
Norway	35.56	32.20	41.21
Peru	55.52	44.90	67.54
Philippines	97.37	94.46	87.88
Portugal	33.70	30.38	37.29
Singapore	40.03	38.31	44.41
South Africa	46.76	50.97	50.92
Spain	26.66	32.01	49.93
Sweden	28.74	28.72	34.47
Switzerland	26.52	22.52	34.44
Taiwan	55.71	60.09	58.25
Thailand	51.96	57.89	68.74
Turkey	54.12	58.48	53.95
U.K. - Buys	74.01	71.47	72.47
U.K. - Sells	25.53	31.83	31.55
U.S. - NYSE	25.87	29.00	29.30
U.S. - Nasdaq	34.50	38.87	40.36
Venezuela	76.41	74.70	81.33
Overall	46.95	47.35	54.25

Source: Elkins/McSherry.

A "basis point" is one hundredth of one percent. Therefore, 10 basis points equals 0.10%.

institutions, pay higher transaction costs, which is one of the main reasons why they are usually advised not to trade frequently.

PROBLEMS WITH TRANSACTION COSTS

The shares of the largest companies should, in theory, be cheaper to trade than others because there are more active buyers and sellers. During the last few years, however, institutional investors have complained about delays in execution and that they have been paying too much in transaction costs on the NYSE for high volume deals in the shares of large companies. Some have even found that they were able to make better deals for the same stocks on NASDAQ and other OTC systems, although these markets generally have higher transaction costs. While commissions for large deals are only a fraction of 1% of their value (while small private investors may pay 2% or more on smaller deals), even a small difference in costs can add up to large sums of money, especially for an institution that is buying and selling every working day. For mutual funds, this is an area of particular concern because higher transaction costs reduce their overall investment performance, the key measure by which their customers judge them.

CLEARING AND TRANSFER OPERATIONS

Once the transaction has been agreed on the exchange floor, the details are reported to record-keeping departments of both parties, who then produce a written confirmation of the details of the deal for their clients and also report the details to the exchange's "clearing" system. "Clearing" is the process by which the exchange reconciles the details of every deal, as reported by both sides in each transaction, and asks the parties to rectify any mistakes. On the major exchanges, the volume of transactions is staggering, and there is always the risk that a broker/dealer may default on payments when they become due. To prevent the chaos that this can cause, member firms generally pay money regularly into a "clearing fund," which will cover losses in the event of a firm's failure.

On most exchanges, the ownership title of a security is transferred when payment is made, usually some days after the transaction occurs. Computerization has led many exchanges to dispense with physical share certificates, although they are still used in some markets. Most securities houses use a bank or trust company as a "transfer agent" that records changes in stock ownership, cancels old certificates and issues new ones. Transfer agents may also redeem shares in mutual funds at the request of a customer. When a transaction has occurred, the transfer agent notifies the "registrar," who keeps a list of all the stockholders of a firm, so that ownership records can be updated. Part of the registrar's job is to ensure that the number of shares in issue tally after each transaction. This is to avoid an accidental watering-down of the value of shares, which would occur if too many new shares were issued after a transaction.

MARGIN TRADING

In the equities markets, trading on "margin" allows the investor to use leverage when purchasing stocks. The huge growth in derivatives in recent years has created many new and sophisticated ways of using margin in investment. The traditional method entails purchasing a number of shares, paying a deposit and obtaining credit for the balance of the purchase price. The credit is provided through the broker, who "hypothecates" the stock by pledging it as collateral for a bank loan to finance the customer's loan. The broker typically adds interest to the bank's interest rate, but the total interest charged to a private investor is often competitive because the broker can obtain a low interest rate from the bank.

Using leverage when purchasing shares is considerably more risky than, say, a mortgage, since such leverage is short-term and subject to share price volatility. Investors who pay the full purchase price limit their maximum loss to 100%; if the share price falls, they have the option to hold on to their investment indefinitely until the share price rises. Purchasers on margin may be subject to a "margin call" if the share price declines. They then have to come up with the money for the loan or the broker will sell the stock in the market at a loss.

To prevent unsophisticated investors from getting into difficulty, many stock exchanges ban or limit the use of margin for direct investment in equities. In the US, during the "Roaring Twenties", there were no restrictions on margin trading, and many small investors used margin in the hope of getting rich quick. Deposits were as low as 10% of the purchase price, and stock prices were very volatile. In the Wall Street Crash of 1929, many margin traders lost everything as prices collapsed. As indicated by Figure 8.8, margin debt has increased substantially. Before 1990 it was less

 TERMINOLOGY

CHINESE WALLS – *The system of policies, procedures and physical arrangements used to manage confidential information. Chinese walls are intended to prevent the misuse of inside information.*

INSIDE INFORMATION – *Confidential and detailed information about financial instruments, which is likely to have a significant impact on the price.*

CONFLICTS OF INTEREST – *Conflicts of interest arise when an intermediary, such as a broker, has incentives other than simply acting in the best possible way for the client. The main ways of preventing conflicts of interest include: disclosure to clients, consent of clients, Chinese walls, and declining to act.*

"CHINESE WALLS" FAIL TO CURB CONFLICTS OF INTEREST IN SECURITIES FIRMS

Information continues to flow between departments at securities firms despite laws designed to prevent potential conflicts of interest and insider trading, according to a new University of Michigan Business School study.

"Our study does not support the logic of the recent deregulation in financial services firms that assumes Chinese walls are effective and appropriate," said H. Nejat Seyhun, professor of finance at the U-M Business School. "Recent deregulation has moved away from complete separation of various functions under separate corporate ownerships and allowed the same firm to engage in multi-service activities provided they are separated by a Chinese wall…"

"But our evidence shows that these walls do not work effectively and that information flows between departments. Chinese walls need to be reinforced and measures are needed for increased monitoring and increased sanctions for violations."

Source: *University of Michigan News Service,* September 2005

than US$50 billion on the NYSE, but by 2004 it had risen to over US$200 billion.

SHORT SELLING

Short selling, or selling something that you do not actually possess, existed before stock markets; in any community of traders of basic commodities, the potential for reducing risk by fixing a future price — or to increase possible gains by speculating on future prices — has been evident since ancient times. If a farmer expected to harvest a large corn crop, he might agree to sell it before the actual harvest if he thought the current price was better than the price at harvest time. With the advent of shares, opportunities for short selling increased. Early speculative booms, such as those that occurred in 17th century Amsterdam, encouraged short selling, which was blamed for the decline in prices during the collapse that followed. Ever since, politicians and loss-making investors have frequently sought to blame short selling for market ills.

Amsterdam experienced two major speculative booms during the 1600s — first, on the shares of the Dutch East India Company, the only company then traded on the Amsterdam market, and later on the tulip market, when speculative activity grew to the point where more contracts for future delivery of tulip bulbs were made than could be supplied.

In 1720, a speculative boom occurred in England as investors scrambled to trade shares in the government-endorsed South Sea

Figure 8.8 — Margin debt on the NYSE

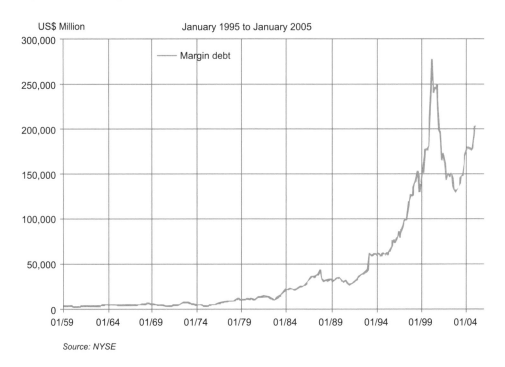

Source: NYSE

Company, which was to enjoy a monopoly of trade in the South Seas, and in the aftermath many prominent insiders were castigated for selling short. A little earlier, France also suffered a speculative bubble in the shares of the Mississippi Company, and short selling was forbidden by royal decree. After the French Revolution, Napoleon continued to outlaw short selling on the grounds that short sellers wanted government stocks — essential to his war effort — to drop in price.

In the US, the time between the late 19th and early 20th centuries was a heyday for professional stock manipulators, for whom short selling was an important activity. In New York, short selling was banned following speculation at the outbreak of the war of 1812, but this was eventually repealed in the 1850s, only to be reintroduced briefly by the Gold Speculation Act of 1864. A run on English banks in 1866 was initially blamed on short sellers and legislation was introduced to prevent the activity.

The "Robber Barons" of that unregulated era were able to pull off staggering maneuvers. For example, in 1869 Jim Fisk and Jay Gould issued vast amounts of new stock for the Erie Railroad, sold much of it short and at the same time withdrew millions from the New York banks, reducing the banks' liquidity. This caused interest rates to rise and stock prices began to fall. The government intervened to improve liquidity, and Gould and Fisk were able to cover their short positions and then to "squeeze" their crony, Daniel Drew, who also had sold stock short but had reneged on their arrangement. As Erie stock soared, Fisk and Gould were able to sell their stock back for a large profit. The following year, the duo attempted a similar maneuver in gold, but were thwarted by government action to flood the market.

Prior to the Wall Street Crash of 1929, other high profile speculators, such as Jesse Livermore, Bernard Baruch, Ben Smith and Joseph Kennedy (the father of the former US president), made fortunes by short selling. One of the worst scandals occurred in 1929, when Albert Wiggin, President of Chase Bank, sold Chase stock short on his personal account and then used money borrowed from the bank to cover. It subsequently emerged that he had sold much of this stock to fellow members of a banking consortium who were attempting to support prices by coordinated buying.

Many of the pre-1929 coups were in no way illegal at the time, and recriminations generally arose only in the aftermath of the collapse. For agonized investors who had lost fortunes, short selling was an easy scapegoat. Time and again, however, official investigations found little evidence that short selling "caused" investment bubbles to burst; often the scale of short selling was relatively small compared with overall market activity and short sellers frequently lost money. The NYSE, for example, found no evidence of a short-selling conspiracy between 1929 and 1931. The SEC, founded after the Wall Street Crash, was initially under pressure to blame short sellers for the economy's ills, but eventually established that the real problems lay in stock manipulation by insiders, and set out regulations that form the basis of today's anti-insider rules.

DERIVATIVES

Derivatives are financial instruments that are "derived" from assets such as equities, bonds and commodities. Derivatives originated centuries ago in the need of merchants, farmers and other producers of basic goods to reduce their risk in the face of unpredictable fluctuations in supply and demand. A coffee producer, for instance, may be unable to predict either the amount of coffee that next year's harvest will yield or what the market price will be at that time. Like any business, the coffee producer has to think ahead for several years and make plans for investment, growth and so on, so a stable, predictable income is very valuable. If the coffee producer can make a contract with, say, a middleman, to deliver next year's harvest at a fixed price, which gives her a profit, then she can make concrete plans for the business, keep her bank happy and be assured of survival. If the actual market price of coffee is higher than her agreed price when the time comes to deliver, the coffee producer is not unduly concerned; she has "hedged" her risk successfully and avoided loss.

The same principle can be applied to financial instruments such as equities, and bonds and can also be based on exchange rates, interest rates and indices. For example, suppose you are heavily invested in equities that you believe have good long-term prospects, but you are concerned that their value may fall in the short term. By purchasing a contract that guarantees you a certain return if the market price of your holdings drops below a certain level, you "insure" yourself against possible losses, assuming that the price is acceptable.

Derivatives make extensive use of leverage, and are therefore attractive to speculators. Speculators are not seeking to reduce their risks by hedging, but to increase their risks — and potential rewards. The difference between speculation and hedging is, in theory, clear-cut, but in practice the distinction has often been blurred. Many high profile disasters such as the collapse of the Barings Bank and the insolvency of Orange County, California, occurred when individuals within the organization speculated using derivatives when they were either supposed to keep within defined risk limits or had been instructed to hedge, not to speculate. Often, the exposure to risk from open derivatives positions are not fully reported in the accounts, and even senior managers may have been unaware of the risks being taken.

HEDGE FUNDS

In recent years, theoretical advances in the valuation of derivatives have led to an explosion in their use, both for hedging and for speculation. Professionally managed funds, known as hedge funds, have proliferated. The term "hedge fund" covers a very wide range of investment activities, and the risks involved depend upon the specific transactions that a given hedge fund takes on. Originally these were restricted to institutions and high net worth private investors who were willing and able to cope with the risks, but more recently they have been adapted for the wider investment market. In some cases, a hedge fund may be involved in highly speculative positions that have little to do with hedging.

 TERMINOLOGY

"NAKED" SHORT SELLING – *Normally traders must borrow stock before they sell it short. But, in a naked short sale the seller does not borrow or arrange to borrow the stock in time to make delivery to the buyer within the standard settlement period. Therefore, the seller may fail to deliver the securities when delivery is due. This is known as a "failure to deliver" or "fail." Some argue that naked short selling contributes to market liquidity when broker-dealers engage in such practices in order to make a market in a security so that the security may have a regular and continued pricing. Therefore, naked short selling is not a securities regulation violation in the US if it is done for that market-making purpose. However, if it is done for the purpose of manipulating the stock, then in the US it is a serious securities law violation of the Exchange Act.*

"I'm looking for a hedge against my hedge funds."

"Structured products" are another area of innovation. These are generally tailor-made agreements that bundle several different kinds of risk together into a form that superficially resembles a bond. An investor may purchase a structured product that is designed to protect her main investment portfolio against short-term or medium-term risks. The key problem is in assessing the value of these risks and deciding on a fair price for such "insurance." A company that is under pressure to perform consistently every quarter, for instance, may need such insurance, while an investor who can afford to ride out volatility over many years may perceive it to be too expensive.

Derivatives are a strong growth area in financial services, offering both profit opportunities to financial institutions that are struggling to compete in the more conventional markets and new career opportunities to young professionals. For the investors who purchase these contracts, however, the key questions remain: "Do I need to hedge?" and "What is it going to cost?"

CASE STUDY: LONG TERM CAPITAL MANAGEMENT

Despite the current popularity of hedging and derivatives, there is a sizeable body of professional investment opinion that they, in the words of one fund manager, "are like giving whisky to an alcoholic." In other words, despite the many assurances that it is possible to use derivatives in a disciplined manner to reduce risks, the temptation to take on greater and greater risks is very great, and could cause serious damage to the markets. Derivatives "nay-sayers" like to point to the collapse of Long Term Capital Management (LTCM), a hedge fund that was bailed out in 1998 to prevent a potential financial panic.

LTCM was founded in 1994 by a group of entrepreneurial senior financial traders who recruited the top "rocket scientists" in the derivatives field to help them, including two Nobel Laureate academics Myron Scholes and Robert Menton who had developed methods of valuing and modeling these arcane instruments. The initial capital was raised from financial institutions and wealthy people, many of whom were Wall Street professionals, who were willing and able to take large risks in the hope of gaining large rewards.

LTCM's goal was to identify and exploit short-term value differences across many types of financial securities across the world using sophisticated analysis. For example, if they thought that, say, yields on German government bonds were likely to converge with the yields on French government bonds, they would buy bonds from the country with the higher yield and sell short an equal amount of bonds from the country with the lower yield. If the assumption of convergence was correct, the result would be a small "guaranteed" profit. To increase these profits, LTCM made extensive use of leverage, which is widely available for derivatives.

Using highly intricate models involving many transactions, the company sought to find as many of these "arbitrage" opportunities as possible. During the first two years of trading it had considerable success, earning annual profits of more than 40%. As competitors entered the game, however, price mismatches began to diminish, and LTCM's profits fell. Under pressure to perform well, the company sought to take on more risk during 1997, committing itself to a labyrinthine series of interlinked contracts that left it exposed to change.

LTCM's models relied, like all models, on certain assumptions — specifically, that there were "normal" trading conditions, and that these would continue. During 1997, market conditions around the world became "abnormal" (for example, many Asian economies went into a nosedive during the Asian currency crisis), LTCM's assumptions were incorrect and it suffered heavy losses; the firm did not want to get out of the markets at once because this would entail even greater losses.

The following year, the situation worsened, and the firm is alleged to have had potential losses of $80 billion. Regulatory pressure was put on some of the firm's creditors to bail it out to prevent a crash that could have spread around the world; this action attracted much criticism at the time, since it seemed to fly in the face of the free market economics that the government was promoting. However, the creditors took control of the firm and supplied it with sufficient cash for it to unwind its contracts and avert a general financial crisis; many regard this as a healthy response to the problem.

Figure 8.9 — Harvard University professor Robert C. Merton, 53, speaks to the media at Harvard in Cambridge, MA, on 14 October 1997. He was awarded the 1997 Nobel Economics Prize, along with Myron S. Scholes, for developing a pioneering formula for the valuation of derivatives. The formula is used daily by traders and investors to value stock options in markets throughout the world.

Source: AFP Photo

OPINION
TIME BOMB DERIVATIVES

Warren Buffett on derivatives in his annual letter to shareholders, March 2003:

"We view them as time bombs, both for the parties that deal in them and the economic system... Essentially, these instruments call for money to change hands at some future date, with the amount to be determined by one or more reference items, such as interest rates, stock prices or currency values... Unless derivatives contracts are collateralized or guaranteed, their ultimate value also depends on the creditworthiness of the counterparties to them. In the meantime, though, before a contract is settled, the counterparties record profits and losses -- often huge in amount -- in their current earnings statements without so much as a penny changing hands... Errors will usually be honest, reflecting only the human tendency to take an optimistic view of one's commitments. But the parties to derivatives also have enormous incentives to cheat in accounting for them. Those who trade derivatives are usually paid (in whole or part) on 'earnings' calculated by mark-to-market accounting. But often there is no real market... and 'mark-to-model' is utilized. This substitution can bring on large-scale mischief. .... In extreme cases, mark-to-model degenerates into what I would call mark-to-myth... Both internal and outside auditors review the numbers, but that's no easy job. For example, General Re Securities at year-end (after ten months of winding down its operation) had 14,384 contracts outstanding, involving 672 counterparties around the world. Each contract had a plus or minus value derived from one or more reference items, including some of mind-boggling complexity. Valuing a portfolio like that, expert auditors could easily and honestly have widely varying opinions."

Buffett concludes: "The derivatives genie is now well out of the bottle, and these instruments will almost certainly multiply in variety and number until some event makes their toxicity clear. Knowledge of how dangerous they are has already permeated the electricity and gas businesses, in which the eruption of major troubles caused the use of derivatives to diminish dramatically. Elsewhere, however, the derivatives business continues to expand unchecked. Central banks and governments have so far found no effective way to control, or even monitor, the risks posed by these contracts."

OPINION
GEORGE SOROS ON LTCM

"When the markets were shaken by the Russian situation, a lot of the normal relationships between different markets were thrown off - say, the relationship between the prices of corporate bonds and treasury bonds. When these relationships get out of line, they can be a profitable opportunity because eventually they can be expected to return to normal. But this time they did not return to normal or, at least, not soon enough. The analytical system that Long-Term Capital Management used to exploit such opportunities works 99.9 percent of the time. But because they had borrowed so heavily, that very unusual deviation of the markets, which might occur 0.1 percent of

the time, caused them almost to run out of capital.

If Long-Term Capital had been forced to liquidate, the deviations from the normal behavior of bonds and other investments would have been even greater and the effects on the banks would have been even worse. That is why the New York Federal Reserve intervened. One really interesting thing is that it showed how faulty are the methods banks use to assess and manage risks."

Source: *Jean-René Giraud, The Management of Hedge Funds' Operational Risks, EDHEC, April 2004. The International Financial Crisis. - An Interview with Hedge Fund Manager George Soros*

SUMMARY

There are many stock exchanges around the world, often with different rules, subject to different tax regimes and facing different legal requirements. They also vary widely in size and importance. The NYSE is the world's most important stock exchange, listing about 3,000 major US companies, such as IBM and GE. Many large foreign firms are also listed on the NYSE, mainly through American Depositary Receipts. Like the other major markets, the NYSE has stringent criteria for listing, mostly relating to the size and strength of the company.

Many unlisted securities have traditionally been traded outside the official stock exchanges in the "over-the-counter" (OTC) markets. In the US, the OTC is very large. NASDAQ, established in 1971, is a computerized trading system for several thousand of the best OTC shares, including Microsoft and Intel. NASDAQ, together with most of the rest of the OTC market, is a "principal" market, where dealers "make a market" by holding an inventory of shares and offering continuous prices at which they will buy or sell.

Market-makers, known as "specialists" on the NYSE, are "wholesale" dealers in specific stocks who guarantee to buy or sell these stocks at all times to ensure liquidity. They make their profit on the spread. On many exchanges, the market-maker/specialist is the sole market-maker for designated stocks, unlike in NASDAQ, where there are many market-makers for the same stock.

Brokers buy and sell stocks on behalf of their clients, earning a commission on the transaction. Dealers buy and sell stocks on their own account. Although a broker may also be a dealer, they cannot do both in the same transaction.

The most common type of order is a "market order," where the investor instructs the broker to buy or sell at the best price available at the time. There are many other types of orders used, such as stop orders and limit orders, which are price-dependent.

Once a transaction has been agreed, the details are reported to the exchange's "clearing" system. "Clearing" is the process by which the exchange reconciles the details of every deal, as reported by both sides in each transaction, and asks the parties to rectify any mistakes. To prevent the risk that a broker/dealer may default on payments when they become due, many exchanges have a "clearing fund," which will cover losses in the event of a firm's failure.

- Trading on "margin" allows the investor to use leverage when purchasing stocks.

- "Selling short" is to sell a financial security that you do not own by borrowing shares from a securities house.

- Derivatives are financial instruments that are derived from assets such as equities, bonds and commodities.

Financial derivatives can be based on equities, bonds, exchange rates, interest rates and indices. By purchasing a contract that guarantees you a certain return if the market price of your holdings moves past a certain level, you can "insure" yourself against possible losses — this is known as "hedging."

Professionally managed hedge funds have proliferated in recent years. The term "hedge fund" covers a wide range of investment activities; they do not only deal in derivatives. Some hedge funds take highly risky positions that are in no way a "hedge" against loss.

1. Are all stocks equally liquid?

2. Why do transaction costs matter?

3. What are the risks of using margin?

4. Is short selling good or bad for markets?

5. How might an apparent hedge actually increase risk?

6. What is the significance of "Chinese walls"? Why might they not be effective?

7. You receive a newsletter promoting very high potential returns from penny shares; how would you investigate these claims?

8. A small foreign firm wants an American listing. Which exchange is it most likely to approach, and why?

9. You purchase 32 shares on the NYSE. Is this an odd lot or a round lot?

10. You are quoted $15.00/$15.25 for a stock. What is the spread?

11. I'm a market-maker. My bid price is $20. Am I buying or selling?

FINANCIAL STATEMENTS

THE FIRST SOURCE

Stock exchanges and capital market regulators the world over make it mandatory for companies to publish audited financial statements, which are often the first source of information that investors may have about a particular company. Ideally, the financial statements, the core of a company report, should tell you a lot of what you would need to know about a company's past performance, a major element in evaluating its stock price. In reality, however, they represent a compromise between what the company wants to tell the public, the nature and effectiveness of the prevalent auditing standards, and the level of transparency that institutional investors and regulators can enforce in a business culture.

The three main financial statements are:

• Balance sheet

• Income statement (called the "profit and loss" in some countries)

• Cash flow statement

These provide the key materials that an investor may need to understand the company and its financial health. Of course, there are other important elements such as the notes to the accounts, the chairman's statement, corporate governance statement, etc. However, even these statements don't tell you about the company's future performance. In addition to analyzing the financial statements, valuation entails research of the company's industry, the management, the customers, the suppliers, etc.

ACCOUNTING PRINCIPLES

There is no single, generally accepted theory of accounting. Different countries, industries and companies use very different methods to obtain the information they need. This creates challenges for all participants — company managers and directors, investors and stock analysts. Ironically, continual changes in accounting standards, and the struggle to make accounts more transparent, have made understanding company statements more difficult.

NEWS CLIP
IN SEARCH OF A RELIABLE AUDITOR

As ebullient executives toasted Bank of China's initial public offering last week and breathless investors chased its shares higher, one group sat purring contentedly in the background. Gratified by their lucrative role in the $9.7bn flotation were auditors from PwC, who had knocked the bank's books into shape. They had surpassed rivals at KPMG, which audited China Construction Bank for its $9.2bn IPO last October. But PwC itself is likely to be trumped by Ernst & Young if, as expected, Industrial and Commercial Bank of China launches a $10bn-$15bn offering in September.

The upshot is that three of the "big four" international accounting firms – the fourth is Deloitte – have sewn up three of the finance world's other "big four": China's giant former state-owned lenders. The fourth, Agricultural Bank of China, is a long way from reaching the stock market. International firms monopolize the auditing not just of banks but of the whole gamut of Chinese companies listed outside the mainland. Their dominance is explained by the trust overseas investors and bankers put in their rigour, experience and geographical reach.

But the perception that big-four work is a cut above that of domestic accounting firms demands closer examination today, not least because their influence – for nationalistic reasons – has become a source of discomfort among some policymakers in Beijing. The audit process is always shrouded in secrecy because of its potential influence on share prices, making it near impossible to do a scientific comparison of local and international firms. But the conclusion from interviews with Chinese companies, accountants and regulators is that the clear blue water thought to separate the big four and local firms is in reality a narrow swamp.

(con't)

In the capital markets, the prevailing view is that the big four are streets ahead at doing so, in terms of professionalism, technical ability and their independence from clients. For that reason, Citic Frontier, a Hong Kong brokerage that last year surveyed 150 mainland stocks in Hong Kong, labelled the handful of companies that use a non-big four auditor as "the suspicious six".

... PwC, meanwhile, is facing demands for a reported Rmb200m of compensation from Waigaoqiao, a Shanghai-listed property group, for allegedly failing to discover that company funds deposited with a broker were being misused, according to state media. The case is due to be heard by an official arbitration commission and PwC says it has confidence in its audit work and believes the allegations are unfounded.

.... Dishonest accounting is unavoidable, perhaps, and sometimes undetectable in present-day China. But if that is true, it means the biggest gap in the audit world is not between the international and local firms. It is between the big four's promise of a consistent global service and their ability to deliver it on the ground.

Source: *Financial Times, Barney Jopson,* 7 June 2006

Even if a single international standard for accounting were agreed, there would still be many cases where managers and accountants would have to use their judgment in deciding how to treat various account items. There are a number of general principles that accountants apply:

Historic Cost:
Should assets be shown at their original cost ("historic cost accounting") or at the current market price? Historic cost accounting may seem very conservative — for example, if a company bought an office block 50 years ago, it may be worth considerably more today, if only because of inflation — but the original cost does provide a more objective measure than opinions on current market values, which may vary widely. The trend in new accounting rules seems to be toward revaluation of assets so that they reflect the current market value.

Materiality:
Faced with a huge and unmanageable mass of accounting data, accountants have to make decisions on which items they should examine in detail, particularly when conducting audits. For example, it is impractical for an auditor to spend time, tracking down how every paper clip has been used. For this reason, accountants decide which items are "material" (i.e. important) and which are too minor to be worth examining in detail and therefore "immaterial." Usually regulators leave it to the auditors to use

their judgment in fixing "immaterial" items. This means that in a small company, an auditor will regard much smaller items as "material" than in a big company.

Conservatism:

If in doubt, accountants say they prefer to choose the "safest" figure, recognizing profits only when an invoice has been issued, but accounting for losses early, as soon as they have been foreseen. However, a number of accounting firms have been put out of business recently because of their efforts to make companies' financial health look good by hiding or even falsifying accounting data. Since managers pay the accountants and select them in most cases, there are worries that not all accountants practice conservatism in the face of opposition from managers.

Managers are eager to build value, so they tend to have an optimistic view of the worth of company assets and are reluctant to admit losses until they are clearly unavoidable. This tension between accountants and managers can cause misunderstanding among investors; during bull markets, investors who want stock prices to increase often lobby for overly optimistic valuations. However, conservatism may also cause problems — for example, at times of corporate acquisitions, companies might undervalue their assets.

Substance:

Through arrangements, such as leasing assets, it may be possible to disguise a company's liabilities "off-balance sheet" or to hide profits to avoid tax (such as pricing the transactions between related companies artificially low). Accountants prefer substance over form in their treatment of such items.

Consistency:

Where possible, a company should stick to the accounting methods and policies that it has always used, treating a given type of transaction in the same way in each reporting period. This enables readers of the financial reports to make meaningful comparisons and assess the company's performance over time. New markets and activities may sometimes require a change, and this should be explained in the notes to the financial statements. Although such changes are usually legitimate, a company that frequently adopts new policies and methods may be attempting to commit fraud.

Realization:

Accountants prefer to recognize profits only when they are realized and not earlier. Some prefer to recognize profits only after goods are delivered and paid for. If profits are accounted for when invoices have been issued, what if a customer makes a reduced payment, or doesn't pay at all? To deal with these possibilities, accountants make "provisions," adjusting sales and profit figures downwards. This may be done by a blanket percentage for smaller items, but large sales that are doubtful may be examined carefully.

Going Concern:

Finally, accounts are usually prepared on the assumption that the company will remain in business as a "going concern," meaning it is assumed that any raw materials a company owns will eventually be manufactured into salable products. The "going concern" assumption gives higher values than would be the case if the company collapsed. Many investors do not appreciate that during a liquidation, company assets are often sold off at a fraction of what the company paid for them because of the need to raise cash quickly.

GLOBAL ACCOUNTING STANDARDS

Efforts are underway to establish a truly universal set of accounting standards. From January 1, 2005, the 7,000 listed companies in the

NEWS CLIP

THE WORLD'S FASTEST-GROWING ECONOMY IS SUFFERING A MASSIVE SHORTAGE OF ACCOUNTANTS

A massive shortage of accountants in China is threatening to act as a brake on the world's fastest-growing economy.

"The demand for accountants is so high – not just among domestic enterprises, but many foreign enterprises setting up in China – that there will be a shortage of accountants for the next 10 years," said Beijing-based Ernst & Young partner Clive Saunderson.

It is estimated that China has less than 50% of the 300,000 qualified accountants it needs.

Source: *Accountancy Age*, 23 Jun 2005

European Union had to ensure that their financial statements conformed to International Financial Reporting Standards (IFRS). In the US, a different version of GAAP (Generally Accepted Accounting Principles) is in use, but many US-based multinationals have subsidiaries that will have to conform to the new global GAAP standards.

The creation of a single international standard is highly desired by many, since it makes the accounts of companies in different countries easier to compare, and should, in theory, give companies better access to capital and better relationships with their shareholders. However, many groups with vested interests resist it. One of the biggest controversies is the move towards "fair value" accounting, which is favored by both US and European regulators. Fair value is broadly defined as "the price at which an asset or liability could be exchanged in a current transaction between knowledgeable, unrelated willing parties," but in practice this is difficult to define. Although the International Accounting Standards Board (IASB), which promotes the global standard, tends to favor a mathematical model to establish fair value for assets and liabilities that do not have a clear market price, critics argue that some of these "hypothetical" valuations may be unreliable, and that a clear distinction should be made between those valuations that are dependable and those that are imprecise.

ACCOUNT NOTES

Company reports usually contain extensive notes explaining the financial statements. Professionals regard these notes as important and often turn to them first, before reading the rest of report, since they contain vital information about how the statements have been constructed. For example:

- Accounting policies and practices — because of the choice available to companies in how they treat many items in their accounts, it is essential to understand their policies.

- Details of the company's current and deferred taxes, which may be due in many different tax jurisdictions.

"I can assure you, madam, that our commitment to transparency will never inhibit our willingness to kick ass."

STOCK OPTIONS SCANDAL HEATS UP

MANHASSET, N.Y. — An upsurge of criminal charges and financial reporting delays stemming from the stock options scandal is putting even more heat on the electronics industry.

Some companies face delisting from stock exchanges, while others face growing scrutiny from shareholders, some of whom are filing suits. In addition, stock prices for some companies fell as shareholder distrust heightened.

The U.S. Dept. of Justice came down hardest on communications company Brocade Communications Systems Inc. and software vendor Converse Technology Inc.

On Thursday, two former executives of Brocade, former president and CEO Gregory Reyes and former vice president of human resources Stephanie Jensen, were hit with a 12-count indictment for scheming to backdate stock option grants to give employees favorably priced options without recording necessary compensation expenses.

Both executives were charged with securities fraud by the U.S. attorney's office and the U.S. Securities and Exchange Commission (SEC) on July 29— the first formal charges brought against companies implicated in the stock options scandal.

On Wednesday, the U.S. Justice Dept. charged three former executives of Converse with scheming to manipulate the granting of millions of dollars of stock options grants to themselves and their employees, between 1998 and 2002.

According to a Justice Dept. statement, the executives issued misleading financial statements to the company's shareholders and the investing public regarding the true value of the options grants.

Source: *http://www.eetimes.com*

- Pension plans are often sizable, and many regulators require details of the assets they hold and whether they are over-funded or under-funded.

- Stock options for managers and employees, including details of how these are accounted for and the effect of the method on reported results.

ANNUAL REPORTS

In most countries, in addition to the audited financial statements, an annual report contains a number of written statements:

- The directors'/chairman's reports
- The auditor's report
- Corporate governance report
- Environmental report
- Management discussion and analysis

The chairman's report is intended to set out, in general terms, the recent performance and current prospects for the company, and to comment on economic and political issues affecting the company. It is often a blandly optimistic piece of PR, but may contain useful comments relating to serious matters. It may refer to changes in board membership, the key activities of the company, key events in the previous financial year and new strategies and objectives.

The directors' report contains more detailed information about the main activities of the company and its subsidiaries, and any important changes that have occurred during the period of review. It should comment on the information given in the financial statements, in particular:

- Revenues and profits
- Exceptional items
- Taxation
- Foreign currency issues
- Borrowings
- Changes to fixed assets
- Research and development activities

The report may also give details of the names of the directors and their loans, salaries and shareholdings in the company.

Recently, reports have also begun to include information on:

- Political donations
- Employees and their working conditions
- Company environmental policies
- Corporate governance of the company
- Willingness of the auditors to continue to audit the firm

AUDITOR'S REPORT

Publicly traded firms must be independently audited by a qualified accountant. For large companies, this is normally done by a team of accountants employed by one of the major international accountancy firms.

The objective of the audit is to provide shareholders with independent assurance that the accounts have been prepared in accordance with legal requirements and "best accounting practice" and that they present the information in a true and fair manner. Auditors cannot check every single transaction in large firms; they make a high level review of the company's accounting policies and controls, and make detailed spot-checks in certain areas, particularly new activities and critical transactions. It remains the board's responsibility to manage internal accounting controls.

Every so often a large company collapses and fraud is discovered. When this occurs, there is intense criticism of the auditors, but this is not always justified. Although accountants expect to detect instances of fraud, the aim of an audit is not primarily to detect fraud but to give a "reasonable assurance" to outsiders that the accounts are accurate. However, cases such as the collapse of Robert Maxwell's Mirror Group Newspapers and Enron have demonstrated that auditors can be deceived by determined fraudsters or even co-operate with them.

There are ongoing efforts to reform the way in which audits are conducted, and to educate users of annual reports about the precise nature of the respective responsibilities of auditors and directors. Some professional investors, however, remain concerned that in big business, the interests of the managers who employ them overly influence the auditors.

Normally, the auditors' report is "unqualified," meaning that it gives the standard assurances of the validity of the financial statements. A report that is "qualified" in any way by, for example, a statement that certain activities could not be verified, is generally regarded as a "red flag" by the financial markets and the company will be pressed to clarify the issue.

CONSOLIDATED ACCOUNTS

Many large companies are actually groups of companies, each with their own sets of accounts. The annual report of a corporate group will generally contain income and cash flow statements for the group as a whole, but with a balance sheet for the consolidated group and also for the holding company that controls the other firms within the group.

A group often contains companies that are not wholly owned, and the way in which such firms' accounts are consolidated usually depends on whether they are managed or controlled by the group. The exact definitions vary from country to country, but in general:

- A subsidiary is a firm in which the group has a majority shareholding and exercises control over its operations.

- An associate is a firm in which the group has a significant, but not controlling, shareholding and exercises influence over its operations.

- An investment is a firm in which the group owns some shares, but does not have significant influence over how it is run.

Profits from associates and investments are usually simply recorded as items in the income statement and balance sheet of the consolidated accounts. The results of subsidiaries, however, are included fully consolidated first, and then the proportion due to the other shareholders is subtracted from earnings.

THE BALANCE SHEET

The balance sheet is a "snapshot" of the assets and liabilities of a firm at a given point in time. The net assets of a company are "due" (as a liability) to the shareholders, as owners of the business; these figures, which are listed on separate sides of the statement, must always match ("balance").

ASSETS = LIABILITIES + SHAREHOLDERS' EQUITY

NEWS CLIP
ENRON WHISTLEBLOWER

Enron whistleblower Lynn Brewer says, "The number of whistle-blowing reports has increased from 6,400 to 40,000 a month, two years after the passage of the Sarbanes-Oxley legislation. Clearly, it is not deterring what's going on.

"The key to Enron's failure was that every day, when the Enron stock was going up by a dollar, most of us were making thousands, if not millions of dollars a day, because our own income was tied to Enron's stocks going up... Some days, I was making US$20,000 to US$30,000. So there was complacency on everybody's part to sort of look the other way from what was really going on."

"While blowing the whistle inside the company and telling senior management what was going on, I was also cashing in on stock options, which made me equally guilty with everybody you read about in the news.

"Sadly enough, it was that willingness to look the other way by 20,000 people, (that) it went on for as long as it did and ultimately, it imploded."

Brewer said she was able to sell out all her stock options because under Enron's severance package, one had to cash in on the stock options within 60 days of leaving the company.

Source: *The Edge Daily* September 5, 2005

Figure 9.1 — Balance Sheet Example

ASSETS	US$ '000	LIABILITIES	US$ '000
Current assets		**Current liabilities**	
Cash and cash equivalents	49,695	Trade and other payables	125,916
Trade and other receivables	88,810	Current income tax liabilities	341
Inventories	9,390	Borrowings	22,819
Derivative financial instruments	1,120		149,076
Financial assets at fair value through profit or loss	33,388		
Other current assets	2,119	**Non-current liabilities**	
	184,522	Borrowings	63,249
		Deferred income	476
		Retirement benefit obligations	1,213
			64,938
		Total liabilities	214,014
Non-current assets		**EQUITY**	
Available-for-sale financial assets	5,142	**Capital and reserves attributable to the Company's equity holders**	
Investment in associated companies	34,972	Share capital and share premium	529,373
Property, plant and equipment	450,134	Treasury shares	-
Intangible assets	63,220	Other reserves	5,597
Deferred income tax assets	5,892	Accumulated losses	(5,102)
	559,360	Shareholders' Equity	529,868
Total assets	743,882		743,882

A company may list its assets on the left side of the balance sheet, and its liabilities and shareholders' equity on the right side; alternatively, it may show assets at the top, followed by liabilities, with shareholders' equity at the bottom.

ASSETS

The assets of a company include the following:

Fixed assets (or non-current assets) – The assets that the company uses to run its business. In general, the value of fixed assets is determined by how much these assets cost the company less the rate of depreciation for that particular asset. In some circumstances they may be revalued (for example, if the value of a building has risen substantially). The rate of depreciation is used to spread capital investments over the expected useful life of the asset. Fixed assets include physical property, such as plants, vehicles and equipment, and also "intangibles" such as trademarks and patents. Fixed assets are therefore broken down into several sub-categories, such as:

- **Tangible assets** – These include land and buildings, sometimes noting whether they are freehold or have long or short leases. Associated legal fees, interest payments, landscaping, construction and demolition costs may be included here as part of these assets, and are thus "capitalized." Buildings may be revalued periodically at market prices. Industrial plants, machinery, fixtures, fittings, tools and equipment are also included in this category.

- **Intangible assets** – This category includes "goodwill," patents, trademarks, brand names and other intellectual property. If the asset has a limited life, such as a patent, it may be depreciated. Development costs may or may not be capitalized, depending on the firm's policy and its home country's regulations. Increasingly, there are strict rules over the types of intellectual property that can be listed as assets — one of the main tests is whether such property can be sold, and whether it has a clearly definable market value.

- **Investments** – Minority shareholdings in other companies that are not part of the group, and other investments, such as buildings and financial securities, which are held as investments and not used for the business.

Current assets – These are assets that are likely to be held for the short term, such as inventory, cash and outstanding debts from customers.

They are subdivided as:

- **Stock/inventory** – Inventory (known as "stock" in the UK) consists of finished and unfinished products to be sold by the company, as well as raw materials. In general, inventory is valued at either its cost or its realizable value, whichever is the lower figure. The valuation of inventory relating to long-term contracts poses particular problems, which should be explained in the notes following the statements. Another problem occurs with goods that are held on consignment; these should normally be indicated as such, and the terms explained.

- **Debtors/receivables** – Mainly the money owed by customers, but there may also be other items, such as inter-group debts, money owed by company directors, and pre-payments such as insurance premiums.

- **Cash** – Includes cash held on company premises and in bank accounts, credit card vouchers, checks and similar items.

CAPITALIZATION AND AMORTIZATION/ DEPRECIATION

The extent to which companies can capitalize various expenditures and record them as investments, rather than as operating expenses, varies between countries and accounting regimes and between different industries in the same country. This means that a company's capitalization policy requires detailed scrutiny because one of the easiest ways to show an increase in profits is to defer recognition of expenses as capital costs and amortize them over a long period of time.

The rules governing capitalization exist because the stakeholders need to know the difference between money paid out to operate the company and money invested to generate future growth. Once the expenditure has been recognized as a capital cost, it should be amortized, or "depreciated," over the expected useful life of the equipment or other asset. So if an asset cost $10 million and its expected useful life is 40 years, it would be amortized as the same amount

each year according to the "straight line" method of depreciation. On the other hand, a semiconductor fabrication plant might decide to amortize its equipment over five years or less because rapid technological change will make this equipment useless after this period. This semiconductor company might also have a rude surprise from an unexpected new technology that made all of its investment virtually worthless in two years. Thus, the rate of amortization can change in some businesses, making for wrenching declines in profitability by forcing companies to recognize investments as expenses faster than they expected.

Besides obvious assets like buildings or machinery, other investments can be capitalized, though the rules governing capitalization vary with the accounting regime. Some of these other investments could be:

- Software: under most accounting rules software can be capitalized once "technological feasibility" has been reached and all the planning coding and testing activities have been completed to assure that the software will do what it is supposed to do. There is leeway in this area and companies have been known to use it both to capitalize quickly — because they want to increase profitability right now — or slowly, because they want to increase profitability with capitalization close to the time the product reaches the market, signaling to investors the new product's impact on the bottom line.

- Interest costs: in the US and some other countries, interest paid on money invested in assets can be capitalized so long as the written-off cost of the asset does not exceed the market value of the asset, less the cost of the sale.

- Direct mail costs: can be capitalized if the company has a track record of using direct mail and has a good historical reason to know the return it will receive on this sales and marketing activity.

- Money invested to prevent future environmental liabilities: can be capitalized in some countries.

The examples above show just how broad the definition of assets has become. This means it is important to examine companies' capitalization policies carefully before arriving at an assessment of their assets, especially when comparing companies that apply different policies.

For an analyst, the main question should be whether expenditures on assets can create shareholder wealth. Aggressive capitalization policies can be dangerous because the company could be sending the wrong signals to the market by showing more profitability than it should. Changes in capitalization polices can be warning signals, even though they may legitimately reflect changes in the business and financial environment.

Companies under stress may try to capitalize as much of their expenses as they can and seek to extend amortization periods for as long as they can to inflate the size of their reported assets. The longer the amortization period, the longer the asset stays on the books, keeping up the company's book value.

A company that tends to keep assets on the books for too long is creating an overly optimistic picture of shareholder wealth. Given the complexity of large companies, a rule-of-thumb solution used by analysts is to divide the company's total assets (except for land) by the rate which it depreciates every year and compare this figure to those of similar companies in the same industry.

LIABILITIES

Liabilities, like assets, are also divided into current and non-current liabilities, depending on the length of time before they must be discharged.

Current liabilities – These include accounts payable (money the company must pay in the coming financial year for goods or services it has received), taxes it will have to pay during the year, pre-payments it has received from customers and other financial obligations due during the current year. Often, the largest item in this category is money owed to suppliers, since this is effectively a free short term loan from the suppliers to the company; many firms make strenuous efforts to maximize this source of funding.

Long-term liabilities – These include long term debts, obligations stemming from pension agreements, deferred tax payments that are not due during the current year and other longer term financial obligations such as bonds that the company has issued.

Shareholders' equity – The final category on the "liabilities" side of the balance sheet, this represents the amount shareholders have invested in the company's stock, adjusted for operating the company's profits or losses since it began. It may also include "reserves," which may be distributable to shareholders as dividends, or "undistributable," such as an increase in the value of a fixed asset such as a building.

GAUGING SOLVENCY

At the crudest level, companies fail when they run out of cash to pay their creditors. Whatever the underlying reason for the failure, the crunch comes when there is no money to pay a large debt. In private companies, especially smaller ones, it is possible for the firm's management to reach this stage without foreseeing the danger. In public firms, which are much more carefully regulated, the danger signs should be evident far in advance, but if the management makes an effort to hide the problem it can be difficult to detect. In most countries, it is illegal for any company, public or private, to continue to trade when it knows it is "insolvent" (which means that it does not have enough cash to pay its debts).

An important test for potential insolvency is the company's use of leverage — how much is the company borrowing as a proportion of its capital. Suppose a couple buys a house for $1,000,000 with no down payment and borrows the money for a relatively short period (say 10 years). The couple is 100% leveraged, and will probably not be able to repay the loan out of their income — a recipe for trouble. Although consumer lenders are often prevented by law from making such a dangerous loan, even if they are prepared to take the risk, the situation is different for businesses.

Once a business has reached a stage where it can obtain many different types of credit, it has a choice about the amount of leverage it takes on. While different industries typically use different levels of borrowing, highly leveraged companies should generally be treated with caution; just like our house-buying couple, they may not be able to make the payments on their loans. A ratio of debt to equity of 1:1 or less is generally regarded as acceptable, although a more conservative figure would be 0.5:1. Higher debt to equity ratios may be explained away by companies — there always seems to be a convincing rationale — but unless the company knows that it can escape its debts, it is increasing the risk of insolvency when it increases its leverage.

Debt to equity can be broken down to compare long-term debts with long-term assets, and short-term debts with short-term assets. The short-term measure looks at the ability of the company to pay off its current creditors, such as suppliers, and short-term lenders, with its current assets, such as its stock, the money owed by customers and its money in the bank. If the proportion of current debt to current assets is more than 2:3, it is a bad sign. Remember that current assets are sometimes valued rather optimistically, and may be worth far less than their book value if they have to be sold in an emergency. There are, however, vast, well-established companies that allow their current liabilities to exceed their current assets by a wide margin, confident in their power to keep their suppliers waiting for payment should the need arise.

THE INCOME STATEMENT (PROFIT AND LOSS)

The income statement, or profit and loss account, is conceptually the most easily understood of the financial statements; it shows the profit or loss for the period covered by deducting the company's expenses from its income.

- Profit is the surplus of revenue over costs for the period; it is not the same as cash flow. A fast-growing company can make profits but still suffer a negative cash flow because it has not yet collected money from sales to customers, but has incurred costs in producing its products and services.

There are several possible formats for the income statement and, as with the other financial statements, a company has some freedom in the terminology it uses. This can be confusing at first, especially if you are attempting to compare the income statements of different firms. Figures 9.1A, 9.1B and 9.1C show three formats from real companies, the first two US-based, and the third from the UK:

As you can see, the terminology and formats used in the three extracts differ considerably. Nevertheless, each of these statements is doing the same job, which is to give the total sales figures and subtract expenses, broken down into various categories, to come up with the profit that the company has earned for the period.

Figure 9.1A — US company income statement - example 1

Net Sales (See Note 1) ....
Cost of sales (See Note 1) ....

Gross Profit ....
Advertising and promotion expenses ....
Other selling and administrative expenses ....
Amortization of goodwill ....
Restructuring and other charges ....

Operating Income ....
Interest expense ....
Interest (income) ....
Other non-operating (income) expense, net ....

Income From Continuing Operations Before Income Taxes ....
Provision for income taxes ....

Income From Continuing Operations
Discontinued Operations (See Note 14) ....
Gain from discontinued operations, net of tax ....

Income Before Cumulative Effect of Change in Accounting Principles ....
Cumulative effect of change in accounting principles, net of tax ....

Net Income ....

Income (Loss) Per Common Share — Basic
Income from continuing operations ....
Gain from discontinued operations ....
Cumulative effect of change in accounting principles ....

Net income ....

Weighted average number of common shares ....

Income (Loss) Per Common Share — Diluted
Income from continuing operations ....
Gain from discontinued operations ....
Cumulative effect of change in accounting principles ....

Net income ....

Weighted average number of common and common equivalent shares ....

Dividends Declared Per Common Share ....

Figure 9.1B — US company income statement - example 2

Revenues:
    Subscriptions ....
    Advertising ....
    Content ....
    Other ....

Total revenues[a] ....
Cost of revenues[a] ....
Selling, general and administrative[a] ....
Merger and restructuring costs ....
Amortization of intangible assets ....
Impairment of goodwill and other intangible assets ....
Net gain on disposal of assets ....

Operating income (loss) ....
Interest expense, net[a] ....
Other income (expense), net ....
Minority interest income (expense) ....

Income (loss) before income taxes, discontinued operations and
    cumulative effect of accounting change ....
Income tax provision ....

Income (loss) before discontinued operations and cumulative
    effect of accounting change ....
Discontinued operations, net of tax ....

Income (loss) before cumulative effect of accounting change ....
Cumulative effect of accounting change ....

Net income (loss) ....

Basic income (loss) per common share before discontinued
    operations and cumulative effect of accounting change ....
Discontinued operations ....
Cumulative effect of accounting change ....

Basic net income (loss) per common share ....

Average basic common shares ....

Diluted income (loss) per common share before discontinued
    operations and cumulative effect of accounting change ....
Discontinued operations ....
Cumulative effect of accounting change ....

Diluted net income (loss) per common share ....

Average diluted common shares ....

Figure 9.1C — UK company income statement - example 3

Turnover
Cost of sales

Gross profit
Selling, general and administrative expenditure
Research and development expenditure

Trading profit
Other operating income/(expense)

Operating profit
Share of profits/(losses) of joint ventures and associated undertakings
Profit on disposal of interest in associate
Product divestments
Profit/(loss) on disposal of businesses

Profit before interest
Net interest payable

Profit on ordinary activities before taxation
Taxation

Profit on ordinary activities after taxation
Equity minority interests
Preference share dividends

Earnings (Profit attributable to shareholders)

Basic earnings per share
Adjusted earnings per share
Diluted earnings per share

Profit attributable to shareholders
Dividends

Retained profit

The key entries in an income statement are:

- **Total sales** (also called "turnover" or "total revenues"). It is called "net sales" for reasons the company explains in the accompanying notes — an allowance has been made for rebates and returns of products. Total sales is the money that the company received during the course of trading.

- **Cost of sales**. This is the money the company spent on producing its goods and services, and normally includes labor and raw materials.

- **Gross profit.** This is the remainder after "cost of sales" is subtracted from "total sales." It is an important figure because it indicates the basic profit margins. The higher the gross profit margin, as a percentage of sales, the more money the company has to develop its business.

- **Operating income** (or "trading profit") is the profit gained by the company's ongoing operations. It is equal to earnings before deduction of interest payments, income taxes and other financing costs or income generated outside normal activities, such as foreign currency gains.

- **Depreciation** is a way of spreading the purchase cost of a fixed asset over its useful life. This is a paper transaction that affects the calculation of profits. The main reason for doing this is to prepare for the day when these assets wear out and must be replaced. There are several ways of calculating depreciation, and different methods may be used for different assets; for example, hi-tech equipment may have to be depreciated rapidly because it will soon be replaced by new technology, while patents have a known life fixed by law (20 years in many countries).

- **Net profit** (or "net earnings", "net income," or "profit attributable to shareholders") is the "bottom line," giving the profit that the company has earned for its shareholders. Some of this money may be distributed as dividends or can be earmarked for reinvestment in the business.

- **Retained earnings** is the proportion of net profit that the company is keeping to reinvest in the business. Although in theory some mature businesses may be unable to grow and have little need to retain earnings, most listed companies do retain the majority of their profits.

WHAT THE INCOME STATEMENT DOES NOT TELL YOU

The income statement talks about the profitability of the company, and provides an insight into its income and expenses. However, it often does not give a detailed breakdown of the profitability of individual products and services, which is normally regarded as sensitive information and is not revealed to outsiders.

THE CASH FLOW STATEMENT

The main aim of the cash flow statement is to provide readers with the information they need to examine the reasons for any rise or fall in the amount of cash in the company during the period reported. This information does not appear in the income statement.

Reasons for a rise in cash flow include:

- The company is collecting its debts more quickly

- The company is paying its trade creditors more slowly

- The company has sold a fixed asset

- The company has raised new finance from its shareholders

- The company is making increased profits

- The company's inventory is decreasing

- The company has borrowed cash

Reasons for a drop in cash flow include:

- The company is extending more credit to its customers and/or collecting debts more slowly

- The company is paying its suppliers more quickly

- The company has invested in fixed assets

- The company is trading at a loss or decreased profitability

- The company has increased its inventory

- The company has increased its dividends

- The company has repaid loans

These events may all be a normal part of business operations and none of them may be indicative of poor performance in themselves; they do, however, raise further questions about how the markets are changing and the firm is being managed. For example, a one-off increase in inventory purchased very cheaply may mean that the company has taken the opportunity to buy cheap materials, but a trend of ever-increasing inventory holdings may indicate weak management or problems in the supply chain.

The categories appearing in the cash flow statements vary from firm to firm and country to country, but generally include:

- **Operating activities** – cash generated in the normal course of trading (this includes an "add-back" of depreciation, and any changes in working capital). Usually, this reconciles the net income (as shown on the income statement) to the actual cash used in operating activities.

- **Returns on investment and servicing of finance** – dividends received by the company and interest paid and received.

- **Taxation** – payments and pre-payments of taxes on sales revenue and capital gains. In countries that charge VAT sales tax, this is included in "operating activities," not here.

- **Capital expenditure, acquisitions and disposals** – assets bought or sold by the company.

- **Equity dividends paid to shareholders**

- **Financing activity** – receipts and repayments of the capital sum of loans. Cash flow from shares, bonds and other types of corporate financing are shown here.

CASH FLOW ANALYSIS

In analyzing a cash flow report, it is important to determine how it was calculated.

The two methods of doing so are:

- The direct method represents the actual inflows of cash from customers or other factors and the outflows to employees, suppliers, taxes and the like. These direct method reports then have to be reconciled with the company's income statement.

- The indirect method starts with the income statement and reconciles this to real income with provisions for factors such as depreciation, amortization, taxes and other factors.

Cash flow reports indicate the stage of a company's development. Start-up companies typically exhibit negative cash flow as they are building the business in the hope of future profits. Successful young growth companies are typically operationally cash flow positive, but still expend large amounts of capital as they need to get going. The positive cash flow in these companies usually does not cover the company's cost of capital nor provides the means necessary for the next stage of growth. In growing companies that are not in the retail industries, cash flow from sales typically lags behind income since more sales are recognized in the current period than cash from a lower sales level in the previous period.

Once the growth pattern is more established, companies might still need to raise money for growth, but the rate of depreciation is closer to the capital used to finance expansion. In well-established, profitable companies, cash flow from depreciation and amortization cover the company's capital needs. The real winners, and there are not that many of them, cover all their capital needs from positive cash flow from operations without the need for depreciation and amortization.

Cash flow reports allow outsiders to catch the signs of trouble — for example, when companies cover deficits in cash flow from operations by selling fixed assets, then shareholder wealth is being eroded. When the proceeds from the sales of fixed assets are not re-invested for future growth, management may be struggling for air. The lack of capital expenditures can also be another warning signal because companies that don't invest are often sitting on their laurels and could be overtaken by a hungrier competitor.

One could assume that the management of a public company will try to maximize profits in its financial reports. This is not, however, always the case. In companies that have been through a leveraged buyout, the new majority owners may try to minimize net income to decrease taxes and free more resources to service debt. The cash flow report of such a company will typically use a large part of the operationally positive cash flow to service debt.

Cash flow reports are usually divided into three sections: Operations, Investment and Finance. The first is obviously the key element in measuring a company's prospects because it measures how much cash the company generates from operations. Most companies do not, however, separate the report into cash flow from continuing operating and discontinued operations. This can be misleading because one would want to deduct the impact of one-time cash inflows, just as one deducts them from the income statement.

Another common problem with the report on operations is taxes. Typically all income tax payments are entered as outflows in the operations report. One cannot tell how much of these taxes were paid on income from operations or from financial or investment activities. Taxes on discontinued operations would also appear here, also distorting the real operational picture.

Another factor than can distort cash flow reports, particularly in emerging markets, is the wide variety of tax breaks, outright grants, hidden or open subsidies for R&D, incentives for plant location and other perks available for companies acting in accordance with a country's industrial development strategy. There is nothing wrong with these breaks. Intel, for example, uses its tremendous clout and prestige to shop between various countries for the best tax break and other incentives before deciding where to set up a new fabrication plant.

The first problem is the way in which these incentives might appear, or not, in the cash flow report and its notes. The second problem is that many of these incentives are time-delimited and may worsen as a result of changes in government policy. Understandably, many of these incentives have strings attached to them such as a requirement to continue operations in the given location for a number of years, a factor that greatly affects management's operational flexibility. Analysts seeking data on the basic viability of a company have to uncover all of these incentives and discount their effects on operational cash flow to see whether a company is generating real cash or if it is the result of a hidden government subsidy.

Yet another issue than can confuse operational cash flow reports, particularly in software companies, is the company's capitalization policy. As noted elsewhere in this book, management has fairly broad latitude is deciding when to capitalize software under development. Companies that capitalize quickly will usually show stronger cash flow than companies that recognize expenditures on software development as expenses because the capitalized costs move to the investment section of the cash flow report while the ensuing amortization charges are a non-cash event that does affect operational cash flow. This is particularly true about software, but it also applies to any area in which management has more flexibility in capitalizing expenses.

Companies usually record the purchase and sale of debt or equity in the section of the cash flow report dealing with financial activities. Yet, dealing in trading securities, usually in a shorter time frame, can be recorded under operational cash flow. This too is an issue to be removed from the operational cash flow figures if one has to understand the core viability of a company.

The main guideline in looking at operational cash flow is to seek sustainable inflow of cash that the company can use. Obviously this means that one has to be attentive to all non-recurring events in the cash flow report in the same way these issues are usually treated in the income statement. The same applies to both inventory and accounts payable. Sudden changes in these figures can signal that management is trying to change the cash flow picture.

Analysts or regulators can usually only detect the more blatant forms of earnings management, such as unreasonable write-offs or a fishy revenue recognition policy. Quite often regulators uncover the details of over-creative earnings management only when the company is in deep trouble. However, the market tolerates a certain amount of earnings management and even applauds it. For example, one company reported earnings exactly one penny per share above analysts' predictions for 13 consecutive quarters! The probability of this happening without some form of earnings management is low indeed. In good quarters, large corporations routinely "store" positive business developments when they expect rough news ahead so they can continue to project the kind of stable growth the market loves.

COMPANY EARNINGS ANNOUNCEMENTS

Stock markets relentlessly punish companies that do not meet analysts' expected earnings figures. It is not that analysts make very accurate predictions; they are often late in recognizing trouble, and their forecasts are usually more accurate when a company is prospering and is happy to share its information with them. But analysts are usually the only bellwether the market has, and downward deviations from their predictions nearly always cause stock prices to tumble.

EARNINGS MANAGEMENT

Earnings management is the process by which management "manages" items in the company's financial statements to give the best impression to the markets. The tricky game of meeting expectations lies at the heart of earnings management. In complex businesses, management often has considerable leeway in the way it reports the top line of a company's revenues. Analysts must scrutinize accounts carefully and do their own research to ensure that they are not being given too rosy a picture of company revenues.

"Our stock just went up ten points on the rumor that I was replacing you all with burlap sacks stuffed with straw."

Earnings management involves tweaking the entire range of the company's financial statements, from earnings recognition policies, depreciation methods and depreciation timetables, deciding how much charges to allow for uncollectible receivables, estimating write-downs for investments, decisions on future liabilities as a result of litigation or environmental regulation, decisions of the length of amortization for goodwill or other intangible assets, and estimating the charges to make as a result of restructuring inside the company. Common problems include "channel stuffing", when a company forces products into its distribution channels, often on generous credit terms, so it can pump up sales figures artificially.

The reasons for earnings management vary with each company. They may arise from a contract that was not closed at the expected time, causing a shortfall in revenue; a debt-to-equity ratio that violates the covenants attached to the company's bonds (which may cause bondholders to demand immediate repayment or to demand higher interest on new bonds to compensate for higher risk); a sudden peak in revenues that management believes cannot be repeated in future quarters; or even a strong desire to reach targets linked to management's compensation schemes.

REVENUE RECOGNITION

As business becomes more complex and the difference between products and services has become increasingly blurred, revenue recognition has become an area in which management has considerable leeway in the way it reports the top line of a company's revenues. Both investors and analysts must pay far more attention to the fine print of financial statements.

Some accountants argue that revenue should not necessarily be recognized when a customer pays for the goods. If somebody buys an annual subscription to a swimming pool, the fee can be recognized gradually during the whole period of the subscription because the owner of the swimming pool has not finished delivering the service until the end of the year. Alternatively, if a machinery vendor gets an order for a machine from a reputable customer and ships it under an agreement calling for payment within 90 days, the revenue can be recognized when the machine is shipped and not when payment is received.

Rules for revenue recognition differ in various countries and among industries. Software is one of the most problematic industries because of its elusive and intangible nature, and also because the dividing line between products and services is so hard to draw.

In general, however, there are a few guidelines for revenue recognition that are true under most accountings regimes:

> **Fixed Price:** The transaction in question has a fixed and agreed-upon price. This is particularly true of subscriptions of various kinds that can be cancelled without any penalty to the subscriber or of goods whose final price is pegged to any extraneous element. If any elements of the price can change, there must be adequate provisions for the flexibility under a separate heading in the financial statements.

> **Shipping Date:** This is ostensibly the simplest criterion, saying that revenue should be recognized only when goods leave the company's warehouse. But in many cases this is often abused because there are so many ways in which companies can ship goods without actually having made a sale.

> **Sales Agreements:** There normally is a final sales agreement under the normal standards used by the company and in its industry. In most cases this is a purchase contract, but there are industries like the diamond trade, for example, in which oral agreement is the accepted norm. The agreement must stipulate the cost, quantity and time of delivery. Some sales agreements stipulate that the vendor will continue to hold on to the purchased goods. In these cases, called "bill-and-hold sales," there can be a long list of conditions for allowing recognition of such sales, starting with the fact that the customer assumes ownership of the goods and asks, for a good business reason, for the goods or services not to be delivered until a specified date.

> **Rights of Return:** This is a gray area, yet of critical importance, especially with smaller firms that deal with more intangible goods.

Some software is sold with almost unlimited rights of return, allowing buyers to basically first test the product and then see if they wish to pay for it. On the books this might look like a sale since it is governed by an agreement and the product has been shipped, but many software firms have recorded such sales as real transactions and then have to restate their reports when the sale did not materialize. In larger companies with a free-return policy, there must be a provision for returned goods in the financial statements that should be based on historically accurate rates of return.

Collectibility: Companies cannot know whether all customers will pay their bills. However, shipping to a company in known financial trouble, or shipping goods with the understanding that the vendor will arrange financing for the transaction in the future, are not real sales and should not be recognized as such.

Services: Some businesses cannot operate with these criteria, particularly in services and in contracting transactions. In services, the rules are usually simple — revenue should be recognized gradually throughout the period in which the vendor is obliged to render the service. In practice, however, there is a lot of leeway, particularly when the vendor is obliged to render services over a period of time as part of the purchase agreement of a product. A car manufacturer, for example, might offer some free services for its vehicles for a number of years. The service part of such a transaction should be recognized over the period of the guarantee. In a new model, however, the company would have to make an estimate that could be wrong about how much of the revenue should be deferred because it would have no data on the car's reliability.

Contracts: Revenue recognition in contracts is usually spread over the lifetime of a contract using the percentage of completion method, pegged to the costs the vendor incurs in completing the project. This too leaves a lot of leeway for management since it can assume costs with very long financing arrangements in order to recognize contract revenue earlier.

HOW TO BE SKEPTICAL ABOUT REVENUE RECOGNITION

Companies must reveal their revenue recognition policy in their financial statements. This is the first step. The question that should be asked is whether these policies are conservative or aggressive relative to the local accounting regime and to other companies in the same industry.

Other common problems are:

Channel Stuffing: In one famous case in 1993, a US contact lens maker informed its distributors, just before the end of the financial year, that they would have to buy up to two years of inventories immediately or lose their distributorship. Most of them complied after they were told they would not have to actually pay for the lenses until they sold them. The company showed a marked increase in revenues, which it subsequently restated after the case was exposed. Channel stuffing is a particular temptation to executives who work in countries where companies are judged by quarterly results. It often is the prelude to more dubious forms of earnings management.

Related Companies: Sales to companies in which the vendor has a direct interest should be reviewed carefully. The question to be asked is whether the sale might have taken place if the companies involved did not have this direct relationship. There is nothing inherently wrong with such transactions, but they do require a higher level of disclosure on the part of the vendor who recognizes these sales.

Side Letters: One of the hardest issues to trace is "side letters" that accompany a purchase agreement. These "side letters" do not appear in the usual channels of the company's accounting procedures, but they can, and in many cases do, substantially change the

---

NEWS CLIP
CHANNEL STUFFING REARS ITS UGLY HEAD

A raft of companies has taken to channel stuffing to artificially increase their top-line sales. The practice, which can take on many forms, basically amounts to pushing unwanted products onto distributors, VARs (Value Added Resellers) and retailers, and counting those shipments as sales. The practice is dubious because the products simply sit unsold in a warehouse, destined only to gather dust or, worse yet, to be returned at a later date.

Because little or no money ever changes hands, the Securities and Exchange Commission (SEC) and various accounting governing bodies seriously frown on these antics, preferring that a sale not be booked on a "sales-in" basis, but rather when money changes hands and goods move to a third party on a "sell-through" or "sales-out" basis.

Source: *VARBusiness.* 6 May 2003

OPINION
MANIPULATING EARNINGS

Management has so many ways to manipulate revenue recognition that outsiders have to rely on the evidence that must turn up, sooner or later, somewhere in the company's financial statements.

The first indication that revenue recognition might be too liberal is often in accounts receivable. Sudden surges in the level of accounts receivable in proportion to sales are usually an indicator that something has changed in revenue recognition. Another good indicator is any increase in the length of time these accounts

receivable are due. Untoward increases in both figures indicate that the company is possibly striving to keep revenue figures up despite a declining business environment.

Yet another good indicator of problematic revenue recognition is an overlarge disparity between revenue and cash flow. In a growing company, cash flow very often lags behind revenues. But sudden increases in the relative proportion between sales and cash flow can indicate that not all of the revenues were recognized in a timely manner.

nature of the sale. Such "side letters" can offer far more generous return rights, for example, than those that appear in the contract. In most cases, the existence of such "side letters" is revealed only after legal or regulatory authorities find other reasons to investigate the company.

 SUMMARY

A company's balance sheet, income statement and cash flow statement are the first sources of information for an investor. But accounting practices differ and these statements offer only limited help in evaluating a company's prospects. In addition, auditors and company managers have conflicting objectives. Investors should be aware of the specific practices the company follows, what its statements do not reveal and how profit and revenue are recognized to be able to assess its present condition, gauge solvency and predict future prospects.

1. Could there be something very wrong with a company that shows tremendous profits and little cash?

2. What would make you suspect that something could be wrong with the company's accounting practices even though its balance sheet, income statement and cash flow are all quite fine? What loopholes will you look for?

3. If a company's financial statements show it in the pink of health but the market is steadily pushing down the value of the stock, what could be the reason?

4. Company X has two subsidiaries in different industrial sectors: A and B. The company has 32 million ordinary shares in issue.

Subsidiary A

	2002	2003	2004
Sales	$57m	$58m	$58.5m
Operating profit	$3.2m	$2.3m	$3.1m

The subsidiary has debts of $10 million repayable over 5 years at a fixed rate of interest of 6.5%.

Subsidiary B

	2002	2003	2004
Sales	$72m	$76m	$100m
Operating profit	$3.5m	$5m	$6.3m

The subsidiary has debts of $15.0 million repayable over 8 years at a fixed rate of interest of 7%.

The share price is currently $11, down from $23 two years ago.

- What do you think a fair price for the share would be, based on the company's recent trading history?

- Would you recommend that the company spins off one of its subsidiaries? Explain your reasons.

- Subsidiary B has substantially increased its sales, but its profit margin seems to have fallen. Is this important? Where would you look in the accounts to find more information about why this is occurring?

- If the two subsidiaries were separate companies, what would be a fair price for their shares, in your opinion?

5. Company Y has earnings of $500m on which it pays 10% tax. Company Z is of equal size in terms of assets and sales; it has earnings of $630m on which it pays 30% tax.

- Which company has the more profitable business? Why?

- Can you think of possible reasons why the tax burden of the two companies is different?

SECURITY ANALYSIS

10

The historic, current and projected future earnings of a company impact its share price in the market. Companies that have a history of good and growing earnings and that are expected to continue growing earnings will tend to have rising stock prices. Companies whose earnings are expected to fall are more likely to have a declining stock price. Stock prices can also accentuate actual company earnings results or economic activity, so that when company earnings are expected to rise by, say, 10%, the stock price might move up by 20% or 30%. The opposite is true when negative earnings numbers are expected or announced — a 10% decline in earnings might result in a stock price fall greater than 10%.

However, the valuation of companies is one of the most difficult tasks due to the complexity of variables that determine the future price of a stock. This is in marked contrast to bonds, where future cash flows and terminal values are known, and so precise figures can be reached (although assumptions on risks are still made subjectively). We cannot know for certain what the future earnings of any equity will be. At best, it can only be an educated guess. This uncertainty does not prevent large numbers of value estimates from being published. Figures are often presented with unjustifiable confidence in their accuracy, and many investment decisions are made using published valuation data without knowing how these estimates have been arrived at.

While estimates of value have many important applications in the financial markets, they are also used as a broker's or company's sales tool. It is easy to paint a rosy picture of the performance and future prospects of a company by selecting the valuation measures that show the firm in the best light. For this reason it is important not to accept valuations at face value and, in any discussion, to establish common definitions of the measures under review.

Valuation models have become increasingly complex, and there are now models that incorporate many inputs into their calculations that may actually increase, rather than reduce, the potential error. Complex models may seem impressive in terms of the amounts of quantitative data they process, but this is no guarantee that the results will be more accurate. In fact, a sound principle of valuation is to choose only those variables that determine the company's true asset value and its earnings.

USES OF COMPANY VALUATIONS

In spite of the many problems and pitfalls, company valuations are essential to a number of financial operations in addition to investing in stocks listed on the stock exchange. These operations include:

- Mergers and acquisitions: The firm acquiring must try to arrive at a good estimate of the value of the firm it is buying — there is considerable evidence that firms often over-pay. Questions arise over the extent to which the merger adds or detracts value from the combined firm. Stockholders of both firms must consider whether or not to retain their holdings after the merger.

- Management policies: In recent years there has been a considerable effort to analyze the business operations of firms to identify "value adding" and "value detracting" activities, and to find quantifiable links between these and the firm's share price. While these efforts

NEWS CLIP
ANALYST'S OBJECTIVITY?

One report stated how New York's Attorney General released a pile of e-mails from a broker research analyst that show a big gap between hype and reality. The broker had a five-point scale for rating shares. The bottom two scores meant the price would fall, but they were not used. The e-mails revealed that the analysts actually hated some of the stocks they were recommending. One firm, an Internet services company, was given the best rating, but privately the analysts said it was a "powder keg" and a "piece of junk." Though its share price fell from $261 to just $14, the analysts never recommended selling it. A high-speed Internet company was rated "accumulate" or "buy," but the team called it "a piece of crap."

This brokerage firm also did investment banking business and there was supposed to be what they call a "Chinese wall" between two sets of people. The share analysts are there to advise the investors, while on the other side of the wall, the bankers make money advising the companies who issue the shares. The wall is there to stop the obvious conflict of interest. It seems that's not how it worked in practice.

have sometimes borne fruit, such as when GE's market valuation leaped following its announcement of substantial savings achieved by its "Six Sigma" efficiency program, there is, as yet, no fully satisfactory method for measuring this.

METHODS FOR VALUING COMPANIES

There are a number of approaches to valuing companies, including:

- Measures of relative value, which base their estimates on comparisons of the market prices of similar firms and how these prices relate to factors such as earnings, book value and sales.

- Discounted cash flow and dividend discount models, which estimate value by modeling future cash flows, dividends growth and risk.

- Asset value calculation — Calculating the net assets (assets minus liabilities) of a company by summing up the estimated value of such items as real estate, inventory, buildings, intellectual property, brand names, etc, and subtracting all liabilities such as bank loans, outstanding payments.

RELATIVE VALUE MEASURES

There are a number of measures that relate a company's financials to the market price of the firm's stock. Price/earnings, price/sales and price to book value are all relative measures that are commonly used in equity analysis. These are popular basic measures, but since they measure relative values, they tend to reflect the market mood and will usually generate numbers that are closer to market prices than those produced by discounted cash flow models.

However, relative measures can be easily misinterpreted and manipulated. Their apparent simplicity may disguise a number of difficulties that can cause significant errors. For example:

- Relative measures tend to follow the market in undervaluing or overvaluing firms and sectors.

- The assumptions made are not explicitly stated, and it is important to discover what these are in any given case; it is not good practice to accept at face value relative measures supplied by others.

- Important factors affecting a company's value, such as risk and cash flow potential, may be ignored in these measures.

THE PRICE/EARNINGS RATIO (P/E)

The basic definition of the price/earnings ratio is:

P/E = market price per share / earnings per share

Thus, a firm with a P/E of, say, 16, would take 16 years, at its current rate of earnings, to generate the equivalent of its market value.

The appealing simplicity of the P/E ratio makes it one of the most widely applied measures in the equity markets, but there are several difficulties. First, there is more than one way to calculate P/E:

- Current P/E uses the earnings per share declared for the most recent financial year.

- Trailing P/E uses an average of previous periods' earnings.

- Forward P/E uses the expected earnings per share in future financial years.

These variations can produce startlingly different results. Furthermore, even the definition of "market price per share" can vary; although it usually refers to the current price, some analysts choose to use an average price over the preceding quarter, six months or year.

Earnings per share figures must always take into account the total number of shares outstanding and also the additional shares that may be outstanding if warrants, share options for employees or directors, or convertible bonds are converted into shares. This can be adjusted for by calculating P/Es based on "diluted" earnings. Dilution is often only a rough estimate, however, since it treats stock options that are deeply in the money and only slightly in the money as equivalent.

As Figure 10.1 illustrates, the P/E variants can produce markedly different results for the same firm. It is essential, therefore, to establish which measures have been used and also to ensure that like is compared with like.

When comparing the P/Es of different firms, there are two other principal sources of bias:

- Average P/Es for a group of companies are usually calculated as a mean average. There may be a few companies in the sample that have unusually high P/Es due to low earnings. If these figures are used in the calculation of the mean average, the result will be higher and may not be a good representation of the group as a whole. Calculating the median average for the group will produce a more meaningful result.

- Some firms in the sample may have no earnings, in which case their P/Es cannot be calculated. If these firms are excluded, it may produce a bias towards profitable firms. One solution to this problem is to add the prices and EPS for every firm and calculate the aggregate P/E.

Figure 10.1 — Typical difference between P/E variants

	12 Month Trailing P/E	P/E FY1	12 Month Forward P/E Ratio
Mean	18.71	18.74	18.79
Mode	15.00	10.00	10.00
Median	16.32	15.88	14.71

COMPARING MARKETS

There exists wide variation in average P/Es in markets around the world. While it may appear that countries with low average P/Es are undervalued and countries with high P/Es are overvalued, this is not necessarily the case. There are some general points to remember when making such comparisons:

- Markets with high expected growth rates are likely to have higher P/Es, since investors are willing to pay a high price for shares in companies that have a higher earnings growth rate because they expect lower P/Es in the future.

- Markets with high interest rates are likely to have lower P/Es because the reciprocal of the P/E is the rate of return an investor expects — for example, a P/E of 10 is similar to an interest rate of 10% and a P/E of 5 is similar to a interest rate of 20%.

- Markets with high perceived risk are likely to have lower P/Es. Investors are less likely to buy stocks in such markets and more like to sell, thus pushing prices down so that the "P" of the P/E is lower.

- Markets where companies earn higher returns, on average, are likely to have higher P/Es. Investors are more likely to buy stocks in such markets, thus pushing up the P/E.

COMPARING FIRMS WITHIN A SECTOR

The classification of firms into sectors can sometimes be quite arbitrary, especially in this era of rapid business change. Different firms in the same sector may have very different growth rates, risks levels and business mix, and so may be difficult to compare.

As well as the sources of bias already mentioned, there are also potential problems from using data in company accounts, such as:

- Mergers and acquisitions – Companies enjoy a range of choices in the way they state earnings following an acquisition, which can have a strong effect on the P/E.

- Many firms have choices over whether to declare items as capital expenses or as operating costs.

PRICE TO BOOK RATIO

Investors who are looking for a bargain often pay close attention to a company's book value, or better yet, its net asset value, which is the difference between assets and liabilities as stated in the accounts. Net asset value becomes necessary since the book values reflected in accounts are often historical values and may be substantially different from current market values. It is not unusual, for example, to have a real estate holding in the balance sheet of a company valued at the original purchase price, even though that purchase was made many years ago and now, in current market conditions, it has appreciated substantially in value.

NEWS CLIP
SEPARATING BROKER RESEARCH AND INVESTMENT BANKING

In 2003, investigations into wrongdoing on Wall Street climaxed when ten securities firms agreed to pay $1.4 billion in fines and change the way they do business by separating stock market research from investment banking.

This ended an unfortunate period for an industry that was accused of deceiving investors with misleading stock market research oriented to generating investment banking fees.

Two analysts who followed boom-and-bust sectors of the late 1990s were named in the investigations. One covered Internet stocks, while another was a telecoms analyst. They were barred from the business and ordered to pay between $4 million and $15 million in fines.

The firms agreed to (1) cut the links between stock research and investment banking, (2) compensate analysts based on the accuracy of their stock picks, and (3) reform how initial public offerings were distributed.

Some of the regulators termed the firms' research as "fraudulent." This could open the banks to lawsuits from shareholders who could seek monetary damages to compensate for their losses because they followed the firms' investment advice.

In many countries, including the US and UK, the value of an asset is shown in the accounts at the price paid for it, less an annual downward adjustment known as "depreciation." This means that book value is unlikely to be a close approximation to the value of the assets if they were to be sold off piecemeal. However, book value does tend to be a relatively stable number, and is useful for comparisons between firms operating under similar accounting rules.

The interest in low price/book ratios has a long pedigree. Benjamin Graham (1894–1976), widely regarded as the founder of stock analysis as a formal discipline, used low price/book ratios as a major screen for his stock picks; he demanded that price should be less than 66% of book value. Such a low ceiling is likely to capture only companies with little growth potential. Graham understood this, but, scarred by his experience of the Wall Street Crash of 1929, preferred to invest in such companies, saying they were "like cigar butts with one or two good puffs left in them."

Countries such as France and Germany allow firms to state higher book values. Also, some industries, such as financial services and technology, may value assets differently or may not hold many tangible assets.

Price to book ratio can be defined as:

P/B ratio = price per share / book value of equity per share

Points to check:

- Some analysts use the average book value over the previous 12 months, while most use the figure published in the most recent annual accounts. Use either measure, but make sure you use it consistently for all firms in the sample.

- There has been a recent trend in the US for firms to buy back some of their stock, which returns cash to stockholders but reduces the firm's book value if these shares are cancelled. If a firm's P/B is rising, check for stock buybacks.

- In mergers and acquisitions, the P/B of the combined firm may change dramatically, depending on the accounting policies used. This may make P/B ratios difficult to compare.

A number of studies during the 1980s and 1990s found a strong link between low price/book ratios and higher-than-average returns. If this link holds true in the future, the preference of bargain-hunting "value investors" for low P/B firms may be well rewarded.

PRICE/EARNINGS TO GROWTH RATIO (PEG)

The PEG ratio is often used in valuing high-growth firms. It is defined as:

PEG = (P/E) / expected growth rate per share

Although firms with low PEG ratios are often regarded as undervalued, this is only the case when the firms in the sample have similar dividend rates, risk levels and expected growth. When calculating PEG, make sure that the type of P/E used (current P/E or trailing P/E, but not forward P/E) matches the earnings period (current or trailing).

PRICE/SALES RATIO

Price/sales ratio has a number of attractions as a method of identifying undervalued and overvalued firms because several sources of potential bias are removed. For example, earnings per share and book value of equity are derived from companies' financial reports, and may be calculated differently by individual firms according to their accounting policies, making them difficult to compare. "Pure" sales figures, on the other hand, are more often directly comparable across any sample group of firms.

Sales figures for large companies tend to be quite stable over time, and certainly less volatile than earnings. If earnings fluctuate over a several year market cycle, sales figures may be a better measure to use. Also, new companies and loss-making companies may not have earnings, so P/Es cannot be calculated, but they will still usually have sales figures.

The basic price/sales ratio is defined as:

P/S = price per share/sales per share

The price/sales ratio tells you about sales, but not about profits. A company with high sales may not necessarily have commensurately high profits — in fact, "over-trading," which occurs when a company expands too quickly, often causes margins to fall while sales increase. The companies that are most likely to be undervalued on this measure are those with a low price/sales ratio and high profit margins. Although sales figures are harder to massage, they can be misleading as we have pointed out when discussing recognition of sales.

RELATIVE VALUE RATIO CALCULATIONS

When calculating measures of relative values, check that:

- The ratio being used is clearly defined and is applied in the same way to all firms in the sample.

- The inputs for the ratio (e.g. price, earnings) are calculated in the same way for all firms in the sample.

- The values for the ratio are typical for the market or sector you are analyzing.

- The firms in your sample are really comparable.

Remember that valuations are not absolute, objective figures; they are useful aids to estimating value, but they are not infallible.

ECONOMIC VALUE ADDED (EVA) AND MARKET VALUE ADDED (MVA)

Popularized by Stern Stewart, a New York-based consultancy, as a tool both for management and valuation, EVA came into fashion during the 1990s, particularly as a way of measuring management performance. In some companies, it is used as the main way of calculating management incentives because of difficulties with other compensation schemes. If managers are judged purely by their firm's earnings, for example, they are given an incentive to manipulate an increase in earnings even if such actions are "wealth-destroying" for the company. Other schemes, such as those based on share price or sales and profit figures, are similarly open to such problems.

CASE STUDY: DOES EVA REALLY HELP IMPROVE COMPANY PERFORMANCE?

EVA measures "economic profit," as do other schemes such as value based management (VBM). In recent years these methods have been widely adopted as a means of rewarding managers and are used by major corporations such as Coca-Cola and Monsanto. But do they really help to create wealth for the company? A study by scholars at Southern Methodist University and the Owen School of Management of Vanderbilt University found that there was no significant difference in performance between firms that used such schemes and those that did not. Furthermore, bonuses for managers increased at almost the same rate in companies that did not use economic profit schemes as in those that did use them. This suggests that criticisms that managers adopted economic profit schemes simply as a way of making more money are unfounded. The study concluded that economic profit schemes are no better or worse at creating shareholder value than other executive compensation schemes.

Source: *The Long-Run Performance of Firms Adopting Compensation Plans Based on Economic Profits* by Chris Hogan and Craig Lewis, July 2001.

Based on the concept of shareholder value, the idea of EVA is to measure how much wealth a company has created from the total capital invested in it. The EVA is the calculation of what profits remain after the costs of a company's capital — both debt and equity — are deducted from the operating profit. The idea is that true profit should account for the cost of capital. It is intended to be an objective measure by which any set of companies can be compared, allowing investors to see how well firms are investing their money, adjusting for variations in the cost of capital.

A related measure is market value added (MVA), calculated as:

MVA = market value (total shares issued times the share price) minus total capital

A company with a negative MVA may be profitable, but proponents of MVA argue that since each dollar invested is producing less that a dollar's worth of value at the current market prices, it is actually diminishing the value of shareholder equity, and if the market is reasonably efficient, it won't be long until the market responds to this erosion by slashing the price of the share.

EV/EBIT AND EBITDA
Earnings before interest and tax (EBIT) and earnings before interest, tax, depreciation and amortization (EBITDA) are entries on a firm's income statement that can be used in relative valuation. Using these figures may make companies with different debt levels more directly comparable, since the earnings are used before subtracting interest costs, which will be higher in a more highly leveraged firm. They are often used in conjunction with "enterprise value" (EV), which is the market value of a company's equity plus the value of its debt minus cash.

Measures using EBIT or EBITDA and earnings have become increasingly popular among analysts in recent years because:

- They make it easier to compare firms with different capital structure.

- By excluding depreciation and amortization, firms with different depreciation policies are more easily compared.

- Since it is rare to find a firm with negative EBITDA (firms with negative net earnings are far more common), so more firms can be compared.

Enterprise value/EBITDA is most frequently used to compare firms involved in major infrastructure projects that will take many years to produce a profit, especially when the firms have different depreciation methods and have already invested heavily.

DISCOUNTED CASH FLOW (DCF)

DCF is based on the idea that the value of anything, whether an asset or a company, is the sum total of the cash it can generate in the future, adjusted for the present value of that cash. As is obvious, receiving cash now is worth more than receiving it in the future; the challenge is to estimate accurately the "present value" of a number of expected future payments. In the case of a company, this can be a complex process.

Unlike relative valuation measures, discounted cash flow seeks to arrive at a valuation figure by a detailed examination of a firm from the "bottom up." The calculations can be difficult and require good judgment in the assumptions and estimates that must be made. Although DCF seems to be a more rigorous estimate of value than other methods, because of its complexity many "sell-side" finance professionals use relative value measures such as P/E when making presentations to customers because they are easier to explain. As mentioned earlier, however, investors who do not or cannot make their own detailed estimates of value are vulnerable to being misled, especially during bull markets when relative measures are likely to produce much higher valuations than DCF.

Before examining DCF, let's look at how the present value of a future payment is calculated:

Suppose you have $1,000 now and you can obtain a 5% real return on it per year in a bank deposit.

Value now: $1,000
1st year's interest: $50
Value at end Year 1: $1,050
2nd year's interest: $52.50
Value at end Year 2: $1,102.50

Note that the second year's interest was slightly higher than the first year's, because you also earned interest on the interest you earned in Year 1 (this is "compound interest").

Suppose you are asked to estimate the present value of a payment of $1,102.50 due in two year's time. You can see from the above example that the answer will be $1,000 — in other words, the present value of a future payment is found by "discounting" the interest rate over the period.

Although this can be calculated step by step, there is a simple formula:

$A_o = A_n / (1 + i)^n$
where
A_o is the present value
A_n is the value in n number of years (when it is paid)

i is the annual interest rate

n is the number of years

EXAMPLE

What is the present value of a payment of $1,102.50 due in two year's time? The interest rate is 5% p.a.

$$Ao = An / (1+ i)^n$$
$$= 1{,}102.50 / (1 + 0.05)^2$$
$$= 1{,}102.50 / 1.1025$$
$$= 1{,}000$$

This calculation is easy enough if you are certain of the interest rates you can obtain during the period and that you will definitely receive the sum when promised. This is a "risk-free" situation.

In the real world, however, there may be some risk, especially when time periods increase; you may be confident of your estimate of interest rates over the next two years, but can you be as confident for a period of ten or twenty years? And can you be sure that you will receive the full amount on time? The deal may also be subject to other risks, such as changes in taxation.

DIVIDEND DISCOUNT MODEL

The dividend discount model is a variation on the DCF theme. Let's consider the simplest situation, where an investor wishes to value a very stable company with a predictable growth, a capital structure (equity, debt, etc) that is unlikely to change, and a steady record of dividend payments. The formula for calculating the value, known as the dividend discount model, is:

Fair Share price = next year's dividend / (required rate of return – expected dividend growth rate)

Notice that the discount rate is defined as the required interest rate of return. This refers to the return that rational investors might require to compensate them for the risk of investing in a company. Setting that rate is difficult. While companies tend to be more risky than the "risk-free" rate obtainable by investing in, say, a bank deposit or a government bond, there may be considerable disagreement regarding the exact level of risk, for several reasons. First, it is evident that many investors do not behave "rationally," so their "required rate of return" may vary with market sentiment. Second, "rational" investors may require different rates of return depending on their taxation rates, other investment opportunities, their home country's investment regulations and differences in transaction costs.

Suppose our stable company pays a dividend of $2, investors can obtain a "risk-free" return of 10% from bonds and dividends are expected to grow by 5% annually. Then the "correct" value of the share price would be:

$$\$2 \ / \ (0.1 - 0.05) = \$40$$

If the current share price is less than $40 dollars, then the company is a "buy" if the valuation is correct.

Notice, however, that even small differences in the estimation of the discount rate and the growth rate can result in large differences in the valuation. For example, suppose we set the discount rate at 11%:

$$\$2 \ / \ (0.11 - 0.05) = \$33.33$$

If we keep the discount rate at 10% but change the growth rate to 3%, the valuation changes to:

$$\$2 \ / \ (0.10 - 0.03) = \$28.57$$

There are many ways of estimating the discount rate and dividend growth rate.

Some argue that the dividend discount model is overly conservative because it does not take into account the value of intangibles such as major brand names. Others argue that if the firm really does possess valuable intangibles, these can be valued separately and added to the valuation, and that conservatism may actually be the strength of the model.

So how well does it work in practice? A study by Sorenson and Williamson examined the performance of 150 stocks in the S&P 500 in the early 1980s and compared this with their dividend discount model valuation in December 1980. They found that portfolios of stocks that were undervalued at December 1980 according to the model substantially outperformed the index and portfolios of overvalued stocks during the period. However, basing an investment strategy on dividend payments could have negative tax consequences, especially for higher rate taxpayers. Also it cannot be easily applied to companies that do not have stable dividend payments and growth, such as:

- Restructured companies – during restructuring, a company may sell some assets and acquire others, go public or private, or change its executive compensation.

- Commodity companies and others subject to trade cycles – companies in cyclical industries may experience large changes in sales and profit levels over a period of several years.

- Failing companies – a company that is in serious trouble may be making losses and even suffering negative cash flow.

- Companies with unused patents or licenses – these may be valuable assets without cash flow. Valuations can be made by using an option pricing model or by estimating their market value.

From the point of view of investors, in a publicly traded company, the only cash flow that will ever be received is from dividends (and the sale of stock, if it is ever sold). DCF's dividend discount model is intended to supply a realistic valuation for such investors. Analysts who use DCF to value a company must monitor developments closely to check if any of the inputs (dividend, required rate of return and expected dividend growth rate) should be changed. Events such as a major acquisition or changes in financing can drastically alter DCF calculations. A major challenge in DCF is in distinguishing between fundamental, long-term changes to the company and temporary fluctuations. While DCF offers a sounder basis for valuation in many situations than other methods, only hindsight can reveal whether the assumptions used were correct. As with all valuation, much depends upon the analyst's skill, judgment and knowledge of the companies examined.

While every valuation method has its strong supporters and detractors, none provide absolute certainty and freedom from risk. As we have already seen, stocks are inherently risky, especially in the short term, and valuation figures can easily be used to justify irrational decisions. Nevertheless, all committed investors need to have ways of estimating the value of companies, even if they cannot arrive at exact figures, to help them make investment decisions. Ideally, investors should be able to calculate valuations themselves; relying on other people's figures may lead to major errors if the figures used are not comparable, or if they have been "massaged" to put a firm in the best possible light.

PERFORMANCE MEASUREMENT

The major market indices, sometimes called "the averages," are well-known and quoted continuously in the financial media. Strictly speaking, an index is calculated differently from an average, as we will see below. To the uninitiated, indexes such as the Dow Jones Industrial Average (DJIA), the Financial Times Stock Exchange 100 (FTSE 100), the New York Stock Exchange composite index (NYSE Composite) and Hong Kong's Hang Seng index may appear to be stable and absolute measures that are truly representative of their respective markets, but this is not necessarily the case. Many private investors have the notion that they are simple averages of the performance of all the companies in the market. The reality, however, is very different; indexes are not mean averages, and the way they are constructed and adjusted varies considerably. They are a more refined measurement tool than an average, but to interpret them correctly it is important to understand how they are constructed.

Indexes use sophisticated mathematical approaches to measure the performance of a group of stocks, in general by "weighting" component companies according to their market capitalization. This has the effect of giving greater importance — or "weight" — to larger companies, which, it may be argued, is better than the price-weighting effect of averages, which favors stocks with high nominal prices.

Indexes are useful for tracking market trends since they provide a historical view of a market. They provide the investor with a "map" of where the market has been. This enables an analysis of how the market may relate to various economic and social trends. Indexes are also helpful in comparing various events, such as market crashes, in one country to similar events in another country.

Despite their usefulness, indexes have a number of problems. First is the so-called "calculation bias." Since most indexes tend to be market capitalization-weighted (i.e. a heavier weight is given to the companies with the large market capitalization — number of shares multiplied by the market price), those companies with the highest market capitalization have the largest influence on the index movements. You therefore may have a situation where the large cap stocks are not doing well while the small cap stocks are going up, but the index indicates an overall market decline, which would be misleading. Of course, proponents of the market cap weighted indexes say that such indexes best capture the overall market since they best track the movement of money in the market. Detractors of such indexes say that they would have higher volatility due to the heavy weight of the large cap stocks, since they tend to go up and down as a group. They say that a fairer index would be equally weighted so that the impact of smaller stocks would be better represented.

There is also the matter of "representative bias." Since many indexes tend to be made up of a small number of stocks, they may not be truly representative of the entire market. In addition, since indexes are normally changed each year, with some stocks deleted and others added, a historical chart of any index cannot represent the trading patterns of the same stocks over a long time period. Also, since the stock selection is made by committees, they can make mistakes and pick the wrong stocks for the index.

All investors and investment managers want to know how well their investments are performing, but this is difficult to judge, especially in the short term. A very risky portfolio of investments may produce outstanding returns in one year, for instance, and then plummet in the next. Even very stable companies may perform below expectations during downturns in the economy or in their industry. The picture gets blurred further by many other factors, such as stock splits, new stock issues, company mergers,

mergers of investment funds, radical changes in government and shifts in the global economy.

When judging the performance of any investment, the first task is to decide what to measure it against; should you, for instance, measure it against other companies in the same industry, or companies of a similar size, or the performance of the market as a whole? Faced with many benchmark choices, do you, for instance, select the one that puts the best possible light on the performance of your investment? Do you change the benchmark every year or do you stick to the same benchmark year after year, even if changing circumstances make the comparison less and less meaningful? Do you decide that some political or economic change has ushered in a new era, and that it is useless to make comparisons with any figures that predate the change? Wishful thinking, and the investment industry's natural desire to tell attractive stories about investments they are promoting, may result in very misleading performance data.

There are no simple answers to this problem, but traditionally the first place to look when searching for an appropriate performance benchmark is at the market indices.

DOW JONES INDUSTRIAL AVERAGE (DJIA)

The Dow Jones Industrial Average (DJIA) is the oldest index and provides a long-term perspective of the US stock market. It is sometimes referred to as the "blue chip" index since it includes the largest stocks traded on the New York Stock Exchange. Charles Dow created this original index in 1884 and later created other indexes to monitor what were then considered the high-tech sectors of the day — electric utilities and railroads. By 1928, the number of stocks on the Dow Jones Industrial Average increased to 30.

Unlike most indexes, the DJIA was originally a simple average of the prices of major US stocks. Dow was something of a "chartist," believing that it was possible to base investment decisions on the patterns of price movements, and used the average as a means of promoting his ideas to the general public. With a partner, Edward D. Jones, Dow established Dow Jones & Co. in 1882 as a publisher of financial news. In 1889 he founded *The Wall Street Journal*, which remains the publisher of the DJIA.

Up until his death in 1902, Charles Dow continued to publish a number of different averages, but it was the Dow Jones Industrial Average — often called the "Dow," that became the most widely followed. For many years, it was generally regarded as the key indicator of the US markets, despite the small number of companies used. Today there are many other market indicators in use, but the DJIA is still used, and its supporters argue that it fluctuates in line with other indicators. The number of stocks in the DJIA was increased from 12 to 20 in 1916, then to 30 in 1928, and has remained at 30 ever since.

At first, Charles Dow calculated the DJIA by adding up the prices of his 12 chosen stocks and dividing by 12 to obtain the arithmetic mean. As time passed, changes to the companies began to distort the picture;

for example, when companies "split" stocks. Stock splits naturally result in a share price adjustment to reflect the increase in the number of shares, but the overall value of the investors' holdings is not reduced because they receive newly issued shares; the price of the stock is lowered, often in order to encourage new investment from price-fixated investors.

To adjust for the effects of stock splits and other distorting factors, the DJIA changes the divisor, and it is now no longer simply the number of companies in the average. Factors that have led to adjustment include:

- Stock splits
- Spin-offs
- Rights offerings
- Special cash dividends

Today, the components of the DJIA are chosen by the editors of *The Wall Street Journal*, which publishes a large number of market indices, both for the US and the rest of the world. To preserve continuity, changes are made infrequently to the DJIA, and are most often made after an important change occurs to one of its constituent companies; for example, if a company is taken over. Over the years, some stocks have been dropped from the DJIA and then restored; for example, General Electric, the only survivor from the original 12 published in 1896, was dropped in 1898, brought back in 1899, dropped in 1901 and brought back in 1907. More recently, IBM was dropped in 1939 and only restored in 1970.

The DJIA has acquired a mystique among American investors because of its longevity and popularity, but despite the enthusiasm of its supporters, there is no sound reason to suppose that it is truly representative of the US markets or the US economy as a whole; in fact, it is hard to see what the DJIA does represent, other than the average price of its constituent companies.

Although many market indicators, including the Dow, may rise in anticipation of economic growth and fall before a recession, such movements may not be closely correlated to the economy.

NASDAQ COMPOSITE INDEX

The NASDAQ index is based on common stocks listed on the NASDAQ exchange. It is a market-value weighted index, meaning that each company's stock impacts the index in proportion to its market value, or capitalization (the last sale price multiplied by total shares outstanding). Currently the index is very broadly based and includes over 5,000 companies, more than most other indexes.

In addition to the general NASDAQ indexes, there is the NASDAQ 100 Index launched in 1985. It includes 100 of the largest non-financial domestic companies listed on NASDAQ. It is market capitalization weighted. The companies in the index have a minimum market capitalization of $500 million, and an average daily trading volume of at least 100,000 shares.

Figure 10.2 — Recent changes to the companies included in the DJIA

No.	Date	Added to DJIA	Removed from DJIA
1.	1 Jun 1959	Alcoa Inc.	
2.		Du Pont	
3.		Exxon Mobil	
4.		General Electric Company	
5.		General Motors Corporation	
6.		Honeywell International	
7.		Procter & Gamble Company	
8.		United Technologies Corp	
9.	8 Aug 1976	3M Company	Anaconda Copper
10.	29 Jun 1979	International Business Machines	Chrysler
11.		Merck	Esmark
12.	30 Aug 1982	American Express Company	Johns-Manville
13.	30 Oct 1985	Altria Group	American Tobacco B
14.		McDonalds Corporation	General Foods
15.	12 Mar 1987	Coca-Cola	Owens-Illinois Glass
16.		Boeing Company	Inco
17.	6 May 1991	Caterpillar Incorporated	Navistar International Corp.
18.		Walt Disney Company	USX Corporation
19.		J.P. Morgan Chase	Primerica Corporation
20.	17 Mar 1997	Citigroup Incorporated	Westinghouse Electric
21.		Hewlett-Packard Company	Texaco Incorporated
22.		Johnson & Johnson	Bethlehem Steel
23.		Wal-Mart Stores Incorporated	Woolworth
24.	1 Nov 1999	Microsoft Corporation	Chevron
25.		Intel Corporation	Goodyear
26.		SBC Communications	Union Carbide
27.		Home Depot Incorporated	Sears Roebuck & Company
28.	8 Apr 2004	American Intl. Group Inc	AT&T Corporation
29.		Pfizer Incorporated	Eastman Kodak Company
30.		Verizon Communications Inc	International Paper Company

NYSE COMPOSITE INDEX – NYSE

The New York Stock Exchange calculates its NYSE Composite Index. It is a market-value weighted index and is calculated back to December 1965 with adjustments for capitalization changes. The starting value of the index is $50 and changes are shown in dollars and cents.

VALUE LINE INDEX

Another major average still in use today is published by Value Line; it is based on a list of about 1,700 US stocks, drawn mainly from the NYSE, AMEX and NASDAQ markets. Since it covers a much wider range of shares than the Dow Jones averages, it has a superficial resemblance to an index; because it includes many smaller companies, it has often been regarded in the past as an indicator of what naïve investors were buying and selling, but newer indexes of companies with small capitalizations have appeared that may be better indicators of this.

STANDARD AND POOR'S INDICES

Standard and Poor's is a company that publishes a number of well-known US indices, including:

- S&P 500
- S&P 400 MidCap
- S&P 500 SmallCap

The S&P 500

The S&P 500 is one of the best benchmarks for large-cap stocks and accounts for about 70% of the US market. The performance of the S&P 500 is considered one of the best overall indicators of market performance and a mutual fund manager's goal is to beat it. Unfortunately, the top 45 companies comprise more than 50% of the index's value.

S&P also publishes a large number of other indexes of securities ranging from foreign markets to global hedge fund performance. The S&P 500 is the most widely followed. It is a composite of 500 large industrial, financial, utility and transportation firms that are given a base of 10 dated at the period 1941 – 1943, the relatively depressed wartime market. Because of their large capitalization, the value of these 500 firms adds up to a large proportion of the total market capitalization (over 60%), so the index is often used to represent the market as a whole. The S&P 500 is widely used by investment professionals as a performance benchmark for US portfolios and managed funds.

Recently, S&P indexes introduced a "free float" adjustment to exclude shares held by other listed companies, government organizations and "insider" shareholders. The purpose is to make the index reflect only the shares that are publicly available for investors to buy and sell, since the excluded shares are generally held with the aim of influencing or controlling firms strategically, rather than to maximize investment returns (which is what most "outside" investors, both private individuals and investment funds, hope to do).

MORGAN STANLEY CAPITAL INTERNATIONAL (MSCI) INDEXES

Morgan Stanley Capital International has become a major provider of indexes during the last few decades, providing a very wide range, primarily for use as benchmarks against which to judge the performance of mutual funds and other institutional investment activities. MSCI's indexes include:

- Global, regional and country equity indexes across the world
- Global sector and industry indexes
- Value and growth indexes
- Small cap equity indexes
- Hedged and GDP-weighted indexes
- A wide range of US equity indexes
- Hedge fund indexes
- Fixed income indexes

MSCI aims to provide a more detailed and comprehensive set of benchmarking tools than were available in the past and makes efforts to solve some of the problems investors have in interpreting and following indices, such as:

- Some countries have limits on the size of foreign investors' shareholdings, or on the sums of money they invest. MSCI global indexes take these factors into account, and aim to make each index "replicable" by an institutional investor — in other words, to make it possible for an institutional investor to invest in the same companies, and in the same proportion, as the index while retaining liquidity.

- Efforts are made to ensure that any changes made to the calculation or composition of an index are fully explained ahead of time, and that it is possible for outsiders to follow the calculation of adjustments.

As with other index providers, emphasis is placed on calculating the "free float" of shares that are actually available for trading on the public markets. This is particularly important in countries where large firms tend to be controlled by families (as often occurs in Asia) or where the state has significant ownership in firms. MSCI offers indexes for over 50 countries, and works with Standard and Poor's to establish a standardized system for classification of firms, sectors and industries.

As mentioned earlier, good liquidity is very important for institutional investors, who do not want to become trapped into holding large shareholdings for longer than they wish. MSCI aims to ensure that firms included in their indexes have sufficient liquidity, and monitors this continually.

Figure 10.3 — A trader yells out orders on the floor of the S&P 500 Index trading pit on 31 August at the Chicago Mercantile Exchange in Chicago, IL. It was one of the most volatile days of trading at the Mercantile Exchange, with the S&P 500 down 77.00 to close at 954.00.

Source: AFP Photo

WILSHIRE 5000

The Wilshire 5000 Composite Index follows the majority of US-listed equities and is the broadest measure of the entire US market; it includes companies with headquarters in the US that trade overseas. Like most of the major indices, it now uses float-adjusted weighting as well as market capitalization weighting (but on slightly different rules to S&P). Multiple classes of stock are combined with the firm's primary issue to calculate its market capitalization. Like the S&P 500, the Wilshire 5000 is widely used as a US benchmark by investment professionals. The Wilshire group now cooperates with Dow Jones to have the Dow Jones Wilshire 5000 Total Market Index. It was created in 1974 when Wilshire's founder utilized new computer technology then available to make it possible to collect stock prices and calculate returns on a large volume of stocks. The index was named after the approximately 5,000 stocks that it originally contained, but the number of stocks has grown over the years as US equity issues have grown.

FINANCIAL TIMES INDEXES

This index follows the top 100 UK companies by market capitalization and adjusts for free float, and represents about 80% of the entire market. Component companies change quite frequently. It is often used to represent the entire London market, but purists sometimes prefer to use the FTSE All-Share Index, which represents over 98% of the market.

The FTSE company also produces a large number of indexes to cover markets, and groups of markets, across the world. The most important of these include:

- The Hang Seng Asiatop Index – Produced in partnership with the Hang Seng Bank, the Hang Seng Asiatop Index follows the top 30 Asian companies by market capitalization. Other indexes are produced to follow Asian sectors such as high technology, resources, financial and telecoms.

- The FTSE All-World Index – Covering 2,700 companies around the world, weighted by market capitalization and representing over 90% of the world's investable market capitalization.

- The FTSE Eurotop 100 Index – Follows the 60 largest companies in Europe weighted by market capitalization, and includes a further 40 companies to represent other important market sectors.

DAX – THE GERMAN INDEX

DAX stands for Deutscher Aktienindex, introduced in 1988 by the German Stock Exchange. However, this index may be tracked back to 1959 by chain-linking it to the former Borsenzeitung Index. The DAX includes a family of stock market indices. In addition to the DAX 100 Index there is a midcap index (MDAX) and the Composite DAX (CDAX) subdivided into 16 branch indices. To avoid the obsolescence of the index sample, the base is recalculated annually and the new series of index numbers is spliced to the previous one. The creators of the DAX say that it paved the way for the concept of a total return index to be accepted as a benchmark for the price development of a major stock exchange. Also, the DAX was the first performance index ever to be used as an underlying for derivatives trading.

The DAX follows the top 30 companies in Germany by trading volume and market capitalization. The index sample used for the DAX is selected according to the following criteria:

- Listed for at least three years

- Free-float capital has reached at least 15% turnover

BENCHMARKING PORTFOLIOS

"Evaluating the performance of a portfolio manager is difficult because the large amount of randomness in portfolio returns makes it difficult to distinguish luck from skill. A typical stock portfolio may have a standard deviation of 25 to 30 percent per year. Even very significant performance (say 5% per year) can be distinguished from luck only after a long period.

"A benchmark portfolio is intended to represent the return to a passively managed portfolio. In fact, the benchmark portfolio is a paper portfolio and may not represent the performance of a feasible passive strategy. For example, the trades in the benchmark portfolio may assume execution at some closing price, while actual trades would not execute so well due to the bid-

ask spread. (Interestingly, this is a special problem for equally-weighted indexes that are rebalanced daily, since an equally weighted strategy implicitly buys more of a stock whose closing price is artificially low.) Also, the benchmark portfolio usually assumes no brokerage fees.

"There are also reasons why a benchmark portfolio might understate realistic performance. For example, quoted benchmarks often do not include dividend income in computing returns. Also, security lending fees (to accommodate investors desiring to take short positions) are not included in benchmarks."

Source: *Philip H. Dybvig. Washington University in Saint Louis, lecture 1997, 2000*

- Turnover

- Market capitalization

- Representative of the German economy

CAC – THE FRENCH INDEX

CAC stands for Compagnie des Agents de Change. It is published by the Societe des Bourses Francaises — Bourse de Paris (Association of French Stock Exchanges — Paris Stock Exchange, and includes 40 French companies listed on the Paris Stock Exchange that are also traded on the options market. It is a capitalization-weighted value ratio index with a base date of 31 December 1987 and a base value of 1,000. This is the main index for French stocks, and follows 40 companies chosen from the top 100 by market capitalization and the most active stocks listed.

NIKKEI

There are two main indexes for the Tokyo Stock Exchange, the Nikkei 225 and the Nikkei 500, which follow the largest 225 and 500 companies respectively. Like the Dow, these indexes are not weighted, so may not be representative of the Tokyo market as a whole.

USING INDEXES AS BENCHMARKS

Although many investors compare the performance of their portfolios with a major index, such as the S&P 500, for the comparison to be completely valid, strictly speaking the risk of the portfolio should be the same as the risk of the index. In other words, if the collection of stocks in your portfolio does not have the same risk characteristics as the stocks in the S&P 500, comparing their performance could lead you to draw inaccurate conclusions.

To see why, imagine you have a portfolio of twenty fast-growing stocks — at least, they had been fast-growing for a period before you bought them — and although some of them are components of the S&P 500, others are too small to be included in the index. If your portfolio outperforms the S&P 500 this year, does this mean that your investment strategy is working? Not necessarily — it could simply be that your portfolio is more volatile than the index, and so is likely to produce returns that are markedly above or below the performance of the index.

INDEX TRACKING

With so many investment funds on the market, it is perhaps not surprising that many of them do not outperform the major indices. As we have seen, such comparisons may not be entirely fair, since most funds use investment strategies that involve a different risk level to that of the indices. Figure 10.5 illustrates the problem.

TRACKING ERROR

In recent years there has been growing interest in funds that simply try to match a major stock market index. Index tracking makes a lot of sense from the point of view of the efficient market theory, but in practice many index funds could under-perform the index a little in the long term because of tracking error. Tracking error is the divergence of the price behavior of a portfolio and the price behavior of the benchmark index. Index-tracking funds generally buy the stocks of all the firms listed in a given index in the same proportions that they are weighted in that index. If the index includes thousands of companies, then the fund may only buy a representative sample of them. If the prices of that representative sample diverge significantly from the index, then there may be problems.

MEASURING RISK-ADJUSTED PERFORMANCE

Any investment in equities involves risk, and in investment this risk is often defined as the risk that your actual returns are different from the expected return. So, what returns should you expect from a given stock or portfolio of stocks? To understand how one might estimate the expected return, first consider what you can expect from a "risk-free" investment.

Of course, there are no true "risk-free" investments, but investment professionals generally regarded government bonds issued by the US and UK as being risk-free. In the case of the US, this is largely because of its dominant position as the world's pivotal economy, and in the case of the UK, it is because of its long track record — the government has never reneged on its bonds since it began to issue them in the 18th century, despite many temptations to do so. The same cannot be said for many other countries' government bonds, so they are generally regarded as a little more risky than US and UK government bonds.

Is it unrealistic to say that US Treasury bonds and bills are not entirely risk-free? No. There are many events that could cause a suspension of interest payments or a repudiation of the debt — for example, a massive natural disaster, such as the impact of an asteroid, or violent political change, such as a revolution. These may be very, very unlikely to occur, but since there is a minute chance that they could happen, we cannot say that US government debt issue is 100% risk-free.

Figure 10.4 — An investor at a Taipei brokerage house turns from the computer monitors and signals a share price to other investors in Taipei, 21 June 2004. Despite the fact that Morgan Stanley Capital International (MSCI) raised Taiwan's weighting over the weekend, investors still took profit from earlier gains and pushed the weighted price index down by 12.75 points or 0.23 percent to close at 5,556.54.

Source: AFP Photo

In practice, however, most people accept the assumption that US government bonds and bills are risk-free, and so they are widely used as a benchmark for risk. Suppose you can invest in US bonds for one year and receive a guaranteed return of 5%. Now, let's consider what happens in an equity investment. You calculate an expected return from a given investment and buy the stock. When the time comes to sell, it is quite probable that your actual returns will not be exactly the same as your expected return; if they are slightly lower, or a lot higher, most investors will be satisfied with the results, but if they are considerably lower than the expected return, most investors will feel that they have made an error.

The past variance of returns for any stock can be measured and used to calculate the expected return in the future. This is a useful measure, but it has its limitations; even large, stable companies experience sudden changes to their businesses, and in today's fast-changing world, even multinationals, some of which have greater revenues than the GDPs of small countries, can experience large fluctuations in their profits and stock prices.

VARIANCE/STANDARD DEVIATION

To measure the variance of past stock returns, we calculate the standard deviation.

Figure 10.5 — Percentage of funds outperformed by indices, May 2005

Percentage of Funds Outperformed by Indices	One Year	Five Years
All US Domestic Funds	63.2	58.3
Large Cap	**60.2**	**60.2**
Mid Cap	**63.0**	**92.8**
Small Cap	**61.4**	**64.8**
Large Cap Growth	79.7	64.4
Large Cap Blend	58.8	58.4
Large Cap Value	36.7	52.1
Mid Cap Growth	68.4	97.2
Mid Cap Blend	62.4	86.1
Mid Cap Value	49.1	83.3
Small Cap Growth	90.3	72.2
Small Cap Blend	56.1	60.1
Small Cap Value	18.6	41.6

Source: Standard & Poor's, May 2005

THE CAPITAL ASSET PRICING MODEL

"The CAPM was and is a theory of equilibrium. Why should anyone expect to earn more by investing in one security as opposed to another? You need to be compensated for doing badly when times are bad. The security that is going to do badly just when you need money when times are bad is a security you have to hate, and there had better be some redeeming virtue or else who will hold it? That redeeming virtue has to be that in normal times you expect to do better. The key insight of the Capital Asset Pricing Model is that higher expected returns go with the greater risk of doing badly in bad times. Beta is a measure of that. Securities or asset classes with high betas tend to do worse in bad times than those with low betas. I'd be the last to argue that only one factor drives market correlation. There are not as many factors as some people think, but there's certainly more than one. To measure the state of the debate, look at textbooks. Textbooks still have the Capital Asset Pricing Model because that's a very fundamental economic argument.

If you just take somebody's current investments and project return without any notion of risk, you give them a wildly distorted view of what their future might hold. It may be the best point estimate if you've done it carefully, but they have no notion of how good or how bad it can get."

Source: Professor William F. Sharpe, inventor of the Sharpe ratio Dow Jones Asset Manager May/June 1998, pp. 20-28

The variance and the related standard deviations are measures of how widely spread data is distributed around their mean (average) value. Variance is a way to measure the variability or volatility from the average. It is a measure of risk, since if a stock has a price pattern and history that has high variance, it is thus less predictable and considered more risky. It is computed by taking the average squared deviation of each data point from its mean.

The standard deviation is also a measure of the dispersion of a set of data, since the more spread apart the data are the higher the deviation. The standard deviation can be calculated as the square root of the variance. A stock with a high standard deviation would be considered a volatile stock and thus more risky. With the standard deviation statistics and if we know the mean and the standard deviation of a normal distribution, we can then compute the percentile rank associated with any specific score. In a normal distribution, for example, about 68% of the scores are within one standard deviation of the mean, while 95% of the scores are within two standard deviations of the mean.

SUMMARY

A complex set of variables impact the future price of a stock making it difficult to evaluate the precise impact of each variable. At best, it can be an educated guess. It is better to choose only those variables that determine the company's true asset value and its earnings. Approaches to valuation include measures of relative value, discounted cash flow models and asset value calculations. Relative measures such as P/E and P/B ratios are simple to understand but can be manipulated. They are also inadequate. For example, the P/E ratio alone cannot tell you if a company is cheap or expensive. Even apparently objective measures such as EVA and MVA are not foolproof valuation tools.

While DCF offers a sounder basis for valuation in many situations than other methods, only hindsight can reveal whether the assumptions used were correct. Stock indexes are useful for tracking market trends since they provide a historical view of a market. They too have limitations.

QUICK QUIZ

1. The P/E of a firm looks very appealing. But its P/BV is about one. What conclusions would you come to?

2. DCF analysis of a company is very positive. Could there still be risk of investing?

3. A company has figured in a prominent stock index for the last 30 years. Would you consider it to be safe for investment?

4. Someone tells you that Company X has a P/E of 20 and Company Y has a P/E of 21. What would you need to know before deciding whether the two figures are directly comparable?

5. In *The Wall Street Journal*, you notice that Company Z has no P/E listed. Why might this be? Why might you still invest in it?

6. Company Y's P/BV ratio has risen substantially. Why might this have happened, and what are the implications for its shareholders?

7. Company A is a large, stable firm paying regular dividends. Company B is a fast growing high tech business a tenth of the size of Company A, and pays no dividends. Company C is twice the size of Company B; it has a patchy dividend record and has made losses twice during the last fifteen years. What ratios would you choose to compare their value from an investor's point of view, and why?

8. Why should stockholders care about performance-based incentives for senior executives? From the stockholders' point of view, what should such schemes achieve and avoid, and how?

9. An international manufacturing firm has owned vast areas of land in a South American country for many decades; now that the country has a stable economy and business is booming, you suspect that the value of the firm's land has gone up. How would you value the firm?

11

EQUITY INVESTMENT MANAGEMENT

Conflicting investment approaches abound in the markets, and investors can choose from a very wide range. Institutions, for example, may offer a smorgasbord of funds using different strategies tailored to their customers' appetite for risk, but there is a marketing angle. Just as most stocks are linked to a persuasive story of why they are a "buy," so is every investment strategy. Therefore, mere plausibility should not be sufficient to convince us. The challenge of prudent investment strategy is to select an appropriate strategy and stick to it for an appropriate length of time. This may involve tactical changes, but any strategy must be given enough time for it to prove itself. Switching from one investment fad to the next is likely to result in poor returns.

No one model adequately explains how the markets work, although considerable theoretical progress has been made since the 1960s. Today, professional investors — and many ordinary people — are fully conversant with investment theories and appreciate that although some principles have been established, there are still many points that are controversial, or for which there is no convincing explanation. In the final analysis, we are dealing with human behavior, which is neither quantifiable or predictable.

INFORMATION FLOW

Investors are bombarded with information from many sources, some of it good and some of it bad. It is important to note that professionals in the industry refer to the "buy-side" and "sell-side" relationship, where the investors are the "buy-side" and the brokers the "sell-side." Unfortunately "sell-side", or broker, advice can be vulnerable to bias. Brokers are interested in turnover to generate commissions, so their recommendations to sell or buy come fast and furious. They are also involved in sponsoring or underwriting IPOs and thus may generate research to favor a particular company they are promoting. They also deal on their own behalf or have their own "book" and may want to offload some stock. There have been many cases of sell-side analysts who were alleged to have "pushed" certain stocks not because they sincerely felt they were good investments, but because their bonus depended on how much their underwriting and investment banking department earned on investment banking fees from those firms.

CONFLICTS OF INTEREST

US Congress investigated conflicts of interest among analysts who maintained a buy recommendation for Enron until only a few weeks before its filing for bankruptcy in 2001.

The purveyors of analyst services do not usually share the risk of loss with their customers. Buy-side information is often thought to be more objective, since the institution's own money, or the money of its clients, is on the line. Recent studies have found that buy-side professionals consider sell-side analysts' buy recommendations to have little or no value, and rate their buy recommendations as being the least valuable of the various research services offered by sell-side analysts.

NEWS CLIP
SEC RAPS ANALYSTS

The Securities and Exchange Commission issued an Order in May 2005 instituting public administrative proceedings against the former Heads of Equity Research based upon their failure to reasonably supervise a former equity research analyst with a view to preventing him from aiding and abetting violations of antifraud provisions by publishing fraudulent research. Without admitting or denying the Order's findings, the executives each consented to a fifteen month bar from associating in a supervisory capacity with a broker, dealer, or investment adviser and to pay civil penalties of $120,000 and disgorgement of $1.00.

The Order found that during 2000 and 2001, they were supervisors of the analyst. During thatperiod, they failed to respond adequately to red flags that the analyst had unrealistically bullish ratings and price targets on companies he covered, in particular seven companies. In addition, the executives were aware of potential conflicts of interest posed by the analyst's involvement in the firm's telecommunications (telecom) investment banking activities and aware of the analyst's importance to the firm's telecom investment banking franchise, but failed to respond adequately to specific evidence of investment banking pressure on the analyst not to downgrade the firm's investment banking clients.

Source: *SEC Administrative Proceeding Release No. 34-51713*, May 19, 2005

STRATEGIES

Some of the most successful investors don't restrict themselves to equities alone; they are active in many other investment areas simultaneously. For example, one of the first hedge funds started during the 1970s took complex positions in the equity, bond and derivatives markets across the world, and made heavy use of margin. Between 1970 and 1980 the fund appreciated by 4,200% without ever having a down year. At the time, few Wall Street professionals were well informed about the economic and political changes occurring outside the US, so this fund had little competition and was able to use its superior knowledge to make a killing, using a wide variety of techniques. Highly specialized strategies of this kind exploit "market inefficiencies," and as more investors wake up to their potential, the opportunities for profit tend to diminish. For this reason, some successful investors are often reluctant to reveal their methods until the opportunities have passed. However, the much-publicized methods used by famous value investors are being copied by other investors. Copying a value-oriented investment style looks deceptively simple, but in application it is very difficult because it involves strong discipline and a willingness to devote long hours to studying company accounts and meeting with business people, customers, suppliers and others who impact the success or failure of businesses.

TOP DOWN VS BOTTOM UP

"Top down" investing takes an overview of a country's economy, markets and sectors, and starts by looking at the big picture before examining selected stocks in detail. For instance, if you believe that the GDP of a country will grow strongly over the next few years, you might look at the sectors that are most sensitive to such growth, such as house construction and auto manufacturing, and then use company-specific measures to select the most promising stocks within those sectors, or simply buy a "basket" of the leading companies in the sector.

"Bottom up" investing takes the opposite approach. Individual firms are minutely analyzed in terms of value and growth potential, and the most promising candidates are selected before macroeconomic factors are taken into account.

INVESTING TIMEFRAME

As with companies, investment professionals are scrutinized over very short periods of time. This pressure can have a negative effect. Suppose, for example, you are a fund manager with a coherent long-term strategy of investing in certain volatile types of stock. You know that this makes it likely that at times your performance will be worse than that of other investment strategies, and you state this clearly in the prospectus.

We know that if the expected return is likely to be volatile over the short to medium term, we should not be disturbed if the actual return is similarly volatile. Our fund manager explains all this in every annual report, proposes specific indexes and other measures as appropriate benchmarks, and warns that there will be times when the major markets are likely to perform better than the fund. Despite all the warnings and explanations, the likelihood is that when the fund happens to be performing very well against, say, the S&P 500, short-term money will pour into the fund, even though the fund manager does not regard the S&P 500 as a suitable measure for comparison — the risk/reward characteristics are entirely different. During periods when the fund performs worse than the major market indices, investment money is likely to leave the fund, which may shrink to a fraction of its former size. Rational investors who understand the thinking behind a given investment strategy ought not to behave this way. The performance of any strategy should be judged on its own terms, in the appropriate timeframe, yet often market sentiment does not appear to be rational.

Even investment professionals seem to behave irrationally sometimes. CAPM and other classic investment theories have tended to assume that informed investors behave rationally, yet experience shows us that very often they appear not to do so; the assumption of rationality appears to be flawed.

INVESTMENT CONSTRAINTS

Professional investors also face constraints on many of their activities, especially when they are managing investment money belonging to others. If they are managing money on behalf of a university or a charitable trust, there may be strict limitations on the types of assets they may invest in. For example, some institutional investors forbid their money managers to invest in the so-called "sin stocks" — tobacco, gambling and alcohol — but studies have shown that these stocks tend to outperform other stock categories.

Although hedge funds use leverage, most countries forbid mutual funds from using leverage to any great extent. Although such restrictions are generally intended to encourage conservative investment strategies and prevent drastic loss, in some cases the investment environment has changed so much that such measures may actually be damaging. For example, suppose a trust was set up generations ago in a low inflation era, and the trustees were instructed to keep all investment funds in cash or near-cash instruments at all times. Such a strategy could easily have reduced the value of the original capital substantially in real terms, especially after taxation, administration costs, and payments to the beneficiaries.

We looked at the many illusions, both deliberate and accidental, in analyzing investment returns. To understand why this is so, we need to understand how randomness affects stock price movements.

THE "RANDOM WALK" THEORY

Until the late 1950s, many people thought that if only you could properly understand the patterns in stock price movements, you could predict how they would move in the future. At that time, a young American undergraduate, Eugene Fama, was helping a professor to produce a stock

"Hi. I'm Wendell, Jr. I'm six and I'm fully invested."

market newsletter. Fama's task was to analyze historical price data to devise "buy" and "sell" signals based on recurring patterns in the charts. Fama realized that although you could find repeating patterns in historical data, it was a very poor predictor of future price movements; in other words, past price movements did not seem to be a good guide to future price movements. Later he published an academic paper, "Random Walks in Stock Market Prices," which argued that stock price variations were randomly distributed and therefore unpredictable. Fama was not suggesting that the price of a stock usually fluctuates wildly. In fact, stock prices only rarely change by a large percentage of their value in the short term. Most of the time, the changes are miniscule — often a fraction of 1%.

Random walks are evident in nature; for example, in the flight of a butterfly. To understand how it works, imagine you're standing in a field, and you flip a coin for each step you take. "Heads" you turn right, and "tails" you turn left. After you have taken 25 steps in this way, on average you will be only five steps away from where you started — but it is easy to see why someone might want to predict the points when you were furthest away from your starting point (if you were a tradable asset like a stock!). Fama suggested that the reason for these price changes were that investors' views constantly changed in response to the flow of new information about companies and markets.

EFFICIENT MARKET HYPOTHESIS

In 1970, Fama coined the phrase "the efficient market" to describe his hypothesis that in the major stock markets so many experts are analyzing stocks that their prices reflect all the currently available information. This implies that in such markets, stocks are generally fairly priced, given what is known. In an efficient market, the rational task for investors is not how to beat the market, but how much risk to take in order to achieve a greater or lesser expected return on their investments.

At first, this idea was largely ignored or derided in the financial world, but today it has gained wide acceptance. Much attention has been focused on the degree to which a given market or sector can be said to be efficient.

For example, with the rapid deregulation of foreign markets, there is now much discussion abut whether smaller markets around the world are efficient; if one can identify a market inefficiency, some traders argue, then it is possible to beat that market through superior knowledge. An obscure stock market in a little known country may not have a good system of publishing information in a timely fashion and may be followed by only a few specialists, so, the argument goes, pricing may not be efficient.

According to Fama, an efficient market is one where:

• There are a large number of experts studying the stocks

• Their goal is to maximize profits

• All relevant information is freely available to all market participants

• News reaches all participants simultaneously

While this may be a good description of a major market such as the NYSE, it may not apply to a newer market such as Shenzen in China. Also, a market such as the NYSE may be efficient for the average investor, but offer inefficiencies — and thus opportunities for excess returns — to the professional who has a superior capacity to collate and analyze information, better skills, better access to capital and so on.

By 1971, Fama was qualifying his view of market efficiency, suggesting that it could be separated into three types:

• The "weak" form – Information contained in past prices is fully reflected in the current price of a share. Looking for patterns in past prices to help predict future price movements will not be effective.

• The "semi-strong" form – The current price reflects all information contained in past prices and all relevant publicly available information. Analysis of an industry or a company will not enable an investor,

PICK LONG-LASTING BUSINESSES?

"The first inefficiency [that we look to exploit] is that investors in general tend persistently to undervalue durability in a business. Buffett says: 'Buy shares in a great business.' There's no question that one of the prime characteristics of a great business, in his view, is longevity, or the likelihood that a business is going to be around after you've made the investment, not just for two to three years, but for 10 or 20 years. By and large investors tend to undervalue this crucial and rare attribute. The easiest way to see this point is probably by looking at the opposite, which is the ephemerality of most quoted businesses.

"For example, if you look at the FTSE 100 index and its constituents today, and compare them to the constituents on the first day that the index was calculated in 1984, you realize with a shock that around 75% of the original constituents are no longer there! In 20 years, in other words, a very significant proportion of the largest 100 companies in the UK, have ceased to exist in the same form. A scarily high proportion of that 75% have ceased to exist because they've failed as businesses. It's one of the things that the investment industry, for understandable reasons, doesn't care to advertise too widely. The reality is that most equities and most quoted companies ultimately fail as investments."

Source: *Intelligent Investor Supplement*
October 2003

say, to find a stock that is due to rise because of the application of new technology, since the price will already reflect all that is publicly known about this.

- The "strong" form – The current price reflects all information contained in past prices and all relevant publicly available information and all privately known information (such as "insider information"). This means, for instance, that a scientist who has a special understanding of a technology will not be able to make excess returns consistently because others with a similar understanding will already have bid prices up to a fair level.

The key point to remember is that the efficient market hypothesis does not say that no-one ever earns excess returns; it says that excess returns are randomly distributed, and that, in situations where the strong form applies, no investor will be able to achieve excess returns consistently, except for a very few investors who do so by chance.

As the efficient market hypothesis has become more widely known, it has stimulated interest in index tracking, particularly among private investors in the US. Faced with a vast range of domestic mutual funds of varying quality, many Americans have opted to follow the index rather than the expertise of a money manager on the grounds that if the major US markets are efficient:

- The high cost of analysis and research is wasted

- Investment professionals do not add value to portfolios

- Infrequent trading will produce better results than frequent trading

While these propositions would hold true in a truly efficient market, there is no agreement over the degree of efficiency in any market. Many believe, however, that the major markets are more efficient than the less developed markets.

VALUE INVESTING

Value investing refers to strategies that seek companies with a low stock price compared with the value of their assets. Benjamin Graham, the "father of stock analysis," is widely regarded as the classic value investor, using very strict rules to identify "bargain" stocks. These rules, or "screens" were defined in terms of measurable ratios. In his book *Security Analysis*, Graham set out the ten key measures:

1. The P/E yield (that is, the reciprocal of the P/E) must be at least double the yield of the highest grade bonds (AAA bonds).

2. The P/E must be lower than 40% of the average P/E for all stocks in the market during the previous 5 years.

3. The dividend yield must be at least two-thirds the yield of the highest grade bond.

4. The stock price must be less than two-thirds of the firm's book value, and the book value must not contain values for goodwill and other "intangible" assets.

5. The stock price must be less than two-thirds of liquid current assets (cash and near cash) less current liabilities.

6. The debt/equity ratio must be below one.

7. The firm's current assets must be more than double its current liabilities.

8. The firm's debt must be less than double its net current assets.

9. The firm's growth in earnings per share (EPS) must have grown by more than 7% in the last 10 years.

10. The firm's EPS must not have declined in more than two years during the preceding ten years.

Few firms fit Graham's criteria! A number of studies, however, have found that the strategy would have produced higher returns than the major indexes during various periods. Today, a number of professional investors use this "value" or "bargain hunting" approach, but in general they use different criteria or have adapted the rules differently. Typically these will include some measure of low price-to-earnings and price-to-book or net asset value, but not necessarily as stringent as Graham's; studies of major markets across the world have produced evidence that portfolios of low price-to-book value stocks have produced excess returns in terms of their betas.

Probably one of the most popular screens for value investors is to look for stocks with low P/Es. Again, there is ample evidence that low P/E stocks have outperformed high P/E stocks as a class over the long term. As with most value-based criteria, however, some low P/E stocks are poor performers. P/E is a measure of market expectations about future growth, and a low P/E could indicate that the market does not expect the company to grow strongly in the future or is vulnerable to a number of other risks.

For many years there has been considerable interest in high dividend yields as a screen. Although it is a controversial view, some academics argue that dividend yields imply a forecast of future returns, at least in the short to medium term, and so high dividend yields should lead to higher returns.

There are many problems with this idea. First, a look at the long-term history of dividend yields in the US and the UK markets shows that they are currently very low, but also that there has been considerable fluctuation in average dividend yields that could be interpreted as random movements within a range of approximately 2–8%. Dividend yields may be quite a good predictor of future dividend yields in the short term.

Dividend yields vary considerably from country to country because of differences in taxation, growth opportunities and corporate attitudes to dividends. Broadly, the long-term trend in many countries indicates some relationship between interest rates and dividend yields. This, of course, is to be expected. Dividend yields also vary with the industry with, for example, utilities tending to pay higher dividends.

If an investor buys stocks at a time of high dividend yields, would they achieve above average returns? To define what we mean by "high," we have to look at dividend yields prior to the date of investment rather than

CASE STUDY: ARE FUND MANAGERS SKILLED STOCK-PICKERS?

"We design tests of stock-picking skill based on the subsequent earnings announcement returns of the stocks that fund managers hold and trade... Consistent with skilled trading, we find that, on average, stocks that funds buy earn significantly higher returns at subsequent earnings announcements than stocks that they sell. Funds also display persistence in our event return-based metrics, and those that do well tend to have a growth objective, large size, high turnover, and use incentive fees to motivate managers...

"We naturally begin the analysis by tabulating the earnings announcement returns of fund holdings, but the cleanest and most important results involve fund trades. In particular, for each fund, we track the subsequent earnings announcement returns of the stocks on which it increases portfolio weight over the prior period and the stocks on which it decreases the portfolio weight. Our main finding is that the average mutual fund shows stock-picking skill in the sense that the subsequent earnings announcement returns on its weight-increasing stocks is significantly higher than that of its weight-decreasing stocks. The difference is about 12 basis points over the three-day window around the quarterly announcement, or, multiplying by four, about 47 'annualized' basis points. The contrast between buys that initiate a fund's position in a stock and sells that close out a position is even larger."

Source: *Malcolm Baker, Lubomir Litov, Jessica A. Wachter, Jeffrey Wurgler*
'Evidence from their trades prior to earnings announcements'
Harvard Business School / NYU Stern School of Business/Wharton
September 14, 2004

at all the dividend yields over the long run — this is to avoid adding bias to our definition of "high" by looking ahead to dividend yields after that date, which we cannot do in the real world. Figure 11.1 shows dividend yields in the US and UK between 1900 and 2003. Studies of the world's major markets suggest that although such a strategy is often, but not always, effective in the US and UK markets, it may not necessarily work in other countries. Furthermore, what do you do with your investment money when dividend yields are low — do you get out of equities altogether? If so, will your overall long-term returns be lower than if you had stayed in the market the whole time? This problem affects most "market timing" strategies.

INVESTING FOR GROWTH

Some businesses make higher profits each year, expanding their markets and their market capitalization as they do so. Others make profits without expanding their business, and yet others go on a downward slide. Growth investors look for "great" companies that they can hold for many years and achieve substantial excess returns. Although some firms, such as Coca-Cola and Microsoft, have enjoyed long periods of rapid growth, there is always some doubt over whether such growth can be sustained in the future. It is not very easy to spot a true "growth" stock, except in hindsight. Furthermore, a company may have good prospects for growth, but its stock price may be so high that it discounts all potential future growth, so it may turn out to be a poor investment.

In the 1960s there was a bull market in US stocks, and the consensus on Wall Street was that a group of large-cap stocks, known as the "nifty fifty" were the fast growers. The nifty fifty included companies such as IBM, Xerox, Avon and Eastman Kodak, which few growth investors would select today. At the time, confidence was so high that it was said that the nifty fifty were "one decision" stocks. All an investor had to do was buy and hold, and the returns would be magnificent.

Figure 11.1 — Dividend yield in the US and UK, 1900-2003

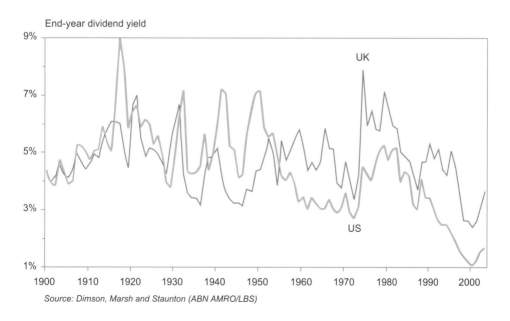

Source: Dimson, Marsh and Staunton (ABN AMRO/LBS)

The oil crisis and high inflation of the early 1970s changed the outlook for the nifty fifty, along with increased competition from companies in Europe and Japan that had recovered from the trauma of the Second World War. While many nifty fifty stocks performed badly, a few continued to expand, such as Coca-Cola, McDonald's and Hewlett Packard, and were joined in the 1980s by massive new hi-tech companies such as Intel and Microsoft, which seemed to some growth investors to have become the new "one decision" stocks.

There are certainly examples of magnificently long runs of growth, such as:

- 100 shares of 3M cost $4,320 in 1946; by 1961 they were worth $210,000, not including dividend payments.

- 100 shares of Du Pont cost $13,000 in 1922; by 1961 they were worth $1,500,000 and had earned $250,000 in dividends.

The problem is that we can only see these results in hindsight; it is not at all clear how an investor in 1922, for instance, would have chosen Du Pont for the long run over other attractive stocks.

If it is hard to select large-cap stocks for outstanding growth in the long term, perhaps the task is easier for small-aps. Figure 11.3 shows the comulative performance of UK small-cap stocks versus the market from 1955 to 2004. Peter Lynch, who ran Fidelity's Magellan Fund during the 1980s, achieved large excess returns by specializing in selecting small-cap stocks that had the potential for high growth, using rigorous techniques of fundamental analysis. Other growth investors have not been as successful. Overall, value investing appears to have more potential than growth investing.

MARKET TIMING

In its simplest form, market timing in equities means switching from stocks to cash and back to avoid periods of low returns from equities and to exploit periods of high returns. This approach involves higher-than-normal transaction costs, especially when done frequently, so any improvement in returns must be in excess of the additional transaction costs to be worthwhile. The improved performance must also absorb the likely increased tax liability from capital gains made when selling stocks at a profit (which does not apply in some countries — many Asian countries, for instance, have low or zero capital gains taxes).

In a completely efficient market, one would expect a strategy of market timing not to work consistently. However, many investors use market timing, either occasionally or as their main strategy, basing their decisions on a number of factors including:

- **External social factors** – When there is a "feel good" atmosphere, consumer spending on non-essentials and luxuries goes up. People eat out more, take more expensive holidays, buy bigger cars and so on. Often this seems to coincide with a period of rising stock prices. Historically, it has been observed that ladies' fashions in the US and Europe have tended to fluctuate according to the economic "feel good" factor. One amusing but problematic example is the length of women's skirts. Stock market lore has it that the length of women's skirts are a good indication of stock market behavior (the higher the skirt, the greater the feel-good atmosphere) and some investors have used this "hemline indicator" as a guide to the future direction of the stock market. If skirts are getting shorter, the thinking goes, then investors are confident and will bid stock prices up.

  Such indicators, of course, cannot be use to make precise forecasts, since such manifestations of consumer confidence may follow behind stock market events, rather than ahead of them.

- **Publicity** – Near the peak of a bull market, many naïve investors are drawn in to buying stocks. Subscriptions to stock market newsletters that recommend "hot" shares tend to skyrocket, stock prices are reported widely in the media and the financial markets are discussed at dinner parties, in bars and at street corners. Conversely, when stock prices are depressed and due for a change upwards, only the most dedicated investors are still in the market and interest in financial matters tends to be at a low ebb. Could this phenomenon be used

Figure 11.3 — Cumulative performance of UK small-caps versus the market, 1955-2004

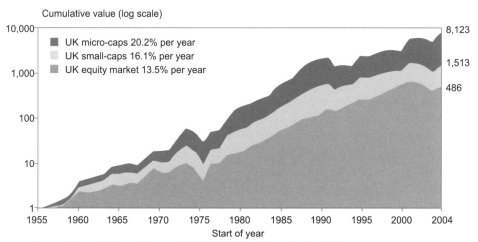

Source: Dimson, Marsh and Staunton (ABN AMRO/LBS) and Triumph of the Optimists, Princeton University Press, 2002.

to predict the bursting of a stock bubble, or a market recovery? Again, it does not appear to offer much precision: it is notoriously difficult to gauge the exact timing of a market collapse or recovery. In a boom, prices may continue to rise to unheard-of levels for months or even years after the pessimists have left the market.

- **Technical analysis** – Technical analysis is devoted to market timing, which it claims to predict, mainly on the examination of patterns. Technical analysts examine price movements and patterns to discern the direction of market and company stock trends. The volume, or number of shares of a company that are bought and sold during a given period, receives a lot of attention from technical analysts. Large, well-known companies tend to have a higher daily trading volume than smaller, more obscure stocks. Although there is evidence that low volume stocks outperform high volume stocks, this may be explained by the difference in risk — low volume stocks are generally small-cap companies, which are riskier and so should generate a better return overall. There also may be a link between high volume and the price momentum from one day to the next; a high volume stock that rises or falls on one day is more likely to continue in the same direction on the following day than a low volume stock.

ECONOMIC INDICATORS

Investors who base their decisions upon their understanding of business fundamentals may also try to time the market. Economic indicators such as interest rates and economic growth are studied carefully.

Interest Rates: If the returns on risk-free government bonds and bills are rising, they become more attractive relative to stocks, since stocks are not risk-free. The idea is that if the risk-free rate goes up, many investors will sell some of their equities and buy bonds, which should depress stock prices. In practice, however, movements in the risk-free rate do not appear to be closely correlated to stock prices.

GDP growth rates: Investors who follow the world's markets commonly compare economic indicators for different countries. Growth rates, measured by the rate of growth in gross domestic product, are among the key indicators used. An investor in, say, the UK, may compare these measures for the UK, US, Japan, Germany and Australia, and may feel that all these countries have highly developed stock markets and are broadly in the same category of risk; the aim here is to forecast which country's market is likely to produce better returns in the short to medium term — say one to three years — and to weight the portfolio more heavily with that country's stocks. A similar process is used to compare less developed or emerging markets. If the Far East is growing faster than Latin America, then the portfolio can be adjusted accordingly. This is an example of a "top-down" approach. Today, we are more likely to see such staggering growth in productivity in the emerging economies, with commensurate growth in their companies listed on local stock markets. During 2004, while the five key developed markets (US, Japan, UK, France and Germany) produced growth rates of 1.7–4.3%, Asian countries in particular, along with Russia, Poland, Argentina, Turkey and Chile, were achieving rates of 5–8.9%, with China in the lead.

Over a longer time span (1996–2004), we can see that as a whole the emerging markets have indeed grown consistently at a faster rate than the developed countries throughout the period, although, interestingly, the rates of growth have fluctuated broadly in tandem with that of the developed countries.

Although the total market capitalization of the emerging markets is still a relatively small proportion of the global total, it is possible that if the emerging markets can continue to achieve superior growth rates in the future, investors in those markets will enjoy superior returns. It may be that China and India, for example, will be the investment success stories during the 21st century that the US was during the 20th.

There are various factors that support the view that the long-term investment prospects for emerging markets are good. Many of the arguments are based on demography. The current imbalance in terms of wealth and population between the developed nations and the rest of the world is remarkable: the lower income countries of the world represent 85% of the total population and control 75% of the world's land.

The major emerging markets — that is, those developing countries that have relatively well-developed stock markets and are "investible" from the point of view of foreign investors — have large work forces that are becoming increasingly highly skilled, yet demand much lower wages than workers in the developed countries. An abundant supply of cheap labor is not only attractive to the multinationals, many of which have relocated manufacturing plants to these countries, but also help to make local firms highly competitive internationally.

There are significant differences in labor costs across the world and this helps to explain why multinationals whose origins are in the developed world have chosen to relocate much of their production to cheaper countries. Cheap labor, however, is not the only important factor — there

"We're expecting stocks to rally but
we don't know which ones and when."

must also be sufficient labor available to support industrial growth, and also to form new consumer markets. Many large firms are finding that markets for goods in the developed world are becoming saturated, and thus are focusing their efforts on developing new markets for their goods in the newly industrialized countries. The number of people aged between 20 and 50 in China and India dwarfs those living in other countries, and represent not only the world's largest supply of labor but also massive potential new consumer markets.

Although the major emerging markets offer great promise for growth in the 21st century, it is not a foregone conclusion that they will all live up to their promise, or that foreign investors will enjoy good returns there.

ASSET ALLOCATION

In recent years, major banks have become prominent in the "asset allocation" advisory business, using a host of fundamental indicators to produce well-reasoned — but not necessarily successful — predictive advice on how to adjust the weighting of an investment portfolio to take advantage of short- to medium-term trends in different markets, sectors and asset types. Briefly, the rationale for doing this is as follows:

- The mix of asset types in a portfolio is based on the investor's financial needs and appetite for risk; for example, it may be appropriate for an investor who is saving money to send her children to university in fifteen years' time to invest in moderately risky stocks in the hope of growth over that period, but it would not be appropriate for her to, say, use the money in currency speculation, which is considerably more risky. The more risk-averse the investor, the more the portfolio should be weighted towards assets with low volatility, such as bonds, and the more risk-seeking the investor, the more the portfolio should be weighted towards assets with high risk-return characteristics. An investor with a high appetite for risk is often an individual who is wealthy and can afford to "ride out" downswings in the market — such a person might choose to be 100% invested in volatile stocks.

- The basic asset types — equities, bonds and cash — have different risk/reward characteristics. At times, bonds and equities may move together for a period (positive correlation), while at others they may move in opposite directions (negative correlation). By measuring the correlation of asset types in a given market over a number of years, asset allocators try to identify different combination assets that have the same level of risk. For example, between 1998 and 2003, a portfolio of 100% global bonds had the same risk as a portfolio comprising of 80% global bonds and 20% global equities (Source: S&P Micropal). There was an important difference, however; the 80% bonds/20% stocks portfolio produced a better return (about 0.4% better), so this was the "optimal mix" of assets.

- As time passes, the mix of assets in a portfolio will tend to diverge from the original recipe, as some investments perform better than others. For example, if your asset allocation was originally 50% bonds and 50% equities, and if equities perform well for a few years, they will exceed 50% of the value of the portfolio. To maintain the original risk exposure, the portfolio should then be "rebalanced" by selling some equities and buying bonds to get back to the 50/50 ratio.

- Another reason for rebalancing is if market conditions change. Suppose, for instance, that 5% of your portfolio is in high-risk Chinese equities and the outlook for these stocks worsens. You sell your Chinese stocks and invest in other fast growing but volatile equities with better prospects in the medium term. This is a form of market timing, and is the chief argument that banks use to justify their advisory services for asset allocation.

So does this kind of market timing work? In an efficient market, one would expect it not to have a very large effect. A report by *The Wall Street Journal* on the performance of US market strategies of this type suggested that they would not have significantly outperformed a strategy of remaining 100% invested in equities at all times, or a portfolio of equities, bonds and bills that was not rebalanced during the period. In less efficient markets, however, it may be possible to achieve better results using this approach, since special knowledge may have more of an effect on performance.

TRADING ON INFORMATION

Although the efficient market hypothesis suggests that all known information that could affect stock prices is contained in the current price, many investors attempt to achieve excess returns by trading on information. Here are a few ways in which this is done:

Insider trading – Illegal in most, but not all, markets, insider trading refers to the investment activities of people, such as directors and underwriters, who have privileged price-sensitive information about a company from time to time. Definitions of what is illegal are often revised, but insiders are generally required to refrain from taking advantage of such information by trading on it before it is announced publicly. Are some insiders able to make excess profits by getting around these rules? It is hard to tell precisely, since such activities are naturally kept secret, but in the major markets stock prices do tend to move significantly before a major announcement is made. This may be due to the alertness of outsiders who read the signs of forthcoming news about a firm, but it is at least possible that this phenomenon is partly due to insider trading.

"Actually, 'Monkey see, monkey do' has served me quite well in this market."

Legal insider trading – People who work for listed companies are not generally prohibited from owning their own firm's stock, so long as they do not abuse privileged information. Nevertheless, in the course of their work, they may often gain valuable insights into business events, particularly if they are in senior positions, and may possibly be able to use these to make profitable trades. Research suggests that this does occur in smaller companies, which are less closely scrutinized by outsiders, making such insights rarer and therefore more valuable. Legal trades by officers of a company are reported to the regulators, normally some time after they occur, and some investors follow these reports closely. For example, it has been found in the US that when insiders hedge the stock they hold in their company by purchasing derivatives, the stock price tends to drop.

Information on earnings – Companies must report their earnings periodically, and if the figures are markedly better or worse than expected, the market reacts promptly, sending prices up on good news and down on bad news. In the days that follow, the price tends to drift further in the same direction. Some professional investors specialize in exploiting the drift, which is more pronounced in small firms than large ones. The excess returns are quite small, and for the private investor, transaction costs are likely to wipe out such gains. But since professionals generally pay lower transaction costs, they may achieve excess returns using this approach.

 SUMMARY

There is a wide range of investing strategies to suit every type of investor. Each approach to investing — such as growth and value — has its own merits. However, investors often make irrational decisions based on illogical expectations because they cannot control their appetite for large profits. Some good investment strategies are deceptively simple, but they require rigorous research of companies. Success of some strategies depends on how efficient the market is.

QUICK QUIZ

1. If you were to pick five stocks today that would be the equivalent of the "nifty fifty," what would you choose?

2. If Ben Graham were alive today, which five stocks would be his favorite picks? Would these be different from the picks of Warren Buffet? Why?

3. Would you prefer an exchange traded fund to a long-term blue chip fund, which comprises of mostly the stocks in the benchmark index to which the exchange traded fund is pegged?

4. On the Ruritanian stock exchange, the stocks of major companies tend to rise and fall in advance of public announcements. There are five foreign analysts who cover the stocks, and ten local broking firms. Ruritania's economy has only recently been liberalized. How efficient do you think the Ruritanian market is likely to be? What kinds of investment opportunities would you look for?

5. John Bigbucks has a portfolio worth $10m. He decides to invest $100,000 in a foreign currency trading scheme that promises big returns. His friend, Sam Smallsum, who has a portfolio worth $10,000, decides to join him with an investment of $5,000. Comment on the risk and asset allocation issues.

6. John Bigbucks is interested in growth investing. He puts $20,000 into each of 30 small-cap/high growth companies. Sam Smallsum invests $5,000 in each of two small-cap/high growth companies. Comment on the risk and asset allocation issues, assuming their

total portfolio values are $10m and $10,000 respectively.

7. John and Sam are looking at two companies, X and Y, that are very similar in terms of size, growth, asset value and debt. Company X has 8 million shares in issue and the stock price is $1.50. Company Y has 25 million shares in issue and the stock price is $0.46. Sam thinks that Company Y is "cheaper". Is he right? Why might he be wrong?

8. Sam tells John he has a hot stock tip from an insider. John says it is worthless because the market is efficient. Which of the three forms of the efficient market hypothesis does John subscribe to?

9. Investment fund A and Investment fund B claim to expose investors to roughly the same level of risk. Investment fund A has produced an average real rate of return of 3% over the past 14 years, against 2% for the benchmark index. Investment fund B has produced an average real rate of return of 9% over the past 3 years, during which time Investment fund A has produced an average real rate of return of 5%, and the benchmark index has grown by an average of 6%. What additional information would you seek before choosing one of the two funds?

APPENDIX:
STOCK AND OPTION EXCHANGES AROUND THE WORLD

I. UNITED STATES
- American Stock Exchange (AMEX)
- Chicago Mercantile Exchange (CME)
- Eurex US (U.S. Futures Exchange)
- Intercontinental Exchange (ICE)
- International Securities Exchange (trading in options)
- NASDAQ Stock Market
- National Stock Exchange (NSX - formerly Cincinnati Stock Exchange)
- New York Stock Exchange (NYSE)
- OTC Bulletin Board
- Pink Sheets (formerly the National Quotation Bureau)
- Arizona Stock Exchange
- Boston Stock Exchange
- Chicago Stock Exchange (CHX)
- Pacific Exchange (PCX)
- Philadelphia Stock Exchange (PHLX)
- San Diego Stock Exchange
- Electronic Communications Networks
- Archipelago (ArcaEx; merged with NYSE, 2005)
- Bloomberg Tradebook (BTRD)
- Instinet (INCA) acquired by NASDAQ in 2005)
- NexTrade (NTRD)
- REDIbook (REDI - merged with Archipelago in 2002)
- Strike (STRK)

II. CANADA
- Canadian Venture Exchange (combination of the Alberta and Vancouver exchanges)
- Montreal Exchange (Bourse de Montréal)
- Nasdaq Canada
- Toronto Stock Exchange
- Winnipeg Stock Exchange

III. EUROPE

- Euronext (combination of the Amsterdam, Brussels, Lisbon, and Paris exchanges)
- Euronext.liffe (including the London (LIFFE) derivatives market, the French derivatives (MATIF) and options (MONEP) markets)
- NOREX (combination of the Nordic and Baltic stock exchanges: Copenhagen Stock Exchange, Iceland Stock Exchange, Oslo Börs and the OMX Exchanges - Helsinki Stock Exchange, Riga Stock Exchange, Stockholm Stock Exchange, Tallinn Stock Exchange, and Vilnius Stock Exchange.)
- OMX (merger of OM [Sweden] and HEX [Finland])

Albania
- Bursa e Tiranes (Tirana Stock Exchange)

Armenia
- Armenian Stock Exchange

Austria
- Wiener Börse (Vienna Stock Exchange and Austrian Futures & Options Exchange)

Belarus
- Belarusian Currency and Stock Exchange

Belgium
- Euronext Brussels (incorporating the Belgian Futures & Options Exchange as well as the Brussels Exchanges)

Bosnia and Herzegovina
- Banjalucka Berza Hartija od Vrijednosti (Banja Luka Stock Exchange)
- Sarajevo Stock Exchange

Bulgaria
- Bulgarian Stock Exchange
- Sofia Commodity Exchange

Channel Islands
- Channel Islands Stock Exchange

Croatia
- Varazdinska Burza (Varazdin Stock Exchange, formerly the Varazdin Over-the-Counter Market)
- Zagreb Stock Exchange (Zagrebacka Burza)

Cyprus
- Cyprus Stock Exchange

Czech Republic
- Prague Stock Exchange (Burza Cenných Papírù Praha)
- RM-SYSTEM: Czech Securities Exchange

Denmark
- Copenhagen Stock Exchange (Københavns Fondsbørs)

Estonia
- Tallinn Stock Exchange (Tallinna Börs; division of OMX)

Finland
- Finnish Options Exchange (FOEX)
- Helsinki Stock Exchange (division of OMX)

France
- Euronext Paris
- Marche a Terme International de France (MATIF) is now part of Euronext.liffe
- Marche des Options Negociables de Paris (MONEP) is now part of Euronext.liffe

Georgia
- Georgian Stock Exchange

Germany
- BÖAG Börsen (merger of the Hamburg and Hannover Stock Exchanges)
- Börse Berlin-Bremen (merger of the Berlin and Bremen Stock Exchanges)
- Börse Düsseldorf
- Börse München (Munich Exchange; incorporating the Bayerische Börse)
- Börse Stuttgart
- Deutsche Börse (incorporates the Frankfurt Stock Exchange)
- Hamburger Börse

Greece
- Athens Stock Exchange
- Thessaloniki Stock Exchange Center

Hungary
- Budapest Stock Exchange (Budapesti Irtiktözsde)
- Budapest Commodity Exchange (Budapesti Arutözsde)

Iceland
- Iceland Stock Exchange (Kauphöll Íslands)

Ireland
- Irish Stock Exchange

Italy
- Borsa Italiana (Italian Stock Exchange, incorporating the Milan Stock Exchange and the Italian Derivatives Market)

Latvia
- Riga Stock Exchange (Rîgas Fondu Birza; division of OMX)

Lithuania
- Vilnius Stock Exchange (Vilniaus Vertybiniu Popieriu Biržos; division of OMX)

Luxembourg
- Luxembourg Stock Exchange (Bourse de Luxembourg)

Macedonia
- Macedonian Stock Exchange (Makedonska Berza)

Malta
- Malta Stock Exchange (Borza ta' Malta)

Moldova
- Moldova Stock Exchange (Bursa de Valori a Moldovei)

The Netherlands
- Euronext Amsterdam (see also Euronext)
- jaarverslag.info (Annual reports of all Dutch listed companies)

Norway
- Oslo Børs (Oslo Stock Exchange)

Poland
- MTS-CeTO (incorporating the Centralna Tabela Ofert - OTC market)
- Warsaw Stock Exchange (Gielda Papierów Wartosciowych)

Portugal
- Euronext Lisbon (merger of Bolsa de Derivados do Porto and Bolsa de Valores de Lisboa - Oporto Derivatives Exchange and Lisbon Stock Exchange) (see also Euronext)

Romania
- Bucharest Stock Exchange (Bursa de Valori Bucuresti)
- Bursa Monetar-Financiara si de Marfuri Sibiu (Sibiu Monetary-Financial and Commodities Exchange)
- RASDAQ (Piata Nationala de Valori Mobiliare)

Russia
- Asia-Pacific Interbank Currency Exchange
- Moscow Central Stock Exchange
- Moscow Interbank Currency Exchange
- Moscow Stock Exchange
- Nijny Novgorod Stock and Currency Exchange
- RTS Exchange
- St. Petersburg Futures Exchange
- St. Petersburg Currency Exchange
- St. Petersburg Stock Exchange

Serbia and Montenegro
- Belgrade Stock Exchange (Beogradska berza)
- New Securities Exchange Montenegro (NEX)

Slovak Republic
- Bratislava Stock Exchange (Burza Cenných Papierov v Bratislave)
- RM-Systém Slovakia (Slovenska Burza Cenných Papierov)

Slovenia
- Ljubljanska Borza (Ljubljana Stock Exchange)

Spain
- Bolsas y Mercados Españoles incorporating the MEFF, AIAF and SENAF and the four equity exchanges:
  - Bolsa de Barcelona
  - Bolsa de Bilbao
  - Bolsa de Madrid
  - Bolsa de Valencia

Sweden
- Stockholmsbörsen (Stockholm Exchange; division of OMX)

Switzerland
- Swiss Exchange

Turkey
- Istanbul Stock Exchange

Ukraine
- Kiev International Stock Exchange
- PFTS First Securities Trading System
- Ukrainian Stock Exchange

United Kingdom
- EDX London (equity derivatives exchange)
- Euronext.liffe (formerly London International Financial Futures and Options Exchange)
- LCH.Clearnet: an ECN
- London Stock Exchange
- OFEX
- virt-x (formerly Tradepoint Stock Exchange)

IV. ASIA & AUSTRALASIA

Australia
- Australian Stock Exchange
- Bendigo Stock Exchange
- Stock Exchange of Newcastle
- Sydney Futures Exchange

Azerbaijan
- Baku Stock Exchange

Bangladesh
- Chittagong Stock Exchange (see also its Internet Trading Service)
- Dhaka Stock Exchange

China
- Shanghai Futures Exchange
- Shanghai Stock Exchange
- Shenzhen Stock Exchange

Fiji
- South Pacific Stock Exchange

Hong Kong
- Growth Enterprise Market
- Hong Kong Exchanges (Hong Kong Futures Exchange, Stock Exchange of Hong Kong)

India
- Bombay Commodity Exchange (formerly the Bombay Oilseeds & Oils Exchange)
- Calcutta Stock Exchange
- Cochin Stock Exchange

- Inter-Connected Stock Exchange of India (Association of 14 regional stock exchanges -- Bangalore, Bhubaneswar, Cochin, Coimbatore, Gauhati (Guwahati), Hyderabad, Jaipur, Madhya Pradesh, Madras (Chennai), Magadh, Mangalore, Saurashtra Kutch, Uttar Pradesh, and Vadodara)
- National Commodity & Derivatives Exchange
- National Stock Exchange of India
- OTC Exchange of India
- Pune Stock Exchange
- The Stock Exchange, Mumbai (Bombay)

Indonesia
- Jakarta Stock Exchange
- Surabaya Stock Exchange

Japan
- Fukuoka Futures Exchange (formerly Kanmon Commodity Exchange)
- JASDAQ
- Nagoya Stock Exchange
- Osaka Securities Exchange (OSE)
- Sapporo Securities Exchange
- Tokyo International Financial Futures Exchange (TIFFE)
- Tokyo Stock Exchange
- Japan Financials (from the yuka shoken hokokusho, the Japanese equivalent of the SEC filings.)

Kazakhstan
- Kazakhstan Stock Exchange

Korea
- KOSDAQ
- Korea Futures Exchange (KOFEX)
- Korea Stock Exchange

Kyrgyzstan
- Kyrgyz Stock Exchange

Malaysia
- Bursa Malaysia (formerly Kuala Lumpur Stock Exchange; parent company of Labuan International Financial Exchange, Bursa Malaysia Derivatives, and the MESDAQ Market)
- Malaysia Derivatives Exchange (Bursa Malaysia Derivatives; merger of the Kuala Lumpur Options & Financial Futures Exchange and the Commodity and Monetary Exchange of Malaysia)
- MESDAQ Market

Maldives
- Maldives Stock Exchange

Mongolia
- Mongolian Stock Exchange

Nepal
- Nepal Stock Exchange

New Zealand
- NZX (formerly New Zealand Stock Exchange)

Pakistan
- Islamabad Stock Exchange
- Karachi Stock Exchange
- Lahore Stock Exchange

Papua New Guinea
- Port Moresby Stock Exchange

Singapore
- Singapore Commodity Exchange
- SGX: Singapore Exchange (Singapore Stock Exchange, Singapore International Monetary Exchange)

Sri Lanka
- Colombo Stock Exchange

Taiwan
- GreTai Securities Market
- Taiwan Stock Exchange
- Taiwan Futures Exchange

Thailand
- Agricultural Futures Exchange of Thailand
- Stock Exchange of Thailand

Turkmenistan
- State Commodity and Raw Materials Exchange of Turkmenistan

Uzbekistan
- Uzbek Commodity Exchange
- Uzbekistan Stock Exchange (Tashkent Republican Stock Exchange)

V. LATIN AMERICA AND THE CARIBBEAN

Argentina
- Bolsa de Cereales de Buenos Aires
- Bolsa de Comercio de Buenos Aires (Buenos Aires Stock Exchange)
- Bolsa de Comercio de La Plata
- Bolsa de Comercio de Rosario
- Bolsa de Comercio de Santa Fe
- Mercado a Término de Buenos Aires
- Mercado a Termino de Rosario (Rosario Futures Exchange)

Bahamas
- Bahamas International Securities Exchange

Barbados
- Barbados Stock Exchange

Bermuda
- Bermuda Stock Exchange

Bolivia
- Bolsa Boliviana De Valores

Brazil
- Bolsa Brasileira de Mercadorias (merger of the commodities exchanges of Goiás, Mato Grosso do Sul, Minas Gerais, Paraná, and Rio Grande do Sul e Uberlândia)
- Bolsa de Cereais e Mercadorias de Londrina
- Bolsa de Cereais e Mercadorias de Maringá
- Bolsa de Cereais e Mercadorias do Estado de Mato Grosso
- Bolsa de Gêneros Alimentícios do Rio de Janeiro
- Bolsa de Mercadoria de Brasilia
- Bolsa de Mercadorias & Futuros (Commodities & Futures Exchange)
- Bolsa de Valores da Bahia-Sergipe-Alagoas: see BOVESPA
- Bolsa de Valores do Extreme Sul: see BOVESPA
- Bolsa de Valores Minas-Espirito Santo-Brasilia
- Bolsa de Valores do Paraná
- Bolsa de Valores Regional
- Bolsa de Valores do Rio de Janeiro (Rio De Janeiro Stock Exchange)
- BOVESPA (Bolsa de Valores de Sao Paulo - Sao Paulo Stock Exchange; integrates the regional exchanges at Bahia-Sergipe-Alagoas, Extremo Sul, Minas-Espirito Santo-Brasilia, Paraná, and others)
- Sistema Integrado de Bolsas Brasileiras (SIBB)
- Sociedade Operadora do Mercado de Ativos (SOMA)

Cayman Islands
- Cayman Islands Stock Exchange

Chile
- Bolsa de Comercio de Santiago (Santiago Stock Exchange)
- Bolsa Electrónica de Chile

Colombia
- Bolsa de Valores de Colombia
- Bolsa Nacional Agropecuaria

Costa Rica
- Bolsa Nacional de Valores (Costa Rica Stock Exchange)

Dominican Republic
- Bolsa de Valores de la República Dominicana

Ecuador
- Bolsa de Valores de Quito (Quito Stock Exchange)
- Bolsa de Valores de Guayaquil (Guayaquil Stock Exchange)

ElSalvador
- Bolsa de Valores de El Salvador

Guatemala
- Bolsa de Valores Nacional

Honduras
- Bolsa Centroamericana de Valores

Jamaica
- Jamaica Stock Exchange

Mexico
- Bolsa Mexicana de Valores
- Mercado Mexicano de Derivados (MexDer) (Mexican Derivatives Market)

Nicaragua
- Bolsa de Valores de Nicaragua

Panama
- Bolsa de Valores de Panama

Paraguay
- Bolsa de Valores y Productos de Asuncion
- Portafolio de Valores

Peru
- Bolsa de Valores de Lima

Trinidad and Tobago
- Trinidad and Tobago Stock Exchange

Uruguay
- Bolsa de Valores de Montevideo
- Bolsa Electronica de Valores del Uruguay

Venezuela
- Caracas Stock Exchange (Bolsa de Valores de Caracas)

VI. MIDDLE EAST
Bahrain
- Bahrain Stock Exchange

Iran
- Tehran Stock Exchange

Iraq
- Iraq Stock Exchange

Israel
- Tel Aviv Stock Exchange

Jordan
- Amman Stock Exchange

Kuwait
- Kuwait Stock Exchange

Lebanon
- Beirut Stock Exchange

Oman
- Muscat Securities Market

Palestine National Authority
- Palestine Securities Exchange

Qatar
* Doha Securities Market

Saudi Arabia
* Saudi Stock Exchange (Tadawul Web)

United Arab Emirates
* Abu Dhabi Securities Market
* Dubai Financial Market
* Dubai Mercantile Exchange

VII.   AFRICA
Botswana
* Botswana Stock Exchange

Egypt
* Cairo & Alexandria Stock Exchange

Ghana
* Ghana Stock Exchange

Kenya
* Nairobi Stock Exchange

Malawi
* Malawi Stock Exchange

Mauritius
* Stock Exchange of Mauritius

Morocco
* Casablanca Stock Exchange (Bourse de Casablanca)

Namibia
* Namibian Stock Exchange

Nigeria
* Nigerian (Lagos) Stock Exchange

South Africa
* Johannesburg Stock Exchange
* South African Futures Exchange (SAFEX)
* Share TRAnsactions Totally Electronic (STRATE)

Sudan
* Khartoum Stock Exchange

Swaziland
- Swaziland Stock Exchange

Tanzania
- Dar-Es-Salaam Stock Exchange

Tunisia
- Bourse des Valeurs Mobilières de Tunis (Tunis Stock Exchange)

Uganda
- Uganda Securities Exchange

West Africa
- Bourse Regionale des Valeurs Mobilieres (Regional Stock Exchange for West Africa)

Zambia
- Lusaka Stock Exchange

Zimbabwe
- Zimbabwe Stock Exchange

INDEX

U

V

W

FORTHCOMING TITLES FOR
MARK MOBIUS
MASTERCLASS SERIES

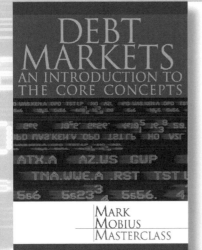

(ISBN: 0-470-82147-7)

(ISBN: 0-470-82143-4)

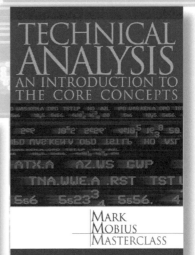

(ISBN: 0-470-82148-5)

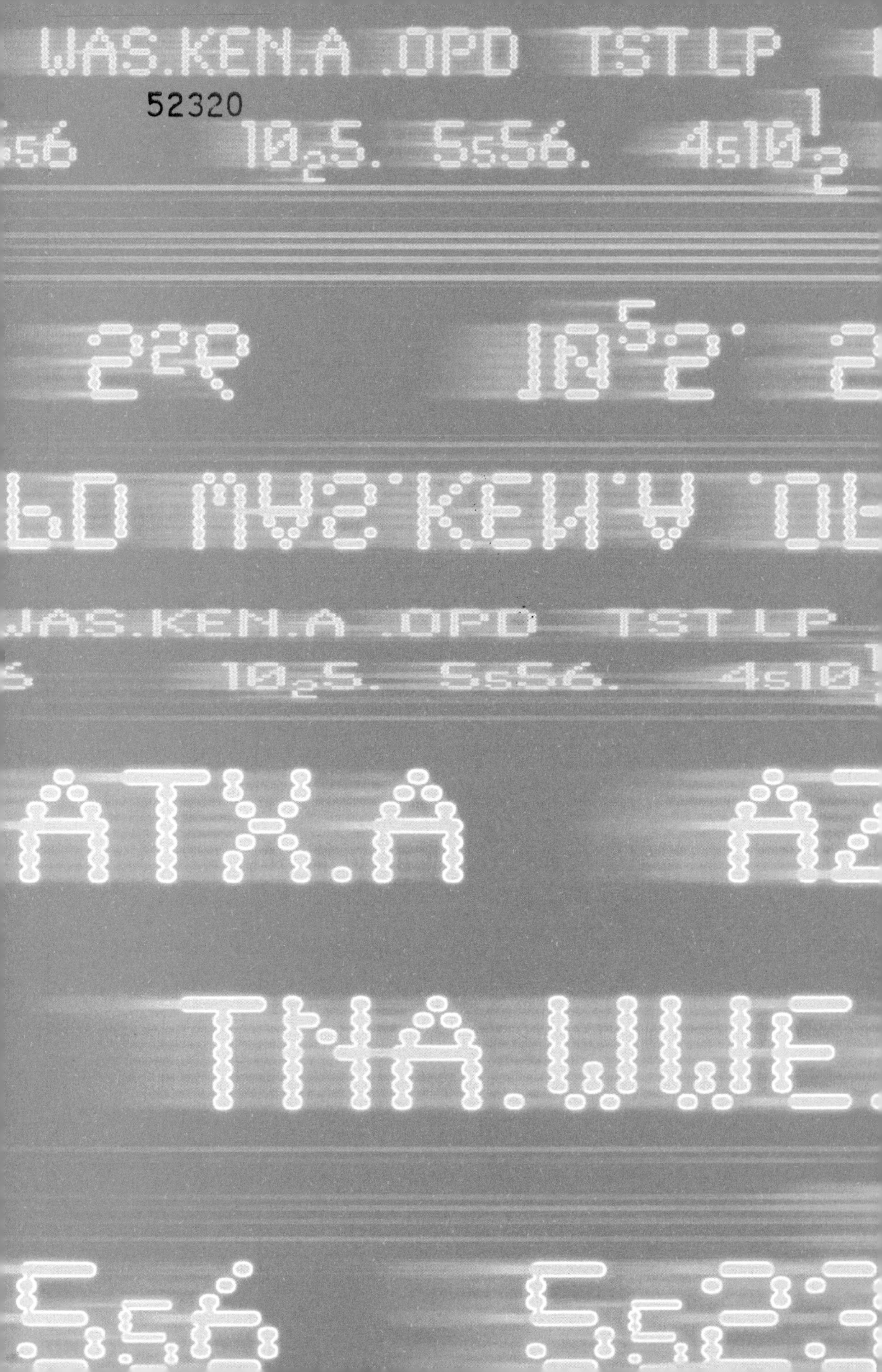
WAS.KEN.A .OPD TSTLP
52320
WAS.KEN.A .OPD TSTLP
ATX.A